A Little Fling

Also by Sam Pickering

Books of Essays
A Continuing Education
The Right Distance
May Days
Still Life
Let It Ride
Trespassing
Walkabout Year
The Blue Caterpillar
Living to Prowl
Deprived of Unhappiness

Literary Studies
The Moral Tradition in English Fiction, 1785–1850
John Locke and Children's Books in Eighteenth-Century England
Moral Instruction and Fiction for Children, 1749–1820

A Little Fling

and other essays

Sam Pickering

The University of Tennessee Press / Knoxville

Copyright © 1999 by The University of Tennessee Press / Knoxville. All Rights Reserved.
Manufactured in the United States of America. First Edition.

The paper used in this book meets the minimum requirements of ANSI/NISO z39.48-1992
(R 1997) (Permanence of Paper). The binding materials have been chosen for strength and
durability. Printed on recycled paper.

Library of Congress Cataloging-in-Publication Data

Pickering, Samuel F., 1941–
A little fling, and other essays / Sam Pickering. — 1st ed.
        p. cm.
ISBN 1-57233-062-7 (cl.: alk. paper)
I. Title.
AC8 .P6645 1999
081—dc21

                                99-6208

For Bill Weaver, my oldest and best friend.
With affection and admiration.

Contents

Preface / IX

Consider the Lilies / 1
Autumnal / 23
November / 36
Surprise / 45
Dysfunctional / 55
A Little Fling / 69
Killing the Bear / 78
Hear No Evil / 90
Numbering / 101
The Traveled World / 112
Profound / 125
Not Enough / 139
A Goer / 149
Most Embarrassing / 164

After Words / 179

Preface

My son Edward is a worrier. For seven years he has spent summers at camp in Maine. This summer he is head boy. His duties are slight. He must set a good example for younger campers and then on Sunday nights light the council fire. Throughout this past year concern about lighting the fire smoldered. "Suppose," Edward said in November, "the bark is damp, and I can't start the fire. What will I do?" In June Vicki and I drove Edward to camp. An old friend, Mook, is a counselor, and I mentioned Edward's fears to him. On July 1, I received a postcard from camp. "Sunday—June 28, 1998," Mook wrote. "It did not rain—the woods were dry—the council fire was high and bright."

"High and bright," I said to Vicki, "that's the way to begin summer." On the front of Mook's card appeared a photograph of the First Congregational Church located at "Sixth and A Street" in "San Diego 1, California." The card was old. Women standing by the church door wore hats. Parked along the curb outside the church were four sedans, all built in the 1940s. "Why didn't Mook choose a card depicting Maine?" Vicki asked, turning the card over and over so it paddled the air. "California fifty years ago and Camp Timanous now? They don't go together." "Only on the page where writers erase and revise do things fit together," I said. "Real life occurs beyond margins." Later that morning I had coffee at the Cup of Sun. Josh and Allison argued about censorship. "I don't give a fart about the First Amendment and free speech," Josh said. "The

Founding Fathers had mothers who would *not* have approved of pornography." I eavesdropped on a conversation two tables away. "I resent it," I heard a woman say, "when family infringes on my public heart space." "California," Roger said, nudging me. "She's visiting from California and lives in San Diego."

Three days later Eliza and I attended the Boombox Parade in Willimantic. On the morning of the fourth of July, WILI, the local radio station, plays patriotic music, and townsfolk march down Main Street carrying radios tuned to the station. Eliza and I took blue-and-white folding chairs and sat in the shade under a maple in Memorial Park. Two college students perched on the curb in front of us, a pit bull squatting on its haunches between them. The dog growled when a flock of children fluttered past on bicycles, American flags flapping on handle bars like wings. The growling made me nervous, and I pulled Eliza's chair close. Shortly afterward, though, the dog threw up into the lap of its owner. Immediately the boys jumped up, and after attaching a leash to the dog, hurried away.

A woman strolled by selling balloons filled with helium. Shaped like dinosaurs and colored red, purple, green, and white, the balloons gamboled lightly through the breeze. "That's my kind of pet," I said to Eliza. "Can I buy one?" Eliza said. "No," I answered. Elections occur this fall, and a gaggle of clucking, smiling politicians led the parade. A state senator rode a lawn mower. Attached to the mower was a garden cart containing a sandwich board. Printed on the board was "I HELPED CUT TAXES." The senator's challenger whizzed along on roller blades, sometimes skating backward and spinning through a logarithm of figures, all the while pulling two grandchildren seated in a Radio Flyer. While supporters of "Koval for Congress" wore short skirts and high-stepped past the park, members of the Lions Club roared. Following the pride of lions was our congressman. He wore khaki trousers, a white shirt, and a red-and-blue necktie. He had been in Congress eight terms, and his stomach jiggled above his belt. Players on teams in the Midget Football League carried signs shaped like goal posts. Printed on cardboard crossbars were the names of sponsors: New England Transmission, VFW, Nassiff's Sporting Goods, and the Willimantic

Policeman's Benevolent Association. Signs shook like branches in a wind. The Connecticut Party observed that "the President Lives in Public Housing." "Poetry Moves the Masses," Curbstone Press declared. While "God is Good. All the Time" at the Light on the Hill Christian Fellowship, the First Church of Christ in Mansfield was an "Open and Affirming Congregation." Kennels of dogs trotted beside their owners, golden retrievers being the most popular species. A square hat sat on the head of a basset. Twirling atop the hat was a fan, its three blades, red, white, and blue.

Ladd's Nursery placed flats of flowers at twenty yard intervals along Main Street. The nursery donated the plants to the town and urged spectators to take them after the parade. I hoped Eliza would pick up scarlet sage gleaming to our right. Instead she selected celosia, or cockscomb, on the left, bringing home twelve small plants, all "Geisha Yellow." She also brought home a New Testament, given to her by a member of the Ebenezer Lutheran Church, the Revised Standard version printed by the American Bible Society. "The Word of God Alive and Active," the cover stated. Printed at the back of the book was a section entitled "Finding Help in the New Testament." Among the entries was "Encountering a Cult." I looked at the reference, the seventh chapter of Matthew, verses fifteen through twenty. Essayists are fuddy-duddies. Few of us embrace change enthusiastically. Consequently I read the King James version of Matthew. "Beware of false prophets which come to you in sheep's clothing," the fifteenth verse warned, adding, "inwardly they are ravening wolves." In essays I spend pages fishing holy waters, trying to pull rainbows out of Glory Pool. I'm not much of a fisherman. I lack devotion; my sentences stray, and I land more snakes than truths. "I'd like to accompany you on a piscatorial excursion," an Episcopal friend of the high, genuflecting variety recently said to me. "What a treat it would be to see a snake in its natural habitat. I only see snakes in church."

Essayists are so commonsensical they make lackadaisical believers, "and worse lovers," Vicki added, hearing me read aloud. Pushing Vicki's emendation aside for a decade, I wondered, as I pondered the selection from Matthew, if I had done right by Francis, Edward, and Eliza. Each child has attended church once, the occasion being his christening. A regular injection of Sunday school might have given them small psychological scars, "not much price to pay," my friend Josh said, "for vaccinating them against the irrational."

Last Saturday when I was not home two men gave Eliza a handful of tracts. "You didn't let them in the house?" I said later. "No, Daddy," Eliza answered, "but they were nice and seemed concerned about my soul. Maybe faith matters." "Jesus!" I exclaimed. "Yes," Eliza said, "that was their point." Later I perused the tracts. One contained an article describing dengue fever. "If there is significant bleeding, doctors may be inclined to recommend a blood transfusion," the article stated. "Some may quickly recommend this without considering the alternatives. However, in addition to being against God's law, this is usually unnecessary."

I dropped the tract into the recycling bag and walked outside the house, something I do when perturbed. Essayists wear habits like hair shirts. Instead of irritating, itch comforts. Change of pasture may fatten a calf and my books, but no matter how long we graze or how exotic the fodder, neither the calf nor I will ever sprout wings. Growing amid the familiar is the good grain of place, hops that so strengthen the mind that it can resist enervating dislocations of change and time. In shade below boulders in the back yard, serpentine leaf miners chewed ghostly trails through columbine, eventually reducing leaves to thin seams of white. Beneath the kitchen window a fledgling cardinal rummaged the husks of cracked corn and sunflower. While color swirled like sherbet through day lilies, berries on tartarian honeysuckle glittered like hard red candy, grains of sugar speckling them silver. On the silverbell by the driveway the upper surfaces of leaves were soft as cotton. From horse balm leaves hung in scrolls. Small, peppery caterpillars sawed through petioles one and an eighth inches above the blades. After rolling and tying leaves, the caterpillars wove silky tents along midribs at the junctures of petioles and blades.

The transfusion of green July invigorated me and, clotting the religious hemorrhage, restored my platelets to rational levels. Although essayists are constitutionally resistant to theological fervor, they are susceptible to poetic inspiration. Good swimmers die in water, and essayists drown in words. No matter that a phrase doesn't pertain to the topic about which I am writing—if I like the phrase, I'll wedge it into a sentence, in the process turning polished paragraphs into puddingstone. Four days ago I received a letter from Chattanooga, Tennessee. In a forgotten play, a man wrote, "I found a verse which would appeal to you. The quatrain is a conversation between a courting couple. The poetry doesn't flow as smoothly as Boreas snorting Zephyrs, but it has an ambrosial rhapsodic tone."

> The moon is shining bright.
> Can I see you home tonight?
> The stars are shining, too.
> I don't mind if you do.

Essays describe parts, not wholes. They don't paint portraits, but sketch earlobes, chins, and foreheads. Yet, a collection of essays, Josh argued two years ago, is a family piece. "The oddments and absurd bits between boards," Josh wrote, "capture the ramper-scamper nature of being and amount to more than the novel's round world. Because readers of novels often submerge themselves in story, they lose life itself, its pauses and reflections, its morning springs and miry clay." Would that Josh were right. Still, much as the early settlers of eastern Connecticut mixed human fat with oil in order to make paint phosphorescent, so I stir anecdotes into essays in hopes of making pages glow. Historians, incidentally, deny that Nutmeggers ever blended human fat with oil, asserting that the only fleshly additive paint ever contained was pork.

Occasionally truth makes Josh bilious, and he swells into tale. "In eighteenth-century Ashford," he recounted, "if a person agreed to leave his body to the Congregational Church, the church contracted to supply the individual and his immediate family with food during famine and parlous times." According to Josh, parishioners wanted to paint the church so it would shine like the pillar of fire that led "the Hebrews through the dark wilderness." Risk accompanied the contract. If a person succumbed to a wasting disease, the church's investment faded away. As a result, in belt-tightening times deacons signed agreements only with large people, generally females in the choir "with some sprawl to them."

Unlike those of Josh, my stories usually describe doings in Tennessee, particularly in Carthage and Smith County, home to my family for a hundred years, 1863 to 1963. Near the end of May controversy erupted in Ankerrow's Café. Discussion boiled over, and neighbors, as Turlow Gutheridge put it, "almost drawed fists and knives." The argument started after Googoo Hooberry asked the lunchtime crowd a question. "If someone told you a dog bit your ear off, would you go after the dog first or would you search for your ear first?"

Early in June a new doctor appeared in Carthage. For a fortnight he drained business away from Dr. Sollows. When the new doctor gave a physical, he checked the pulse in both arms simultaneously, holding the patient's right wrist with his left hand and the left wrist with his right hand. "Two for the price of one," Hoben Donkin said. "The pulse in this left arm is sixty-eight, and that's hunky-dory," the doctor told Hink Ruunt, "but the pulse in your right arm is ninety-three and a half, and you're going to have to take measures." "Measures!" Hink exclaimed later to Turlow Gutheridge. "You should have seen the doctor figure. He counted the pulse in my left arm with the right corner of his mouth and that in my right arm with the left corner. He started simply, saying, 'one, one.' But soon the count was 'five, seven' and before I knew it, 'sixty-eight and ninety-three and a half.'"

The stories that roll clastic through my essays are usually lighthearted. "Don't spend your days," Mother once told me, "like the gloomy dentist, always down in the mouth." I want things to come out happily, and so, as Josh phrases it, I "sugar corpses." The page allows me to sweep and neaten. In life the thirsty farmer has to milk a cow. In a paragraph he can milk a hen. Although I enjoy humor, I don't laugh at actual people. Rarely does an essayist mock the fallen. Essayists know that slippery places lie ahead. Every day I bruise toes against clauses. I see lazy verbs catch on the lips of paragraphs and watch my tone fall flat.

Of course I'm not always cheerful. Level prose doesn't climb hills or mirror feeling. When I confront a weary abuse, sometimes my writing twists upward. Still, I am not a reformer. A sentence can change meaning. Next afternoon may bring a fresh topic. "Why flutter in the net," Josh said, "unless you can embroider new kindness over old crewel?" "Don't run for nothing when you can sit for nothing," the old saying advises. Despite appearing relaxed and uninterested in fashionable doings, I rarely sit. According to a Macedonian tale, the sun sleeps under a white oak every night. While the sun dozes, angels feed it light. Unlike the sun, essayists are rarely spoon-fed material. While my family naps, I roam libraries. As a result I have accumulated ricks of curious knowledge. In Russia St. Basil is the patron saint of swine. Occasionally the material I pack away is useful. In Albania parents warn disobedient children that the Tantarabobus without a tail will eat them. Absence of a tail made the Tantarabobus irritable, I explained to Eliza when she was young, because it prevented him from swishing huge buggy-bumpus flies off his back. The flies laid eggs on the unfortunate Tantarabobus. Once the eggs hatched, the maggots burrowed under the Tantarabobus' skin, causing sores. Instead of infection the sores oozed marmalade. Literature can influence life. Eliza refuses to eat marmalade, a fact that puzzles Vicki, but not me. Although essayists sometimes blight taste buds, and, more often than not, don't manage well when dealing with big matters like religion, they are good with small things and make fine parents, always being willing to drop thoughts in mid-pencil in order to dress dolls in the attic or toss baseballs in the back yard.

In part books reflect authors' personalities. Appetites of writers, literally appetites, Josh informed me, vary from genre to genre. Salads delight poets. "Nothing pleases the poetic graduate of a fine arts program more than tossing iambs and the occasional anapest onto a page fluffy with watercress, radicchio, mandarin orange, a touch of mango, and if the poet is a groovy, free-verse sort, a tuft of cilantro." Not all poets have the same taste. State poet laureates are more conventional gastronomes, those from the East and West addicted to Waldorf salad topped with dollops of Hellmann's Real Mayonnaise, those from the south preferring fruit cocktail suspended in cherry Jell-O.

"And novelists?" I asked. "Novelists, especially compilers of thrillers and mysteries," Josh said, "are as duplicitous as plots. Despite posing outdoors, standing beside grills, hamburgers in hand, such scribblers prefer their food and lives sprinkled with feta, sea-soned the Greek Way." "As for essayists," Josh continued, "although many of the male variety have occasional hankerings for the veg-etarian, all are married to hardy, pop-out-three-children, pig-and-watermelon women, babes who swill red wine and who tolerate the inadequacies of well-read husbands. The wife of the best es-sayist in the nation, if not in Storrs, Connecticut, told me last week that her husband couldn't boil water without scorching it."

"The Central Georgia," an old rhyme states, "burns nothing but coal. / Poke your head out the window and watch the wheels roll." This preface is on its last siding. I now sit on tile surrounding the university pool. Eliza and her friend Tara are swimming. The clock reads eleven minutes after eight. I have been here since six o'clock. I'm hungry, and swimmers keep baptizing me with water. Most readers have enjoyed similar experiences. The next time you accom-pany children to a pool, take a book of essays. This book starts slowly, describing summertime on Vicki's farm in Beaver River, Nova Scotia, twelve miles up the coast from Yarmouth on the Bay of Fundy. At the beginning of September when the family returns to Connecticut and classes begin and seasons change, the rhythm of the essays changes. As days shrink, the essays become shorter and crisper, and at times hard-edged, even cold. While sitting by the pool if you're ever tempted to leap moaning from the high dive, read a paragraph describing peaceful summer. When getting splashed exasperates you, read about damp, green spring. Above all, if woe and wisdom soak your spirits, ponder the dry solemni-ties contained in this book. If you sit back and smile warmly, then my inability to write water to a boil doesn't matter.

Consider the Lilies

The fog swept over the big spruce, wrapping them like wax paper. Here and there thorny limbs snagged rolls, jerking them off spools so that billows unraveled then shredded into wisps. Rain splattered flat over the headland. Slapping trees, water wrinkled through the blueberry field then gathering along the lane gushed toward the house. The rain was the first in a month, and I sat on the porch and watched it frost the landscape. Instead of shining with the tensile strength of beaten steel, the light softened. As water boiled across the headland, the day rotted and dark seams ran crazed across the sky.

Not in a century had southwest Nova Scotia endured such a dry July. Although I welcomed rain, I'd enjoyed the drought. Early in July I roamed the bog behind Black Point. In past summers exploring the bog was unpleasant. The mat quivered, my feet sank, and brown water welled over my shoes. Often the mat itself swelled over ankles and calves, and lifting a leg resembled prying a broken cork out of a wine bottle. Pails of water sloshed into my boots, and instead of raising legs, I often pulled my feet out of boots. This summer the mat was crisp, and rather than watching where I stepped, I studied plants: cotton grass, its three inflorescences white pompons; leather leaf; dwarf huckleberry; and reindeer moss, the brittle wads spongy and scouring. Amid the peat calapogon bloomed. This summer I found a white variety, the rare *albiflorus*.

Finding the calapogon startled me, and flowers I'd hardly noticed for a decade bloomed afresh. Swamp rose bristled along the eastern side of the point. Brooms of tall meadow rue swept through the briars. While Scotch lovage splintered into white behind the roses, in front swamp candles flickered and yellow rattle dried to seed, the pods shaking cindery. White butterflies spiraled above a patch of mustard. The butterflies' wings looked like petals bleached by sunlight, the dark spots amid the white smoldering, the rapid twirling of the insects having momentarily blown the fires out. As rain became a staple of summer conversation, so water often drifted across vision like a mirage. Behind the farmhouse Virginia creeper turned a shed into a green cocoon, the vine's leaves damper than leaves on creeper in Connecticut. Late in the summer, seaside goldenrod bloomed amid rocks at Beaver River. By midday sunlight peeled moisture from the stones like shucks from cobs, and the flowers glistened oily, almost as if they had been buttered.

Early in July cloudberries ripened on Black Point. Yellow and marbled with orange, the berries tasted like apple custard. Later in the month I found smooth gooseberries along the lane running to the bluff overlooking the Bay of Fundy. In a foundation hole on Ma's Property west of the house, raspberries grew big as knuckles. East of the house in George's Field, a thicket of stubby canes roiled around an open well, the berries on them small and as irregular as liver spots. In August I picked blue and blackberries, some days a quart of blueberries after breakfast and then after lunch two quarts of blackberries. Wild mint blossomed at the end of July, and I folded bundles of leaves together and stuffed them into my mouth in front of my lower teeth. On walks I sucked the leaves and with my tongue rolled them back and forth like clumps of snuff.

Essayists are passionate about trifles. In Nova Scotia I was indifferent to worldly matters. During the summer I sauntered wood and shore, preferring still tidal pools to the frothy wash of buying and selling: dipping fingers into silver-spotted anemones; prying shells of surf clams and Atlantic dog winkles out of crevices, or finding bread crumb sponges under ledges, the sponges resembling hunks of batter, the stuff of cakes not salad dressing. Of course ignoring the fret of commerce was impossible. Early in the morning I listened to the radio, and most afternoons during tea I perused the Halifax newspaper. Occasionally I read something ponderable. When women had difficulty giving birth in Newfoundland at the beginning of this century, midwives baked cakes and placed them between expectant mothers' legs. Babies being bundles of appetites, once children smelled the cakes, they crept salivating from wombs. Because the article did not describe the cakes favored by midwives, I whipped up a tray of possibilities. Since diet not only reflects character but can also determine the course of life, I sent several cakes back to the mental oven. The inhabitants of Newfoundland being conventional, at least in intimate doings, I suspected that few midwives tempted infants with fruitcake. Likewise a regimen of devil's food cake would not have augured well for the future while a whiff of angel food might have led to stillbirths. "What cake do you think parents favored?" I asked Vicki. "Pineapple upside-down cake," she said, adding, "Do you know why?" "Sure," I said. "Only someone thick as pound cake wouldn't know that."

Little in the paper rose yeasty as the midwives' culinary practices. Most pages were flatly commercial. In August BMW ran a full-page advertisement. In the middle of the page appeared a reproduction of a portrait of Marie Curie, measuring thirteen by thirteen and a half inches. The winner of two Nobel Prizes, Currie leaned forward and stared intently from the canvas, her left hand pressed against the side of her head. Printed above the picture in heavy black letters was the caption "Would Have Been An Innovative BMW Dealer." "As a BMW dealer," a paragraph under the picture explained, "her ability to innovate would have come in handy." On the radio the next morning a station in Boston advertised the Jaguar XJ6, inviting owners of "luxury cars" 1993 or older—BMW, Mercedes, and Lexus—to visit a dealership and test drive a car. All owners needed, the advertisement stated, was insurance and a valid driver's license.

On Sundays I listened to preachers. One morning a preacher in Halifax attacked "drinking, drugs, gambling, Sunday sports, and nakedness, even in the streets." Twelve miles from our house, Yarmouth is the largest town in western Nova Scotia, the population consisting of eight thousand people. In town are three bookstores: at the mall a small branch of Coles, a chain, then downtown, two religious stores, the Gospel Ship on Brown Street and The Truth and The Life Christian Family Store on Main Street.

At the Gospel Ship I bought a packet of thirty-six "Luncheon Napkins" manufactured in Minnesota for the Graceline Company. "Graceline napkins," a flyer explained, "are tastefully designed for those who appreciate the simplicity, reverence and thanksgiving of gracious table prayer. These distinctive napkins, with appropriate verse and delightful art work, enhance any place setting with their expressions of warm and friendly hospitality." I bought two-ply napkins measuring six by six and three-quarters inches. Stamped against a black background hung with a valence of white was "OUR GOD IS AN AWESOME GOD," the letters of *our* printed in blue and those of *awesome* in yellow. While the remaining four words were printed in white, a pink box resembling a drawer surrounded *is an*. In thick letters one and one-eighth inches tall and an inch and a quarter wide, *God* seemed to leap from the napkin. I had never seen such tableware, and I wondered if Graceline manufactured other divinely inspired paper products. Because goods sold by the Gospel Ship made me queasy, I showed the napkins to a stranger in the County Museum. At ease in religious shallows, she had long sailed on Pentecostal frigates. "Praise the King," she boomed. "When you wipe your lips, you will remember your sins and your conscience will burn." "Amen," I said, close-hauling my mouth and tacking away to an exhibition of samplers.

By the end of summer, however, not only had I gotten my religious sea legs, but I had also purchased salty raiment, albeit purser's slops rather than nankeen. Along with books and tapes The Truth and The Life sold Christian tee-shirts. Rarely does a lapsed Episcopalian rate able-theologian. Indeed only a press gang could force an Episcopalian on board a ship of a doctrinal line. Despite lurching into religious bookstores several times during the summer, I did not make ordinary seaman. Remaining on the main, I rejected several uniforms as suitable only for higher-rated believers. Printed on the front of one shirt were the legs and feet of a boy dressed in jeans and basketball shoes. Rough wear had scuffed the shoes and shredded knees of the jeans. Stamped under the picture was "PRAY HARD," not "play hard." Across the front of another shirt stretched Christ's bare back, a crown of thorns upon his head, his arms splayed, and barbed cuts slicing his shoulders. "To Know What

Real Love Means," the caption below the illustration instructed, "Read Between the Lines." Ill at ease with such ornate rigs, I purchased a simple shirt. Stamped on the front of the shirt was the statement "Hell Ain't Cool." Red and four inches tall, the letters spelling *Hell* shattered near the top into yellow flames. Bits of the flames lapped upward, adding two inches of color to the word.

Last year in one of my essays, Capri Scates burned to death in Carthage, Tennessee. For a day Capri's misfortune furnished the crowd at Ankerrow's Café with matter for lunchtime conversation. "What part of Capri caught fire first?" Loppie Groat asked while slapping mustard on a hot dog. "That's not important," Googoo Hooberry interrupted. "I want to know what happened to his beard. Capri had the longest beard in Smith County." In Nova Scotia I was a busy idler and resembled the fictional characters who inhabit my books. Albeit I didn't ask questions as profound as those posed in Ankerrow's, I rummaged house and days, turning up fragments of the past.

Although each July I imagine discovering a trunk bulging with pirate leavings, I've never stumbled over anything worth much money. Still, in the backhouse this summer I found a bottle blown from blue glass. A fire extinguisher eight inches tall and five wide, the bottle stood on four squat legs and held half a pint of liquid. A plug shaped like a *T* jutted from the top of the bottle. Around the base of the plug glass rippled in circles forming bumpy necklaces. Below the necklaces the glass roughened into a checkerboard pattern of raised edges and low depressions. In the middle of the bottle a flat oval appeared resembling a medallion. Stamped into the glass and circling the edge of the medallion were the words "HARDENS HAND GRENADE." Scrolled across the middle of the medallion was "FIRE EXTINGUISHER." The grenade was a "No.1" and had been patented first on August 8, 1871, and then again on August 14, 1883. The chemicals in the bottle having dried out, I couldn't test the grenade, but I assumed it once contained a blend of salt, soda, ammonia, and magnesium and probably put out a fire almost as fast as a bucket of water.

"When you describe Nova Scotia," a critic wrote me, "I can't see ideas for words." During the school year I force words into thought then staple them to things. Instead of reducing objects to meaning, in summer I find and describe. As I parsed the backhouse searching for matter as clear as nouns, so I studied beach and meadow, hoping that someday I would see what I saw. In contrast to religious doings that led to a press-gang of artificial apostolic declarations, natural things shimmered like simple sentences. Instead of defining, observation of the natural world evoked mood and place. One summer, according to a Micmac tale, a boy was born with a wing rather than a left arm because on the day he was conceived a merlin frightened his mother. In summer I watched birds in hopes that place would take flight. Early in July a white-throated sparrow called from a spruce bordering the bog at Black Point. At first the song ran like an open faucet, but then heat turned a knob and the music dried, the last notes not ringing but splattering like balls of dust. A raft of eiders floated off Bear Cove, the birds' black feathers looking like hunks of waterlogged wood, their white feathers warped, bleached splinters. At high tide black ducks fed below the headland. Tipping over and diving then popping back to the surface, the ducks seemed stones tumbled about by the ebb and flow of waves.

Weather influenced my perception of birds. Not only did ravens sound grinding and hoarse, but they also sounded thirsty. After dusk nighthawks quartered fields, their mouths open, not, it seemed, to scoop up insects, but the cool damp rising from the grass. On the headland I surprised a bittern, the first I'd seen in Beaver River. Swaying into flight, the bird looked like driftwood, fibrous and insubstantial, the white feathers on its neck seams of salt. In the woods behind Ma's Property a ruffled grouse thrashed into flight then settled in a dead spruce, turning itself into a broken limb, its body stretched out of fat, its beak a sharp, dry twig.

Along with the bittern other birds appeared which I'd never seen in Beaver River: in the spruce woods a Swainson's thrush and then on a hazy morning off the headland a northern gannet. Flying west above the beach, the gannet erased fog like a backstroke button a cloud of words, the bird's yellow head collapsing letters, the long black wingtips fading through space like graphite lingering dusty in vision. After rain in August, summer seemed ordinary, and birds appeared in familiar places. One morning at the end of the month, I stood near the cow pond and for two hours watched mixed flocks bustle after insects. While red-breasted nuthatches clicked through birch, boreal and black-and-white chickadees skittered in spruce. Warblers foraged alders, colors flickering, marking the molt of season: blackpoll, yellow, chestnut-sided, myrtle, Wilson's, black-throated green, and common yellow-throat. While cedar waxwings perched atop spruce, robins clucked nervously in underbrush, and a lone junco searched for seeds behind a rock. I was not the only creature watching birds forage. That afternoon a sharp-shinned hawk perched in a spruce beside the pond.

"Wherefore, if God so clothe the grass of the field, which today is, and tomorrow is cast into the oven," Christ asked in the Sermon on the Mount, "shall he not much more clothe you, O ye of little faith?" During summer I paid more attention to scales and palets than to shirts and trousers. Spools of ribbon grass unraveled amid roses behind the barn. The long green and white leaves rolled into butterfly bows. Instead of reducing leaves to ash, sunlight buffed them, turning bows silver, rubbing blue and yellow into white. Meadow fescue swept across the blueberry field, its green stems striped with red, the panicles plaited and falling in a haze, spilling bronze and purple. In damp bruises along the side meadow, slough grass blossomed into racks of combs. At the edge of the blueberry field swamp chess turned white, its keeled scales aground and dry. Tufts of shear grass embroidered the lane while mare's tail wound through the cow pond in a fine crewel. Necklaces of plants surrounded the blue lake behind the outlet at Beaver River, the first string chair-maker's rush, its stems luminously green, behind them the dark shadows of bulrushes.

In August I often meandered down the lane and walked the bluff to Beaver River. To return home I squared the walk, strolling up the dirt road from the outlet to Route 1, where I turned east toward Ma's Property. In August light thinned and resembled fragile, aged glass on the face of a gable clock. Late in the afternoon gulls returned to the lake, wheeling then dropping onto the water like pearls slipping a string. A marsh hawk looped over a pasture, the bird's flight loose then suddenly taunt as it fell toward the ground. On the headland shrubby cinquefoil bloomed. Fat and yellow, the flowers swung across sight like small pendulums. Garish boutonnieres of live forever waved purple beside the dirt road, and from a ditch cattails rose like morning suits. Moths clung to evening primrose. Resembling faded petals, the moths appeared glazed, pale yellow in early morning and just before dusk pink. While seedpods of blue flag were lumpy as fists, those of tall buttercups resembled minute jugs with spigots. One afternoon I walked through the white spruce behind Ma's Property. Tired, I sat atop the trunk of a toppled tree. A small garden of mosses, asters, and wild sarsaparilla clung to the umbrella of dirt raised by tree roots. Amid the plants was mountain wood fern, its subleaflets sharp as Florentine stitches.

Although Solomon may not have been arrayed like the wild flowers of field and shoreline, at times I imagined writing hothouse prose. Occasionally I longed for an exotic life. In my mind I planted smoke trees behind the headland and Nootka cypress along the road, the branches of this last switching like the hair of Afghan hounds. I replaced the tamaracks in the windbreak with European larch. The golden elder beside the barn had aged into weed, so I dug it up and in the hole stuffed a five-stamen tamarisk, its skeletal twigs rosy with flowers. Resembling adjectives, exotic and cosmetic, the plantings did not make my prose or life garish. Consequently I spent a morning transforming the blueberry field into a Victorian garden. Flower beds bloomed like Tiffany glass, and gravel paths twisted ornate as the backs of playing cards. Behind purple bundles of heliotrope, red braids dangled like macramé from love-lies-bleeding. Racks of orange turbans bloomed on tiger lilies, their long stamens laces, the anthers red clasps. Below the lilies stood zinnias, the State Fair Mixture with flowers big as platters, the petals red, yellow, and purple spoons. Scarlet canna lilies sprayed from a round bed, and castor bean turned the legs of an equilateral triangle rickety. While the leaves of canna lilies resembled plumes, those of castor bean seemed grills, yellow veins running wiry through them. Here and there I planted dahlias, my favorite being black wizard, its color dark claret one moment, chocolate red the next.

Transforming people, and prose, is harder than transplanting flowers. When Odometer Hackett was a boy, he left Carthage to seek his fortune. Last year he returned burdened with a big bank account and ponderous airs. "Even if Odo eats his soup with a silver fork," Loppie Groat told the crowd at Ankerrow's, "he's no better than the rest of us." Despite occasional hankerings, I'm more a pansy-and-marigold than I am a tiger-lily or love-lies-bleeding kind of guy. To me simplicity seems perennial, not annual. During the summer Turlow Gutheridge wrote and described doings in Carthage. In June, Omir Beardsworthy attended a family reunion in West Virginia. Family from four states attended the gathering, and the house was so crowded that relatives bunked together. When Omir was told he had to share a mattress with Cousin Willy, he said, "I've done lots of things in my life, but there are some things I won't do. I will not go to bed with a live man or a dead woman."

In 1947 Delima Gimard married Diggory Pickingale and moved to Milk Paws, fourteen miles from Carthage. At the wedding Delima made her cousin Alfaretta promise to visit. Her word aside, Alfaretta did not see Delima again until this past June when the two met at the state fair in Nashville, Delima having won a blue ribbon for butterbeans and Alfaretta a red for watercress. "You promised when I married that you would come see me," Delima said accusingly. "Yes, my dear, so I did," Alfaretta answered. "But just think about the weather we've been having." Near the end of the letter Turlow wrote that Loppie Groat's cat Belle Starr died. Belle was such a fine mouser that Loppie had her stuffed. Afterward Loppie put Belle in the loft in the barn. As a general rule dead cats are not as good mousers as live cats. "Still," Loppie told Turlow, "corpses don't get hungry, and just so long as you move them once or twice a week and then occasionally hide behind the hay and meow, a dead cat will do a respectable job of keeping rodents down."

I read mail beside the road in front of the house. This summer Francis did not attend camp. I set two lawn chairs against the picket fence, and after the mail arrived, we sat in the chairs and chatted. Not long after mail was delivered, tourist buses traveling from Yarmouth to Halifax roared by. Francis and I smiled and waved. Generally tourists waved back. Often we imagined conversation on the bus. "Canada really is the first of frost and the last of pea time," a man said. "People have nothing better to do than wave at buses." "Nova Scotians might be slow," his wife answered, "but aren't they friendly? And isn't it nice to think that we are bringing excitement to their lives?"

Vicki and I are not travelers. Except for driving to Yarmouth to buy groceries, we rarely left Beaver River. On Fridays Vicki dropped Francis and me on Main Street and drove to Sobey's grocery. Francis and I roamed town for two hours before walking out Starrs Road and joining Vicki at the mall. Some days we explored Park and Prince, Carlton and High Streets, studying Victorian houses. Other days we wandered the waterfront, eating muffins at Joshua's and watching gulls drift like snow above the red building that once served as terminal for the Boston and Yarmouth steamship line.

Little happened on our strolls. I complimented gardeners, and one day a young man wearing a tee-shirt with "Jesus Saves" stamped on the chest, handed me a broadside, across the top of which was printed, "Where Does God's Word Say That You Are Going When You Die? Heaven Or Hell?" Suddenly my friend Roger Hibbard popped into mind. A bachelor, Roger is the sort of man for whom femininity holds no attraction. One evening before dinner as Roger was sipping a libation, a telemarketer called. "May I speak to Mrs. Hibbard, the lady of the house?" the man said. "Mrs. Hibbard?" Roger answered, eyeing water beading on the outside of his glass. "Mrs. Hibbard died this morning. She was an absolute bitch, and I am damned glad she's dead. But if you must speak to her, you can telephone Hades. Use the hot line."

Although walks were as circular as paths in my Victorian garden, I planned journeys so that I could visit a lavatory, either at the Ferry Terminal, the Tourist Centre, or at the County Museum on Collier Street. At the Tourist Centre vases of wild flowers stood beside sinks, and the lavatory resembled an arbor. At the museum the lavatory was next to the kitchen, and often the director offered me tea and cake. One Friday in August Francis and I grazed on fudge at the Tourist Centre. The mayor of Yarmouth was present. Each July the town sponsors Seafest, a festival celebrating western Nova Scotia. On the last day a parade winds through downtown. In past years the mayor led the parade, riding in a white Cadillac convertible with cow horns bolted to the hood. This summer the mayor did not appear. When I asked about his absence, he said the car broke down, adding that this was the first parade he'd missed in a decade. "Humph," I responded. "You must have been up to something, some malfeasance of office that so stirred the ire of the citizenry that you dared not risk being seen in public." The mayor flinched. Then after staring at me, trying to place my face, he spun about and walked across the room far from the fudge and lemonade.

At the museum I roamed exhibitions, searching for items with which to bait paragraphs. The great, great-grandmother of Lwood and Psamme Handspiker, Nokomis Brown was the first child born in Milk Paws. Except for a sampler, all traces of Nokomis's life had vanished. Nokomis was good at needlepoint, and at the museum I studied stitches in order to patch Nokomis's sampler together: saw-toothed, four-sided, Algerian eye, rococo, rice, and long-armed cross. Using simple cross-stitched rows, Nokomis, I decided, fashioned a strawberry vine border, each fruit pinched between two rectangular green leaves. The sampler itself was fourteen inches square. Scrolled across the bottom were the alphabet, both in print and cursive; numbers one to ten; Nokomis's name and age, and finally the year, 1884. At the top of the sampler stood a two-story, red-brick house with five windows in the front, a door ornamented with a pair of Gone-with-the-Wind lamps, and then two tall chimneys on the roof, both smoking. Persimmon trees stood on each side of the house, blue and yellow birds perched in branches and dogs sleeping near the trunks, a brown dog to the right of the house, and an orange dog to the left. Below the house appeared a rhyme. "Jesus," Nokomis sewed,

> permit thy gracious name to stand
> As the first effort of a young girl's hand.
> And while her fingers o'er this canvas move
> Engage her tender soul to seek thy love.
> With thy dear children may she share a part
> And write thy name thyself upon her heart.

As the museum supplied ready-to-wear raiment for sentences, so visits furnished actual dress. One afternoon Eric, the director, showed me a necktie he purchased for fifty cents at Smitty's. A warehouse on Prospect Street, Smitty's imported bales of used clothes from the United States. On the front of Eric's tie big-horned sheep perched atop red mountains. Behind the peaks fog lumbered over the horizon. Instead of moisture, however, a menagerie of ghostly animals blew through the haze, most of the creatures large animals of African plain and forest—an elephant, half a lion, a brace of leopards, and the head of a hippopotamus, its jaws spread in a toothy yawn. On my admiring the design, Eric said Smitty's had a zoo of ties featuring scenes from natural history. After Vicki finished shopping, she drove me to Smitty's, so I could animate my tie rack. Alas, only bird ties remained. Wearing red plaid and clutching bagpipes between their wings, a flock of pheasants sailed up the weave of a blue tie. On another tie green and yellow budgies perched in cages, the birds leaning against each other, their eyes pink and almost as big as dimes.

The ties did not molt through imagination. Consequently I left the aerie and examined sport coats. I had not bought a jacket in eleven years, and my wardrobe had tattered, resembling a catbird's nest abandoned to winter and mice. Sartorial fortune smiled on me. On a bar hung a pale blue coat. The coat was my size, forty-three long. Even better, it was on sale, marked down from $4.00 to $2.00. Once tax was included the coat cost $2.30 Canadian, or $1.66 American.

The animals I saw in Beaver River were not cut from an Alpine fabric. Six voles, each the size of my thumbnail, huddled beneath a board. A woodland mouse bounced across the lane. A young hare flattened herself between mounds of sphagnum moss. Three red-bellied snakes dozed under a slab of pressed wood, and a muskrat paddled across the outlet at Beaver River. At dusk a mink slipped down the headland like a shadow and on the beach burrowed into a dead gull and scraped a meal out of the bird's innards.

As the little doings of daily life interest me more than the vibrations of the big world, so small creatures intrigued me more than large. A cuff of blue aphids hung around a stem of meadow sweet. At the top of the stem the larva of a lacewing chewed the cuff. Lower down the stem ants lapped up droplets of honeydew excreted by the aphids. As the ants drank the clear liquid, their stomachs puffed and glowed like amber. Rosy aphids splattered stems of flat-topped asters. Often the aphids bucked, thrusting their hind legs in the air, and from a distance the stems seemed frayed. While looking at aphids, I noticed galls—on the stems of asters ball galls the size of marbles. Often the galls grew above each other in spools, transforming the stems into small bedposts. On meadowsweet spirea pod galls formed along the midribs of leaves. Pods turned leaves dwarfish, the tips of the leaves rising spiked above the galls. I opened a pea-sized gall. Inside I found nine yellow maggots, each with a red line running from its head down through its body. The silk tents of skeletonizers clung to the undersides of leaves on apple trees. Hanging from the ends of some tents were tiny brown pupal cases. I collapsed a tent three-fourths of an inch long and an eighth of an inch wide. Inside were a yellow maggot and its droppings, minute balls of dung clumped together like roe.

If interest measures a person, I don't stand tall. In Nova Scotia I spent more time looking at inchworms than I did fretting about inhumanity. A looper grazed on fireweed. Two and an eighth inches long, the worm transformed itself into a twig during daylight. While its lower legs buckled themselves to the stem of the plant, its upper clasped the midvein of a leaf, the insect's body stretching tight between the two parts of the plant, resembling a strut. After a shower, water balled on the worm before rolling out of symmetry into a small wave, the liquid slipping down the insect just as it did the stem of the plant.

A silver and black inchworm stitched buttonholes across lichens on white spruce. A green looper with a quiver of brown arrowheads decorating its back circled a spike of timothy, the spike bending into a curve and resembling a thin finger and the worm itself a wedding band warped by years. Insects punctuated days with endless commas: bee flies in the woody bog, along the lane marbled spiders inside tents made from bay leaves, and on the headland cranberry bog copper butterflies. While the butterflies whisked over heather, raising wings when they lit so that they looked like yellow speckled leaves, donaciinae beetles sprayed out of grass then suddenly vanished, tumbling quickly to the ground, shredding into small splinters. One afternoon I watched a white mite crawl through hairs on the abdomen of a gray cross spider. Later I followed a red-tailed ichneumon as it crossed the meadow searching the grass for prey. This summer I spent much time gazing at the sky. I enjoyed nights when the moon was full. Some evenings the moon rolled against the horizon and bounced into cirrostratus clouds, breaking them into light. Other nights beveled altocumulus shined like beaten silver. When small cumulus clouds drifted across the sky on clear nights, they tarnished the meadows, for a moment staining the blue fields black.

Usually during summers I roam fields and woods at night. This year I stayed in the house reading, not, however, good books, but oddments. In the 1930s and 1940s, Vicki's grandmother owned the Green Tree Inn in Hebron, just outside Yarmouth. When the present owner explored the attic this spring, she discovered two boxes of books, stored there by Vicki's Aunt Sallie fifty years ago. Most volumes were textbooks used by Sallie at the Columbus School for Girls in Columbus, Ohio, during the 1920s. John Lester, who taught at the Hill School in Pottstown, Pennsylvania, wrote *A Spelling Review* (1923). Lester based the book, he explained, "on a study of the 775 words most frequently misspelled in College Entrance Examinations in English." In the 1920s writing played a greater role in college admissions than did spelling. For students whose parents could sign tuition checks, schools overlooked penchants for putting *e* before *i* after all letters except *c*. Among the books was *The Caravel,* the 1929 yearbook of the Columbus Academy, brother school to the School for Girls. A young man bound for the University of Virginia gave the annual to Sallie. Twelve boys graduated from the school in 1929. One graduate had not decided where to attend college. Four, however, were going to Princeton, two to Harvard, two to Ohio State, one to Yale, one to the Naval Academy, and Sallie's friend to Virginia.

The yearbook devoted a page to each senior. "Last fall," one sketch recounted, "Dave showed admirable spirit in immediately turning out for the football team, but alas—his mother stepped in and offered to give him a new automobile if he didn't play. And Dave, being human, took the automobile; for which we do not criticize him in the least, since anyone in his place would have done exactly the same thing." "In 1921," another sketch began, "a dapper little fellow blessed with a beaming schoolgirl complexion and not very much else entered upon the eight-year stretch at the end of which lies graduation and college." To be specific, Princeton lay at the end of the little tike's stretch as it did that of "the warmest friend" of the opposite sex in the class. When their camps in Maine closed in August, Edward and Eliza came to Nova Scotia. The yearbook intrigued Edward, both the sketches and the names of students. "Ogden Peabody Outhwaite, known to classmates as Ockel," he said, "now, Daddy, that is a name for an essay."

I unpacked the books. Latin textbooks filled a shelf in the study. In his *Beginning Latin* (1919), Percy Oakland Place, professor of Latin at Syracuse, explained "Why American Boys and Girls Should Study Latin," a matter over which I had fussed considerably. Despite my urging them to learn Spanish, the children study Latin. Unfortunately, Place's apologia did not satisfy me. "The study of Latin," he wrote, "is an intensive study of English. Besides its importance for a mastery of French, Spanish, and Italian, the study of Latin fosters habits of persistence, thoroughness, and accuracy; it cultivates the power to understand the thoughts of others and to express one's own. Translating is 'laboratory work in literature,' admirable exercise in expression, insuring steadily increasing power in the use of a varied and rich vocabulary as the great authors, Caesar, Cicero, and Vergil, are successively read."

Mathematics textbooks filled another shelf. In the introduction to *Fundamentals of High School Mathematics* Harold Rugg and John Clark, professors in the Teachers College at Columbia, claimed they used the "scientific method" to construct their book, adding that "the traditional course of study in high school mathematics needs to be completely reconstructed," an event which occurs every decade with students reaping few benefits but also with little damage being done to mathematics. Many early settlers of Massachusetts thought if children ate boiled pigs' brains sprinkled with parsley the children would develop into bright adults. Nowadays people believe that a diet fatty with education nurtures intelligence. As a result industrial education has spread across the country, spewing out clouds of graduates who blow through society, learning rusting their common sense like acid rain. For my part I'm not sure man knows enough to ask the right questions, much less supply answers. When Quintus Tyler told students at the Male and Female Select School in Carthage that a camel could go forty days without water, Billie Dinwidder raised his hand. "That's all well and good, but I've heard that before," Billie said. "What I want to know is how long can a camel go with water."

Seams of thought run through the bindings of books. Occasionally, though, a thought breaks surface, and I pry it loose and glue it to a paragraph. Among the books owned by Sallie was Philip Gosse's *Wonders of The Great Deep; or the Physical, Animal, Geological, and Vegetable Curiosities of the Ocean, with an Account of Submarine Explorations Beneath the Sea*, published in Philadelphia in 1874. In the preface Gosse said he endeavored "to describe, with some minuteness of detail, a few of the many objects of interest more or less directly connected with the Sea, and especially to lead youthful readers to associate with the phenomena of Nature, habitual thoughts of God." Beneath *The Great Deep* lay *The Story of My Heart*, the autobiography of Richard Jefferies, published in 1883. Like Gosse, Jefferies was a naturalist. Unlike Gosse, however, Jefferies found no traces of a creator in the natural world. "There being nothing human in nature or the universe, and all things being ultra-human and without design, shape, or purpose, I conclude," Jefferies declared, "that no deity has anything to do with nature. There is no god in nature, nor in any matter anywhere, either in the clods on the earth or in the composition of the stars." Rather than making Jefferies melancholy, the conclusion cheered him. "This," he explained, "is a foundation of hope, because, if the present condition of things were ordered by a superior power, there would be no possibility of improving it for the better in spite of that power. Acknowledging that no such direction exists, all things become at once plastic to our will."

Would that I possessed Gosse's certainty, for then I could imagine my descriptions of tree and flower revealed more than ease with words. Alas, not only the deity, but all deities have vanished from hill and field. Even worse, Jefferies's comforting belief that man has the capacity to improve both natural and moral life seems naïve. In September I read excerpts from Gosse and Jefferies to Turlow Gutheridge. "Wise men," Turlow said, "can pluck physic out of weeds." Like Jefferies's "things," words are plastic, and if in age of disbelief words cannot reflect awareness of a deity, they can entertain. At the conclusion of the preface, Gosse justified describing small matters in detail. According to Samuel Purchas, Gosse wrote, Nicostratus once found a curious piece of wood, "and being wondered at by one, and asked what pleasure he could take to stand as he did, still gazing on the picture, answered, 'Hadst thou mine eyes, my friend, thou wouldst not wonder, but rather be ravished, as I am, at the inimitable art of this rare and admirable piece.'"

Much as insects intrigued me, so small things amid the books interested me, typically, a bookmark advertising Rand McNally's children's books. On one side of the bookmark appeared a map of the world—Europe, Australia, and islands in the South Pacific colored green; Africa and North America, pink; and Asia and South America, yellow. On the reverse side was a list of Elizabeth Gordon's books, including *Watermelon Pete* and *Granddad Coco Nut's Party,* each costing sixty-five cents, then the Dolly and Molly series, at thirty-five cents apiece, *Dolly and Molly at the Seashore,* and *at the Circus, on Christmas Day,* and *Dolly and Molly and the Farmerman.* Folded in *The New Gradatim* (1895), "An Easy Latin Translation Book For Beginners," was an advertisement for "Penelope Posters." Sold by the New Book Library at 68 East Broad Street in Columbus, the posters were address labels. An inch square, the labels came in rolls of five hundred or a thousand, "gummed and perforated, ready to tear off and affix" to letters. Labels were sold in round boxes, some boxes decorated with flowers, others creating "an embossed leather effect." "An ideal gift," the advertisement stated, "for any occasion, acceptable to both men and women." For women hanging boxes suspended on ribbons were available; for men, a desk stand could be purchased. While a "Hanging Style Box" containing a thousand labels cost $2.50, a "Box with Desk Stand" and labels cost $3.00.

Among the books was *The History of English Literature* written by Reuben Halleck and published in 1900 by the American Book Company. The history belonged to Vicki's grandmother, who wrote her name and address inside the front cover: Margaret Fuller Jones, 1175 East Broad Street. At the beginning of Halleck's essay on Tennyson, sandwiched between pages 462 and 463, was a small card made from rough paper and measuring two and five-eighths by three and five-eighths inches. Scrolled across the top of the card in black capitals was "WILLING WORKERS LYCEUM OF SHILOH BAPTIST CHURCH APPLICATION FOR MEMBERSHIP." Printed at the bottom of the card in cursive were the signatures of the president and the secretary of the Lyceum, "Bro. Carl Guienna" and "Sis. Mary Chapman."

Although membership cost only a dime, Vicki's grandmother did not sign the card. After examining the card, I read Halleck's study of Tennyson. Halleck praised Tennyson's lyricism and "dignity of thought." As example of lyricism, Halleck quoted lines from *Maud*:

> And the woodbine spices are wafted abroad,
> And the musk of the rose is blown.
> For a breeze of morning moves,
> And the planet of Love is on high,
> Beginning to faint in the light that she loves
> On a bed of daffodil sky.

For elevated thought Halleck cited the "Idylls of the King" and quoted King Arthur's advice from "The Passing of Arthur":

> More things are wrought by prayer
> Than this world dreams of. Wherefore, let thy voice
> Rise like a fountain for me night and day.
> For what are men better than sheep or goats
> That nourish a blind life within the brain,
> If, knowing God, they lift not hands of prayer
> Both for themselves and those who call them friend?
> For so the whole round earth is every way
> Bound by gold chains about the feet of God.

The two quotations, I thought, explained both why Vicki's grandmother pondered joining the Lyceum and why she did not sign the card, the lines from "The Passing of Arthur" urging her toward a life of prayer and its muscular consorts duty and high seriousness, the lyricism of *Maud* so celebrating soft beauty for beauty's sake that it weakened the will, elevating melodious days above action. "How do you know that's true?" Vicki said at dinner after I showed her card and book. "How do you know the card even belonged to my grandmother?" "I know it," I said. "People who write know things." "Crap," Vicki said.

"Men are believed," Turlow Gutheridge once said, "as they are beloved." A bachelor, Turlow was unaware that among human females domesticity produces skepticism faster than their mates father children. In books, though, lurks entertainment more satisfying than connubial doings. In one box were four copies of *The Century Handbook of Writing,* written by Garland Greever and Easley S. Jones and published in New York in 1924. Because the handbook was sensible I brought two copies back to Connecticut. *Borned,* the book stated, was "a monstrosity for *born.* 'I was *born* (not *borned*) in 1899.'" While *disremember* was "not in good use," *used to could* was "very crude." Under the category "Barbarisms, Improprieties, Slang" was "language strained or distorted for novel effect." Instead of "ate at a good restaurant," the user of vicious slang "performed the feed act at a bang-up gastronomic emporium." Instead of "hit into centerfield," a baseball player "bingled a tall drive that made the horsehide ramble out into center garden." I jotted the phrases down, thinking them "corking," this last word damned by Messrs. Jones and Greever because it led "to a mental habit of phonographic repetition, with no resort to independent thinking."

In the essay on Tennyson, Halleck quoted two stanzas from "The Palace of Art." Ancient tapestries hung from walls in the palace. Across one tapestry "angry waves" broke against "an iron coast." "You seem'd to hear them climb and fall and roar rock-thwarted," Tennyson wrote. The stanzas brought to mind a tale told by Karen, a friend in Port Maitland. Thirty years ago Karen's brother Jim committed suicide. He left a note saying he had leaped into "The Churn," a savage inlet near Yarmouth where tides whipped around rocks and shattered into undertows. Karen said her brother tied a weight to his waist because, she explained, "the rope or whatever he used cut him in two." Only the lower half of the body washed ashore. But, Karen recounted, "we knew who it was." Jim never wore a belt or socks and did not carry a wallet. The body was shoeless and sockless, and the back pockets of the trousers were empty. The shoes, Karen said, resembled a pair that Jim had brought home a week earlier. "We searched his room for them, but they were gone. Also the trousers had been bought at the store where Jim purchased all his clothes." "We couldn't tell much," Karen continued, "from the legs themselves. They had been in the water a long time, and crabs had gotten to them. Without the trousers and shoes, you understand, a person would have been forced to look twice, or maybe more, before he realized they were legs."

I understood. The ways of going are various. The day before Karen described her brother's death, I found a dead dance fly in the woods. Sap had leaked from a pitch tube in a spruce onto wild sarsaparilla. On one leaf the pitch shined like water. The fly must have seen the droplet and lighting on the leaf to drink gotten stuck. As the insect struggled, it sank into the pitch, the fast whirl of its airy waltz slowing to an amber drowning. Eight days before Edward and Eliza came to Nova Scotia, I discovered a cecropia moth caterpillar on an elderberry. Three and one-quarter inches long, the caterpillar bulged like a stack of green transformers, black hairs bursting electric out of yellow, red, and blue tubercles. Along the sides of the caterpillar narrow spiracles opened, at first white and sparking, but later reminding me of windows stretching along an airplane glowing in an evening sky. Tachnid flies lay eggs on cecropia caterpillars. After hatching the maggots bore into the caterpillars' bodies. The pupae graze on a caterpillar until they reach full growth. Then they chew out of the caterpillar and drop to the ground, in the process killing their host. The eggs are white, and I studied my caterpillar carefully, so that if a Tachnid fly laid eggs on it I could flick them off. The caterpillar intrigued Eliza, and on arriving in Beaver River, she named it Hank. After a week, however, the caterpillar grew so fat that Eliza changed the name to Montelle. Unlike Hank, which smacked of hard days riding twigs and rounding up leaves, Montelle seemed sybaritic, a name for a couch insect, one that lolled about, plates of greenery stacked around him.

For four years I managed the affairs of my father's brother Coleman. For three of the years Coleman lived in a nursing home in Houston. On August 27, the manager of the home called and told me that Coleman had died. Early the next morning I found Montelle falling off the elderberry, his body bent double, his thoracic legs dangling, only the anal proleg and the last two pairs of abdominal prolegs clutching a twig. Green oozed from Montelle's head, and his body appeared crumpled, his skin sagging like a suit tossed on a wire coat hanger. A pair of shield-backed bugs scurried across his back, and I wondered if they had sucked life out of him. I brought Montelle back to the house. "Oh, no," Eliza said when she saw him, "first Uncle Coleman, now Montelle."

In August Francis, Vicki, and I spent a day in Annapolis Royal. In the graveyard stood the tombstone of Isabella Runciman. She died at thirty-eight in 1834. "She was an affectionate partner and sincere friend," the stone declared. "Her husband mourns her departure, with four small children who do not feel their loss." My children never met Coleman, and Montelle meant more to them than a great-uncle. After breakfast I wrapped Montelle in a scrap of dishcloth, and Eliza and I buried him in the side meadow. The next morning on a small spruce I counted eleven spider webs shining like silver doilies. Water boatmen drifted across the cow pond; a blue and black darner dozed on pickerel weed, and web worms spun a nest in an alder. Fall was in air and on mind. The time had come to return to Connecticut. That afternoon I arranged Coleman's funeral on the telephone. "Mario, can we put this on my charge card?" I said. "And what card would that be, sir?" he asked. "MasterCard," I said. "That's just fine," Mario answered. "You should have charged everything on Visa," Vicki said later. "Uncle Coleman is traveling to a new country." "Did you get airline miles for putting the funeral on your charge card?" Francis asked. "No," I said. "I don't have that kind of card."

A week later we returned to Storrs. Waiting for me was a questionnaire from the funeral home. Sketched on the front of the questionnaire was a vase of canna lilies. "We wish to extend our sincere sympathy to you," a paragraph stated. "It was an honor and a privilege to be able to serve you during this difficult period, and in order to be of service to others we would greatly appreciate your assistance." A list of questions followed. "What influenced you to use our facilities?" question nine asked. Under the question was the phrase "recommended by," followed by five choices: relative, clergy, doctor, hospital, or friend. A choice of six reasons came next: family served previously, knew staff member, church affiliation, advertising, reputation, and location. Until I reached the eleventh inquiry, I wrote "not applicable" by the questions. This question, however, made me pause. "The appearance of the deceased was," the entry stated, "Excellent," "Good," "Fair," or "Poor." "Good Lord," I said aloud and wrote "peaked." But then the paper lilies sprouted, and I drew a line through "peaked" and wrote "sufficient unto the day."

Autumnal

In September I read Thomas Hood's ode "Autumn."

> I saw old Autumn in the misty morn
> Stand shadowless like Silence, listening
> To silence, for no lonely bird would sing
> Into his ear from woods forlorn.

That afternoon I roamed wood and meadow. Although flowers on Joe-Pye weed had begun to unravel into yarn, monarch butterflies hovered above the plants, wings snapping brightly. A green anglewing basked in a sand pit, and a milk snake dozed under a board. Dusty finches ripped seeds from Canada thistle. Moss draped over a stump like a caftan, navel cap mushrooms wedging through the fabric like coins. While tiger moth caterpillars grazed across milkweed, tufts of black, white, yellow, and orange hair sweeping over their backs like headdresses, earwigs chewed seedpods into long houses. Virginia creeper screwed itself around a plant. Clinging to the creeper was a pandorus sphinx moth caterpillar. The caterpillar had pulled its head and the first two segments of its body into the third segment, making the segment bulge like the end of a toilet plunger.

Hood's silent English autumn did not resemble fall in New England. Scarlet rained through red maples. On sour cherry trees glazed fruits tinkled, and fragments of yellow hung like refrains on spicebush. Late in October I returned to the woods. Storms had scrubbed leaves from trees, leaving branches dark and rinsed. Nights were chilly, and fall was aging into winter. Nevertheless, the forest was not silent. Titmice and chickadees foraged gossipy through scrub. A chipmunk hurried across a ditch, leaves sizzling under foot. Blue jays perched in the tops of trees, their calls swaying, no longer smothered by leaves. A red-tailed hawk slid from a limb and skidded down a ridge. Juncos scurried over corn stubble while a Cooper's hawk glared at me from a white oak.

Instead of diminishing, season changed. Even the broken land behind the sewerage treatment plant seemed whole. Bundles of fruit bent silverberry to the ground. Leaves on sweet fern dried into fragrance, black oozing oily across them in pools. On quaking aspen and large-toothed popular leaves rowed the air. Cones of scouring rush shined pale blue above gravel. Deptford pinks flickered in grass, and heath asters bristled yellow and white. While cattails burst into ticking, pine cone galls ripened on silky willows. Phragmites sifted the light, the dying leaves pinching yellow from the air and the plumes appearing rags thick with silver polish. At dusk the reeds turned brown; moist chill seeped into hollows, and for a moment as I walked home, autumn seemed old and silent. By the kitchen door, however, the clematis which Vicki had planted in June was blooming, its blue and white flowers youthful as Willow plate.

People stumble into habits of thought much as they do of speech. For me September has long ended summer, the beginning of a new semester not a start but the continuation of an academic year, one during which both days and classes turn wintry. I have taught so long that I doubt not only the promises of education but education itself. Blood, as the saying puts it, follows the vein, no matter the clots raised by schooling. "Poor folks have poor ways, and rich folks damn mean ones," Hink Ruunt said recently, "and nothing you do in the classroom will change that." Because I question the effects of education, each fall the story of a Harvard entomologist comes to mind. The man studied fleas for two decades, finally teaching them to jump when he said "hop." After the fleas learned to obey the command, the scientist sliced off the insects' legs. Immediately the fleas stopped jumping, no matter how loud the scientist yelled. After analyzing data for twenty-six months, the scientist concluded that the reason the fleas ceased hopping was that they heard with their legs. "Once the specimens' tibias were removed," the scientist wrote in the *New England Journal of Medicine,* "they were deaf. Although I spent a year trying to teach *Pulex irritans* sign language, I was not successful."

Of course matters are often not what they seem in odes, in the lab, or even in the classroom. In September Edward entered high school. At ease with numbers, Edward enrolled in third-year mathematics. At the end of September, I asked about the class. "It's all right," he said, "except students work in groups, and since I'm younger than anyone else, I have to work alone." "Alone?" Edward's teacher said at open house the following week. "Edward's not alone. He studies with a girl, sometimes two girls." Suddenly schooldays like autumn seemed joyous, not forlorn.

Instead of appearing shadowy, misty morns and evenings were crowded with full-bodied doings. "How does Isabelle like her new school?" I asked the mother of a sixth grader. That morning the biology teacher explained reproductive matters in lurid detail. At the end of class the teacher promised to review the material the next day. "A review!" Isabelle said to her mother. "How could you forget anything so horrible?" Although birds might not carol across stanzas of autumnal verse, birds accompanied by their metaphoric consorts, bees, transformed classrooms into musical hothouses. One morning a student asked me to criticize a poem she wrote. I read two stanzas then stopped. "Where do I put my breasts when I want to play ball?" the first stanza asked. Although not punctuated, the second stanza was cut from the same foundation cloth:

> I come from you petting me and offering
> To sew my blouse
> Through my tears I smile
> A blouse aside
> Your mouth searches
> Hungrily for my breasts
> Love's still closed eyes moist from
> Still closed crying

Don't worry
A kitten can't see yet either
Loves-child's man hands
Cradle my head—suckle my tit.

"Jennifer," I said, "do you know about the man who agreed to sleep in a haunted house after folks gave him a frying pan, a rasher of bacon, a jug of whiskey, and ten dollars?" Jennifer hadn't heard the tale. Just after the man cooked the bacon and while he was lifting the jug to his mouth, a black shadow tumbled down the chimney and said, "It ain't but us two tonight." "By God, it won't be but you one," the man exclaimed dropping the whiskey and crashing through the door shouting, "rabbits, foxes, flying squirrels, out of the way. Let somebody run what can run!" With that I heisted myself out of my chair and hurrying through the door dashed down the hall, leaving Jennifer to extract symbolism from the story.

No matter how fleet, a person cannot escape the fecundity of autumn. Three weeks ago nights turned cold. Vicki brought my red jacket down from the attic, and I wore it to the university library Thursday night. I read in the library until eleven-thirty then strolled home across campus. Besides cold, revelry and music were on the breeze. As I crossed Gilbert Road, wind whipped down the hill, and I cinched the collar of my jacket around my neck. I didn't consider weather long because as I stepped off the curb, a window crashed open. A girl stuck her head outdoors and shouted, "Hey, you in the red jacket. You want to fuck?" How common, I thought, hurrying into the shadows. "There no hope for such animals," I muttered on the way home. A night's rest often changes hasty perception. In the bright day, especially that of an autumn morning, the irritations of cool evening often vanish. As I pondered the greeting over breakfast, the invitation no longer irritated. Indeed it seemed rather appealing. Although a little too natural to be charming, the invitation went down easily with Earl Grey tea, granola, and a banana.

Dawn rises twice for no man. Such meaty courses are not standard scholarly fare. For the next two weeks I worked late in the library. Although I wore the red jacket and walked home, always managing to cross Gilbert Road precisely at eleven-thirty, the invitation was not repeated. Other happenings, however, kept fall vital. This past summer one of my students worked at Johnny Appleseed's Farm in Ellington, selling peaches and apples. In September she gave me a peach as big as a grapefruit, a Crestheaven, "the last peach of the summer," she said. She also gave me a brochure describing the farm because, she added, "I know you'll write about it."

For the scampering generations autumn is gathering season. Searching for food, animals wander from summer's keeps. During the year a groundhog lived under the back stoop of the Kappa Kappa Gamma sorority house. When I cycled home from the English department, I often saw girls feeding the groundhog carrots. One Wednesday in the middle of October I discovered the groundhog dead in the road. On getting off my bicycle in order to stuff the animal into a trash can, I noticed something that made the season sing. By the groundhog's head lay a long-stemmed red rose.

Until the November rains, asphalt furrows remain lumpy with bone and hide. Although automobiles harvest animals every October, individual autumns differ from each other. During the past decade I lost interest in football. Autumn is now soccer season. This fall Eliza played on a team of twelve- and thirteen-year-old girls from three towns in eastern Connecticut: Willington, Ashford, and Mansfield. The team reached the quarter-finals of a tournament, and I spent Saturdays driving across the state. In part I carted players because parents know I am the slowest driver in town. "Once you get behind Sam," a parent said, "relax because you won't be going anywhere fast." One Saturday early in October I left home at 12:45 in the afternoon and after picking up Christine, Eleanor, and Kara headed for Danbury. I got home at 8:34 that night. While I drove, the girls played "the marriage game," an indoor, counting-out version of plucking petals from daisies to see whom one will marry, a rich man or a poor man, for example, or where one will live, in a big or a small house. One game predicted that Eliza would marry a wealthy man, live in a log cabin, ride a tricycle to work, and have a butler. I was the butler, expenditures for college having so depleted my savings that I had to earn my keep in old age.

Each summer I send Eliza to camp in Maine for seven weeks, and I heard Eleanor ask about camp. "Did you make lots of friends at camp?" "Yes," Eliza said, "but none of them would be my friends at school." Camp costs forty-four and a half times the royalties I earned this year on ten books, and Eliza's response made me blink. But then a big truck rumbled past in the left lane, and I thrust camp back into summer and shutting ears and pasting eyelids open studied traffic.

The girls played at Kenosia Park. Next to the park was a small lake. Before the game I walked around the lake. A fisherman hunched silently in a rowboat, and two mallards foraged amid cattails. Friends told me that western Connecticut differed from eastern Connecticut. A person often finds what he expects. Three men stood on a sandy beach, behind them golf balls piled like leaves. Instead of whacking balls down a fairway or scooping them out of the rough as is customary in the environs of Mansfield, the men knocked balls into the lake. Exotic habits of strange cultures intrigue me, so I watched the men for eight minutes. Not once did they speak, this despite two or three of their shots bouncing like stones skipped across water by a dreamy boy. Unlike the golfers, parents of Danbury girls seemed ordinary, resembling those of us from Mansfield who had trekked across the state. An offside call exercised a man, and he yelled at the referee. "For heaven's sakes," I said, "this is just a girls' game." "Just a girls' game!" a covey of mothers on the sideline exclaimed, before adding, "now you're offside!"

The following Saturday Eliza's team played a team from Wallingford. City girls are linguistically more advanced than country girls. Eliza marked the best player on the Wallingford team. Not only did the girl slam the ball into the goal, but she also slapped words about. When the referee called a foul on her, she shouted, "That's bullshit! You suck!" The referee gave the girl a yellow card, and for the rest of the game she dribbled words about properly. "That girl," I said to Eliza after the game, "was a little outspoken." "Outspoken!" Eliza exclaimed, "she cussed the whole game." "But, Daddy," Eliza continued, "I'm afraid I used the f-word a lot myself. I stood behind the girl and said 'f—— you.' Only I just whispered because I was frightened that if she heard me she would beat me up."

The next Sunday I drove the gang to Sherman, fifteen miles north of Danbury. I left at 7:30 and got home at 4:02. Eliza dashed into the lavatory, and at 4:11 we were on the road to Ashford for a second game. We returned home at 6:53. I arrived in Sherman an hour before the game. To kill time I bought coffee at the American Pie Company, a bakery near the post office. I sat on a bench outside the bakery and while drinking the coffee studied natives. More than miles separates the eastern from the western part of the state. On my saying "good morning," a woman stopped, stared at me, then said, "you must be from out of town." When I spoke to another woman, she lowered her right shoulder and bashed through the bakery door. I was still on the bench when the woman left the bakery. After looking at me then the girls, she said, "I thought you were selling something."

Each autumn I receive much mail. Many letters come from people who read my books. In October a man sent a present from Missouri. "A token of my esteem," a card explained. Squatting deep in a box was a chamber pot. From the bottom of the pot stared a watery eye, letters resembling an eyebrow hanging over it reading, "I SEE YOU." "A local pharmacist in Johnson City, Joe Peavyhouse, now deceased," a Tennessean wrote,

> once told me about the time a portly woman came into his drugstore to have a prescription filled. This happened in the thirties when pharmacists brewed mixes in back rooms lined with apothecary jars. The jars contained mysterious potions that supposedly cured everything from gout to consumption. Joe told the woman that the medicine she wanted had to sit a while after being mixed and couldn't be bottled immediately. The woman refused to wait and demanded the medicine. Reluctantly, and against his better judgment, Joe poured the liquid in a bottle, stuck in a cork, and handed the potion to the woman. Just as she got to the front door, the cork blew out and hit the ceiling. The contents of the bottle spewed over the woman's hand and ran down to the floor. The woman looked at the mark on the ceiling and watched while the rest of the medicine boiled out of the bottle. Then she turned back to Joe and shouted, "Lord have mercy. If I'd 'a-took a dose of that medicine it would've blowed my butt off."

As autumn days grew shorter and colder, tales simmered on my desk. Arriving late in October, the letter from Tennessee brought story to a whistle. The next day was Sunday, and since Eliza's team lost in Sherman, I attended church in Carthage. Prayer doesn't chop corn off a hillside. Only after crops are in barn and silo did farm families fill the Tabernacle of Love. For Slubey Garts autumn was planting and fertilizing season. "Words," he told Turlow Gutheridge, "make good manure." Once the harvest ended outside, Slubey plowed the congregation, his sermons cutting long, deep furrows. "Autumn," he said, "is the time to pull snakes out of milk houses, to squash moths in beehives, to spray cucumbers for cutworms, plums for curculio, and potatoes for Colorado beetles. When the soul is distempered, suffering from wolf teeth, saddle galls, blind staggers, epizootic, and the heaves, there ain't much the Celestial Veterinarian can do, aside from easing the final foundering."

On Sunday Slubey's sermon turned over so many paragraphs that ladies rolled down their stockings and slumping back in the pews dreamed of harvesting lunch at home. "Take care before Take Care knocks at the door," Slubey warned parishioners. "The flat road doesn't climb Heavenly Mountain. Before the lazy man gets to glory, worms will bore into iron, and stones will grow hair." Instead of struggling against sin, foolish Ishbosheths thought they could creep into Heaven through Paradise Alley. Alas, Gabriel and Haniel, Michael and Raphael didn't linger in the dark to fit golden slippers on folks. "No," Slubey said, waving his right arm like a scythe, "the only person in the alley is cross-eyed Sally, leaning against a doorway, a red light blinking above her head." People in Smith County, Slubey declared, believed in God but forgot the Devil. Carthaginians didn't worry enough about sin. "Go downtown," Slubey said, "and you'll see fellows around the courthouse, sitting on rails, taters by the hands and possums by the tail."

Slubey's plow was always bright in autumn, turning over story as well as poetry. After the death of his wife, then Belle, his favorite bird dog, Everyman, Slubey recounted, left Tennessee and traveled to No Graves. As soon as Everyman crossed the border, he searched for a puppy to gun train, assuming that since the dog would live forever, he'd never again have to concern himself with

point and flush. Everyman soon discovered a breeder. The breeder
lived with his aged father. After showing Everyman a litter of pup-
pies, the breeder invited his prospective customer to dinner, serv-
ing leg of lamb. After dessert Everyman thanked his host, saying,
"This has been a wonderful meal. But where is your father? I've
heard that he was quite the dog fancier, and I'd like to meet him."
"You just ate his right leg," the breeder answered. "The rest of him
is on a shelf in the pantry. This country is called No Graves because here dead people are eaten, not buried."

At the end of the story, Slubey told the congregation they were
mortal. "Even if you were raised on Methodist pie," he said, "you
have to earn a ticket to Glory. You want to be on that mourning
train when it pulls out of the graveyard, the Queen of Galilee calling 'All Aboard,' the ram's horn blowing, Thrones cutting the
pigeonwing, and Seraphim singing 'Little Rosewood Casket' and
'I'm All Wore Out a-Toiling for the Lord.'" "Hallelujah Orange
Blossom Special!" Slubey shouted. "You want to be there when the
cars rumble over Sunbeam Trestle and sweep under the White
Gate. You want to frolic in the Pool of Bethesda, prayer splashing
blue about you, psalms rising to your lips like pearls."

In autumn Slubey sowed salvation throughout Smith County.
One Tuesday he traveled beyond Dugget, stopping at every shack
in White Lady and Devil's Bellrope. Near Guess Creek he asked
an old woman if she had heard how Jesus died. "Is He dead?" the
woman said. "Lord have mercy. I didn't know He was dead. I don't
take no newspaper, and if you lived back in these coves you
wouldn't know much about it yourself." "Tell you what I'm going
to do," the woman said, sucking on a wormy pipe. "Just as soon
as you leave I'm going to pray about it. I believe in letting the good
Lord take care of such things."

In Carthage autumn was visiting season. The same day Slubey
journeyed to Guess Creek, Ezreelite Blodgett visited Image of
Christ Lord God Brown. IOC, as neighbors dubbed him, had been
sick all summer and had lost so much weight that he looked like,
as Turlow put it, "a deserter from the graveyard brigade." IOC's
ribs resembled barrel hoops with horse hide stretched across them,
and the months in bed caused his feet to swell and fingernails to

turn white. "When he wiggled his fingertips," Loppie Groat said, "all I seen was maggots. And his feet was worse. They looked like purple kidneys and affected my digestion something awful. I don't think I'll ever be able to eat kidneys and eggs for breakfast again." Although Ezreelite was deaf, he provoked IOC to words, something none of the sick man's previous visitors accomplished. "How are you making out?" Ezreelite asked, pulling a chair close to IOC's head. "I'm dying," IOC whispered. "Well, thanks be to God," Ezreelite said, hanging his head over the bedside table and spitting tobacco juice into an ashtray. "Who's your doctor? He's worked a blessed miracle." "The Angel of Death," IOC answered, lifting himself on his elbows. "Now get out of my house." "An excellent practitioner, none better for the pip. He done my cousin Sawyer Blodgett proud when borers got to his molars. Not only that he cured Sawyer's bull Peggy of the horn ail, not to mention the rheumatics. What medicine has he prescribed?" "Poison!" IOC said, sitting upright and shouting. "Praise God," Ezreelite answered. "That's the very Bread of Life. A dose of that will make an old sawhorse prance like a two by four. Just follow the doctor's directions. The first time I took suppositories I washed them down with Dr. Pepper, and they didn't do me no good at all. But then once I switched to Royal Crown things began to mend. Of course I bloated and suffered something fierce with the wind, but that's just the way medicines do you. When you buy eggs, you buy shells, too." According to Turlow, Ezreelite would still be visiting and talking if IOC hadn't jumped out of bed and run hollering out of the house. "All the sickness blowed out of him by words," Loppie Groat said. By the end of the week, IOC was sunning himself on the courthouse steps, chewing handfuls of grapes, hoping they would ferment in his stomach and turn to wine, nothing fancy, he explained to Loppie, "just a young Beaujolais, or if the temperature climbs high enough, a full-bodied red, perhaps a Bordeaux or a Zinfandel."

After harvest farmers devoted time to maintaining homes and selves: repairing tools, mending fences, and visiting physicians. Faith doctors studied seasons, if not medicine, and began appearing in Carthage at the end of October. The first to arrive was Madame Exodius, known in Nashville as Hamena, the Turkish Fortune-Teller. Born after twins and the seventh daughter of a seventh daughter,

Madame Exodius was a Planet Reader and Magnetic Healer. Among her possessions were, a poster declared, "The Palestine Wonder Charm, an Osiris Talisman, the Pillow of Cupid, Buds from the Garden of Gilead, a Jar of Silver Paradise Sand, and a Pot of Japanese Tokay Beads." "Born with second sight and with a veil," she could remove spells and warts, restore lost loves, cause speedy marriages, determine lucky stars, and "scientifically foretell all business transactions." The madame traveled the country in an enclosed wagon. A statue of St. Expedite stood on a table inside the wagon. When diagnosing a patient, Madame Exodius burned green candles at the foot of the statue. Usually she sold patients nostrums, vials containing Dove's Blood, Florida Water, or the Essence of Three Knaves and Two Kings. Sometimes, however, she wrote prescriptions. For Sawyer Blodgett who wanted to kill borers in his teeth, she prescribed a charm. First Sawyer was to recite a verse.

> Mary, the holy, went over the Land.
> She had three worms in her hand.
> One was red, another white
> and the third was black as darkest night.

After saying the verse, Sawyer, she instructed, was to remove his shirt and put it back on wrong side out. Next, she told him, to put his thumbs at the pit of his stomach, one thumb on the right side of his navel, the other on the left. "Then slowly carry them back under the ribs as far as your hips. Do this three times a day for seventeen days, and the worms will dry up and vanish."

Because she stayed only a week in Carthage, Madame Exodius could not be held accountable for the effectiveness of her charms. Indeed instructions accompanying some nostrums seemed purposely complicated. When Sabrisal Nellson stepped out with Sugg, her cousin Leona's boyfriend, Leona became murderously angry. Instead of razoring her way through Sabrisal back into Sugg's affections, Leona purchased a prescription to kill, as she put it, "her second cousin not once removed from harlotry." Ingredients of the charm resembled the list of a Halloween scavenger hunt. "Into powder beat," Madame Exodius instructed, "a dried toad, the little finger of a suicide, the wings of a bull bat, the head of a doctor snake, and the liver of a screech owl. Next cut a lock from the head of stillborn red-haired baby and stir it into the mixture. If the hair does not blend smoothly, add whites from two black eggs and a pint of Italian whiskey. Then let dry. Afterward remove a shroud from a corpse. Cut a square from the front of the shroud and sew the material into a bag. Dump the powder into the bag. Seal the bag, and place it under the pillow of the victim." If the bag was not discovered, Madame Exodius assured Leona, King Hunger would become a boarder in the victim's house and she would waste away. To make the charm work faster, Madame Exodius suggested laying the feather of an Egyptian ibis on the bag then eating a watermelon plucked from atop the grave of a woman killed by dropsy. Shortly after selling Leona instructions for the charm, Madame Exodius herself took flight, at the Smith County line wondrously transforming herself into Sentinella Guzdho, the Great Prophetess, a lineal descendant of Luxor, king of one of the most ancient tribes of Egypt.

Once corn has been chopped into silage, tall tales grow weedy in Carthage. After giving Chalky Varnel a physical, Turlow told the crowd at Ankerrow's, Dr. Sollows called Chalky's wife Revelia into his office. "The strangest thing has happened," the doctor said. "There's a crop of spinach growing on Chalky's head." "My word! That is strange," Revelia said, scratching herself under the left arm. "I planted broccoli." Not to be outdone, Levi Crowell, editor of the *Carthage Courier,* explained the origin of the clearing atop Battery Hill. Ages ago, Levi recounted, a four-legged man was buckled to Battery Hill by his umbilical cord. Hairy and thick, the cord was long, not only stretching twenty yards along the ground but also reaching down into the bowels of the earth where "Mr. Earthquake snored." Always hungry, the man devoured any animal or human that strayed with the radius of the cord. Fond of salad, the man stripped vegetation from the hilltop, making the clearing. "Whatever happened to the fellow?" Googoo Hooberry asked when Levi finished the tale. "He ain't there now." "He died," Levi said. "How?" Googoo asked. "One night while he was asleep," Levi said after a pause, "a giant terrapin bit the umbilical cord in half. Immediately the man shriveled, and drying like a dead spider, blew away." "What happened to the terrapin?" Googoo asked. "I haven't seen a terrapin up there either." "That's all I know," Levi said, drumming the fingers of his right hand on the table. "If you want to know more, you'll have to ask the fellow who told me the story." "Who's that?" Googoo said. "I'm not sure," Levi answered. "But I think he's the guy who told me about the careful turtle who took a hundred years to climb from one step to another. Unfortunately on the first day of the one hundred and first year, the turtle stumbled and flipping over, rolled back down the step. 'Damn it to hell,' he said, after righting himself and shaking the dust off his shell, 'Grandma was right. Haste makes waste.'"

November

At the end of October breezes spooned trees, and leaves stirred through thin days like cereal dumped into bowls of skim milk. By November lawns were grainy. Trees were bare as forks in drawers, and cold bored metallic through evenings, the edges of light keen, not dulled by peeling and coring colanders of greenery. Eliza's soccer season ended; sore throats started, and the dogs spent mornings burrowed under afghans atop their beds. For my part I spent more hours in the house than I had in spring and summer. Suddenly I noticed noise: the abrasive rumble of Francis's rock tumbler in the basement, in the boys' bedroom storms gathering in Edward's stereo, and from the staircase the nasal deflating honks of Eliza's French horn.

Months affect mind as well as body. In spring my interest in politics rarely grows beyond the cotyledon. In November even that glint of embryonic greenness vanishes. As cold burns season to stalks, the lush grand claims of politicians, and educators, appear unseemly. November pares thought into fine gradations, transforming flower to seed. Last Monday at a meeting of the university senate a nice woman read a list of students appointed to senate committees. Students have served on committees for a decade, and each November the senate routinely, and unanimously, approves the appointments. This year I voted against the appointments. The only dissenting vote, my *no* startled the president of the senate. "What?" he questioned. "No," I repeated. Reading, I told a friend later, would serve students better. Adolescents, I explained, had more important things to do than sit in rooms with the middle-aged, saccharine smiles pasted on their faces. "If the senate were really concerned about the welfare of children," I said, "it would appoint parents, the adults who pay tuition, to committees." Unlike May, for example, during which colors wash field and hill, life seems to diminish in November. I have learned, however, to make do with wintry, if not lesser, things. Or as Orpheeus Goforth put it when his wife decamped, "She was unkind, but God is good, and the world is wide." For some people November resembles the mouth of a tunnel which runs narrowing not simply toward the end of the year but of life itself. One Sunday in the middle of the month a stranger telephoned from Ohio. "I don't know you," he explained. "But I've read one of your books, and I want to know how you handle fear." What is in the heart doesn't always rise to the tongue. I almost said, "I scream then run like hell." Season had sunk to the bone, however, and instead of a spontaneous spring answer, I paused before I spoke, giving the man a contemplative November reply. "I read myself out of worry," I said. I suggested that the man read Jane Austen. "Concern for fictional characters will," I said, "probably make you forget self and those fears that chill dark nights."

November lends itself to contemplation as well as fear. Not until the middle of the month do I start the furnace. Out of the habit of turning on heat each morning, I bundle sweaters about myself and doze rumpled and woolly in the study. One afternoon as I slept, I dreamed about Mother. Mother's face was so sharp that it pierced imagination, and I awoke melancholy and deflated. For a moment I dug the past, trying to turn over recollection. The ground, however, was hard. Memory sprouts in spring, when people push through the crust of winter. In summer memory blooms as travel bumps association through bud into flower. Moreover, memory does not transplant well from one climate to another. For a dozen years after I left Tennessee recollection seemed hardy. Now after thirty years in New England, not only has my childhood aged into compost, but the South itself seems an alien landscape, both to me and my children, its Novembers warmer than those in Connecticut and the soil of its doings softer than our till and drumlin. Last Thursday after dinner Francis answered the telephone. Three times Francis said, "I beg your pardon. Would you please repeat that?" On the telephone was a woman from East Tennessee. "Daddy," Francis said later, "I couldn't I understand her. I thought she was Chinese." Resembling an open grave that demands to be fed, gapping memory needs filling. The next morning at the Cup of Sun, I asked Ellen if she thought about her childhood during November. Ellen is from Massachusetts, and I assumed her memories had remained more vital than mine. "It's odd, you should mention childhood," Ellen said. "Last night I looked at my baby book. Mother worried about me when I was little." When Ellen was three, her mother wrote, "Ellen bothers me. She does not ask cause-and-effect questions like other children. At dinner last night, she asked, 'Did you ever marry a rabbit?'" Long hours stretch across the short days of winter, and in the Cup of Sun talk revolves around story. "Imagine a funeral home," I said one morning, "with a sign over the front door, stating, 'Ladies will behave with decorum in the presence of cadavers, no matter how handsome the deceased.'" Neither Ellen nor I is young, and in winter, we mull the fruits of season. As mildew turns blackberry canes blue in November, so illness spots acquaintances. "Asking 'how are you' makes me nervous," I said, "particularly if I haven't seen someone for a time." "Yes," Ellen said, "the person might answer, wiping a tear from her eye, 'the operation was terrible, and for months I've tried to push the whole thing out of mind. But now I know it helps to talk about it.'"

In November sentences don't slip barren from conversation. Instead they fall on pages and sprout into paragraphs. Just before Thanksgiving Loppie Groat met Googoo Hooberry outside the Smith County courthouse. "Did you hear about Hoben Donkin's fishing trip to Reelfoot Lake?" Loppie asked. "He caught a mermaid." "Great God Almighty!" Googoo exclaimed. "A mermaid! What did he do with her?" "Well, you know Hoben's got a fierce palate for swimmers: gar, cooter, muskrat, cottonmouth, bullfrog, mud puppy, just anything he can bundle into a tureen pot with a bouquet garni. In short he ate her." "Oh," Googoo said disappointedly, "I'd like to have viewed her before she was diced and seasoned.

But that aside, what did she taste like?" "You didn't miss seeing much," Loppie answered. "Hoben told me she was a little long in the gills to be a looker. As for the eating, her upper half tasted like pork while the lower half was oily and smacked of mackerel." "I trust the mermaid's appearance did not sour gustatory pleasure," Googoo answered. "No, you can bet your sweet Feinste Nusstorte that it didn't," Loppie continued. "Hoben relied upon culinary artistry to transform the rough upper portion of the mermaid into Braised Filets of Mermaid Strasbourgeoise. Indeed, leftovers furnished ingredients for a snappy curry of Mermaid Belgian, a covey of Mermaid Birds, and a Melton Mowbray pie, not to mention a dish of Sweetbreads Florentine en Coquilles." "And the scaly lower regions below the pelvic fins—how did Loppie prepare them?" Googoo asked. "He poached some bits then baked a hunk or two in milk. But the triumph of gastronomy, the pièce de résistance, was an exquisite Mermaid Marinade," Loppie continued. "Hoben salted a haunch of mermaid after which he put it on ice overnight. The next morning he rinsed and dried the haunch then laid it in a casserole dish on a soft bed of chopped onions and carrots. Afterward he added two sprays of parsley and a smidgen of freshly ground pepper. Next he poured white wine and vinegar in equal amounts into the dish until the liquid kissed the top of the haunch, after which he sprinkled in more chopped carrots and onions. Then he dressed the haunch in a tutu of buttered paper."

"That sounds divine," Googoo interrupted, smacking his chops. "And," Loppie continued, "set the casserole on low heat to bring the liquid to a boil after which he covered the dish and let the mermaid simmer for fifteen minutes." "And grape juices?" Googoo asked, "did the mermaid raise the temperature of Hoben's cellar above fifty-five degrees?" "Not at all," Loppie responded. "With the Strasbourgeoise, he served Riesling Kabinett. With the other faux pork dishes, he served dry, white, medium-bodied Italian wines, a Tocai, a Soave, and a Corvo Bianco. With the marinade he drank Sauvignon Blanc from Touraine. Of course marrying wine to flesh is always delightful. Hoben has ordered a mixed case of light reds, and after his next fishing trip hopes to send a Fleurie or Morgon on honeymoon with roast mermaid in orange sauce."

"There's money to made in mermaid farming," Loppie said after pausing so the wine could age in Googoo's imagination. "Although mermaids occasionally munch worms, they are mostly vegetarian. They eat silage, and they'd certainly be cheaper to raise than cattle, at least cheaper than black Angus. The problem is finding a pair of breeders. You can pull a mermaid out of water, but you can't make her spawn. Still, if we bait our minds, we'll snag something. The dog that runs about always finds a bone."

I have aged beyond cantering. The young coon for running, as the saying puts it, but the old coon for cunning. I've learned to stir without moving. In November a story carried me to Carthage. Early in the month Nephritis Askew's husband Bolling died when the chimney on their house collapsed and crushed him. Nephritis was mending barbed wire in the lower pasture when the accident occurred. On being told about her husband's death by Sheriff Baugham, she dropped her pliers in the front pocket of her overalls, stretched, rubbed the sides of her hips, then asked, "Was Bolling sitting in the red chair when the chimney fell?" The sheriff said he noticed a hunk of red fabric in the rubble, though, he added that he couldn't be sure about the color because "the chimney squashed Bolling's head and blood sprocketed all over the floor." "Shitfire!" Nephritis exclaimed, "I'll bet five dollars those damn bricks broke my pipe. After breakfast this morning I put it on the table right next to the chair." "Pipe?" the sheriff said, "what about Bolling?" "Sheriff," Nephritis said, "I don't mind passing the day with you, but this ain't the time to do it. This fence is talking loud to my eye, and Bolling won't fix it. The only thing he was good at was the hookworm hustle. Last Tuesday I warned him about the chimney. I told him the bricks need repointing. Now I guess he'll never learn."

This November when I wasn't harvesting blighted tales in Carthage, I roamed Mansfield's hills and woods. At the beginning of the month days were chilly but not cold, and I wore a scarf and stocking hat. Climbing ridges, though, made me hot, and after an hour's walking, I rolled the cap into a ball and pushed it back on my head. I wanted to remove the scarf, but poking about so knotted the straps for my binoculars and their carrying case that I couldn't unravel the scarf. Despite the straps' binding me like complex sentences, I hopped the stile of narrative. November was not a diminished month. Behind the sheep barns a pair of American tree sparrows preened in an alder while a cardinal hunkered in multiflora rose, its feathers fluffed, transforming bird into blossom. A bluebird clung to bittersweet, and gold finches flickered through a yellow birch, the sun polishing the trunk of the tree into a sconce. Seedpods dangled from black locust. A flock of pigeons burst into flight, ringing like a carillon. A doe bounced through Joe-Pye weed and clattered into a wood. Polypody spilled down the shoulders of rocks, strings of fruitdots orange beneath leaflets. Patridgeberry trailed across moss, and sunlight sifted through Christmas ferns turning leaves silver.

Beside the Fenton River virgin's bower roiled over swamp dogwood, its seed heads fibrous, resembling clumps of dust pitched up by wind. At the edge of the beaver pond ditch stonecrop had shed seeds, and the tops of the dried calyxes looked like minute red stars. Behind the pond winterberry switched the breeze, the twigs rolling air into berries. Along the hill frost ribs bulged thick from oaks, and nectria cankers blasted sweet birch. Although the disease forced bark into rough petals, the cankers were as wondrous as summer flowers.

As I walked I wanted to urge friends to roam November. If a person sees and listens, season does not diminish. As November followed a pattern, its heavy bituminous clouds initially spewing cindery ice, then at the end of the month dissolving into snow thick as soot, so my days followed a pattern. Instead of mounting an environmental pulpit and waxing preachy, I described the antics of a preacher, something I do every November. Early in the month Obed Eells led a revival at the Pilgrim Rest Here Pentecostal Church in Smith County. A "Free Gospeller," Obed preached barefoot and in a shroud, dressed, as he put it, in the tomb's own chain mail. Six feet four inches tall and with long hair, gathered and bound on both sides of his head so it shook over his ears like horse tails, Obed's appearance startled. When he preached or "wrestled with mourners," he perspired heavily, "the sweat," Hasam Browning declared, "running off him like carrots." Obed's wife Sister

Wanda, or "the Rib," as he addressed her from the pulpit, accompanied him on his travels. Sister Wanda always sat in the first pew, and when congregations settled into undemonstrative moods, she inserted exclamations, shouting "Hark Hallelujah, Honey from the Rock" or "Sweet Wonder Bread" and "Soar Celestial Dove."

During a sermon Obed emitted a menagerie of sounds, mooing like cow, grunting like a pig, barking, quacking, purring, and bleating. When one of the unsanctified criticized the noises, Obed replied that he was a Lion Tamer in God's Moral Circus, adding that he spoke in bestial tongues so that sinners could understand and learn to leap through the fiery hoops that encircled their souls. "But if," he continued, "you cannot gargle such mustard, trap the sounds, throw a net over them, take them home, cook them, and serve them on Sunday as blessings."

Unlike many Pentecostals Obed did not use formulaic phrases or systematic repetition in sermons, mothy expressions such as "Thank you, Jesus" and "Can you feel the fire?" Instead, when inspiration limped, he leaned on rhyme, declaiming, for example, "White potatoes, sweet potatoes, agitators, fornicators" or "Jesus can cure the itch, the stitch, the grunt, the gout—the pains within and the pains without." Obed often tossed the traces of common sense and galloped down Runaway Road to dead ends, using a phrase such as "Mountain Nelly—ten men to hug her, a boxcar to lug her." Frequently, he burst into song, almost none of the tunes religious. In Carthage he sang, "Mary's gone a-milking, a-milking, a-milking. Mary's gone a-milking, dear mother of mine." Occasionally he cantered down shady lanes. During a lull in the moaning at Pilgrim Rest Here, he shouted, "The hair on her dicky-dido hangs down to her knees. I've seen it. I've seen it. I've been *between* it." Slain in the spirit, most of the parishioners didn't notice the words. Still, after this particular rhyme, the Rib shouted, "Little David, pluck your harp." When Obed grabbed his side and gazed at her, she added, "Lock the lion's jaw, Daniel."

Striking phrases exploded throughout Obed's sermons, broadsides, he called them, fired by the Old Ship of Zion or Cardigrams, tapped out by the Great Orator Beyond. "The world is my possum, I shall not want," he began in Carthage. Later, he said, "I'm just a candle burning on the lip of God, lighting the way to Salvation." In the middle of a peroration he lamented that he was preaching to "uncircumcised hearts and ears." "And noses, too," Hasam Browning shouted. "Amen, brother," Obed responded, "newly blown noses, red blossoming above nostrils, warts sharp as thorns on stems."

In his sermon Obed loosed cloven tongues of fire at "Cosmopolites" and "Turkey-bosomed Levites," almost anyone not Pentecostal qualifying for the labels. In particular Obed attacked what he called the Dagon of Episcopacy and the concept of the Trinity, that is, the tripartite divinity consisting of Father, Son, and Holy Ghost. "My Trinity isn't haunted," he testified. "I believe in God the Florist, the Rose of Sharon; God the Geologist, the Rock of Ages; and God the Baker, the Bread of Life." Obed did not limit his criticism to doctrine. In the sermon he called Slubey Garts, owner of the Tabernacle of Love, "Eve's apple squire" and "a necrotic pomonalist." Years ago when Slubey first appeared in Carthage and in my paragraphs, his evangelical fervor resembled that of Obed. Success and pages have mellowed Slubey, however, tempering theological ardor and at times, making him seem Episcopalian. This past spring Slubey celebrated Apple Sunday. One afternoon after church when fruit trees resembled doilies, Slubey blessed Hopp Watrous's orchard. "Winter thunder, summer wonder," the choir sang, after which Slubey chanted, "Stand fast root. Bear well top. Pray God send Hopp a good, howling crop." Although most of Hopp's trees were peaches, and the only apples, Arkansas blacks, Obed damned the fruit as winesaps, the juice of which intoxicated, changing men, he said, into "headless pigs, eaters of snakes, and guzzlers of sin." "Poor Zion," he cried, "lies in great distress. Her altars are broken down. Thorns of ash her groves have overgrown. Her temples are desolate. Her halls are palaces of owls. There Garts doth meet his mate and eat apples in the nests of fowls."

Obed's remarks angered Proverbs Goforth, Slubey's closest friend and deacon of the Tabernacle of Love. Obed was so proud, Proverbs told the crowd at Ankerrow's Café, that "God Almighty's overcoat isn't big enough to make him a vest." Obed had raised his faith on the heads of fools, Proverbs continued, warning listeners that not everyone who carried a knife or a prayer book was a cook or a preacher. Proverbs did not think highly of Obed's oratorical skills either, noting that although a dog had four legs it did not run down four roads at once.

Although Obed's sermons bounced erratically across grammar and meaning, he was a better speaker than Proverbs alleged. Near the end of his sermon at Pilgrim Rest Here, just after declaring, "God stood fast against trial post-mortem marriages," Obed told a creation story. "Before the beginning," he said, Satan tried to overthrow God. The battle thundered across clouds, and smoke darkened the happy realm of light. During the struggle God dodged a bolt of horned lightning and bunged his elbow against one of the seven lamps standing beside the great throne. The lip of the lamp was beveled, and a patch of skin was ripped from God's elbow. After hurling Satan into the deep, God noticed the bit of skin. Seizing golden compasses, God measured the flesh then, Obed said, "spread his brooding wings dovelike over the skin and created Man." No longer standing at the right hand of God, Satan envied "the toy," as he called man. Stretching the links of his chains, he rose from the burning flood and spat upon Man, causing hideous deformities to grow on Man's body. Immediately thereafter a whirlwind rose from the red gulf and sucked Satan back into that dungeon where "hope never comes." God then took pity on Man and turned him inside out, so that the impurities, "the bowels and the lights, the livers and sweetbreads would always be hidden from sight."

Obed has now left Carthage, churned out of the cream of society, Proverbs declared, by his sour tongue. "The mouse knows better," Proverbs said, "than to build a nest in the cat's ear." November is over. December has arrived, and the yard is white with snow. Eliza and Edward are playing basketball, and Francis is learning to drive. The dogs spend more time sleeping than they did last month, and Loppie and Googoo have lost their appetite for por and piscine mermaids. Even I have gone a bit off story, though recently I heard that the day before the chimney fell Nephritis accused Bolling of being the laziest man in Smith County. "Why are you so angry?" Bolling said, glancing up from the red chair. "I haven't done anything." Oh, well, birdfeeder season has arrived. This afternoon I saw a Carolina wren on the suet, the first Carolina wren I've seen in Connecticut.

Surprise

Surprise makes the heart leap. In spring surprise is natural, the sympathetic accompaniment of streams rolling over green stones, leaves unfurling into palms, and warblers snapping yellow through brush. In winter as the evening of one day coils into the morning of the next, pulling gray with it, surprise seems forced. Habit, not paper, wraps Christmas presents, tying them with duty instead of ribbons. As the sky often hangs low above the horizon like a cover clamped over a saucepan, so joy appears confined. Rarely does mood steam free, bubbles clapping spontaneously into song. For the essayist surprise should never go out of season. If surprise wilts, paragraphs darken, and sentences turn moldy. Still, on snowy winter mornings my capacity for surprise is sometimes brittle. Instead of delighting in the unexpected, I think it a nuisance and shovel it aside.

A decade ago a man who was once my student in high school wrote a movie, *Dead Poets Society*. In part the man modeled the teacher in the film, John Keating, on recollections of me. Despite a litany of disclaimers in which I explained the working of fiction, emphasizing that I had nothing to do with the movie, people have insisted on identifying me with Keating. Each year I receive a mailbox of letters, asking, and occasionally demanding, that I solve the educational failings of individuals and school systems. For these correspondents my actual life is a fiction. Rarely does anyone who mentions the movie know that I have written a sentence. Even when I travel beyond Storrs to read from one of my books, someone invariably mentions the film, starting a reel of questions. In *Dead Poets Society* Keating stood atop his desk and taught classes. At lunch in the English department whenever I speak forcibly, Tom says, "Sam, I'm having trouble hearing you. Why don't you hop on the table. That way we'll understand you better." A decade has made me wince at references to DPS, as I now refer to it, not wishing to breathe life into the aging celluloid by naming it, preferring instead to use an acronym as if the film were a disease.

At the end of November I received a manila envelope mailed from a small town in Alabama. Inside were nineteen letters written by tenth graders. In hopes of interesting sophomores in poetry, a teacher showed DPS to her class. Students enjoyed the movie so much that the teacher urged them to write me. "I felt this would add," she explained, "a short letter-writing exercise to the unit as a communiqué to a famous person!" "Nuts," I said, closing the envelope after reading the teacher's letter, "oh, nuts."

Not until the next day did I look at the children's letters. "I'm fortunate enough to be growing up on a catfish farm," I read, and my heart bounded. "Fortunate Enough To Be Growing Up On A Catfish Farm," I said aloud. "What a title for a book!" The next letter almost made me glad people confused tired, ordinary me with Keating. "From the way you were portrayed, you can teach us anytime," John Allan wrote, adding, "I'm just a 15 year old from a flyspeck town in Alabama, and poetry is not exactly abundant." The class attended "The Academy," but, John Allan explained, "it's only an academy in the loosest sense of the word, nothing like anywhere you've taught, I'm sure. No rich kids here!" "Well," John Allan continued, "I've never thought of myself as someone who would like poetry, though I'm not sure why. I love to read and write stories, and I'm pretty good at making up a story as I go along—it comes in handy!" "You bet it does," I said aloud.

Because they were "from the South," several students wrote that they "couldn't relate" to the movie "very much." "If you've seen it," Scotty explained, "you'll notice that it was set in the North with a higher class people, and I'm just a middle class boy who lives in the South." "How are you doing in these cold days of winter?" Benji asked, adding, "It may be a little weird to hear from a person of so little experience in the big cities and schools." Benji explained that he lived in Marion, Alabama, the population of which was almost three thousand. "Where I go to school," he noted, "is a different story. There population is about 6,000."

Instead of writing about their lives, some students discussed the movie. "At first," Johnny said, "I really thought it would be some boring story about some boring story." "How were we to know this movie would turn out to be educational, not just another waste of time film?" Crystal Joy asked. For some members of the class fiction was life. "I'm sorry you got fired at that boys' school," Jody commiserated, before reassuring me, "I'm sure you do just as well at the University of Connecticut though." "I want you to know that I think you are very courageous in the way you teach," Brooks wrote. "My mother is a teacher. Too bad she doesn't teach as interesting as you do." The classroom aside, Brooks's mother was a fine parent. She and his daddy, Brooks said, "have supported me in every sport I play and in everything I do. I think they have brought me up very well."

Several students hunted lessons and, as could be expected, bagged a couple. At the end of the film a frustrated boy killed himself. "I learned," Kristy wrote, "that you should always communicate with your parents and always let them know how you feel about situations. Suicide is not the way to go." The movie "made me realize," Aprille explained, "that when someone commits suicide, it hurts everyone around you. We face decisions and trouble everyday and just because something doesn't go the way we want it to, suicide is the worst decision made." Lindsey said she learned that "poetry comes from the heart, not charts and rules." Lessons, I thought, as I read the letters extracting morals from the film were the compacted stuff of charts and rules. When not pinpointed by the longitude and latitude of convention, truth delights. "For the past nine years," John Allan recounted, "I have yawned through countless poetry lessons. Now I'm writing a bit of it. Buried beneath rhymes, meters, iambic pentameter, and all that stuff, you may fine a gem—even if it only pleases your eye." "Yes," I exclaimed, surprised by the boy's sparkling prose.

Words surprise. On Friday Josh told me a story. A possum

walked into a bar and ordered a shot of bourbon. "That will be three-fifty," the bartender said, handing the possum a check, then adding, "This is the first time I've ever served a possum." "And it will be the last time," the possum said, curling his tail in anger, "unless you charge less." Although I had heard the tale before, I wasn't bored. Details breath life into the hackneyed. As Josh talked, I wondered what bourbon Mr. Possum ordered. Old Crow or Wild Turkey, I decided, for although Mr. Possum had dined on crow and turkey at roadside cafés, he'd always enjoyed them in high-fleshly, not low-liquid, form.

For the person susceptible to surprise, actual story is rarely final story. Real events buff imagination, making details shine. Earlier in the morning before Josh visited, I read an account describing the arrest of a grave robber in Wilton, Connecticut. The thief specialized, the *Hartford Courant* reported, "in burglarizing vaults." Suppose, I thought, laying the paper down on the kitchen table, that the man broke into the tomb of a woman who had just died from apoplexy. A wealthy widow, the woman wore a wedding ring, in the setting of which nested a diamond big as a goose. Unable to pull the ring from the woman's finger, the thief started to saw off her hand. As soon as the blade bit skin, however, blood spurted, and the woman squawked and sat upright in the coffin. "She'd been buried alive," I told Eliza. "Her relatives were so eager to invest their inheritance in the stock market that they rushed her into the grave." "What happened next, Daddy?" Eliza asked. Being able to make up a story as one goes along does come in handy. "They married," I told Eliza. Wilton was old fashioned, I explained. If the woman had not married the man, her reputation would have been ruined. "For a woman to be discovered with a man in her bedroom was a grave social offense. Only marriage could resuscitate the reputation of the fallen." "And the husband? What did he do for a living?" Eliza asked. The woman owned a large estate, I replied, and the man became her gardener. People are creatures of habit. Years of wandering night and tombs determined the husband's horticultural interests. He planted spider lilies, monkshood, stonecrop, incense plant, toadshade, bleeding heart, carrion flower, angel's trumpet, dead nettle, and three varieties of skullcap—hyssop, mad dog, and heart-leaved. He grew two varieties each of iris and day lilies, New Moon and Night Owl, and Mission Moonlight and Haunting Melody, respectively. Rip Van Winkle was his favorite daffodil; Blue Angel, his favorite hosta, and Night Queen, his favorite dahlia. "Did he grow members of the nightshade family?" Eliza asked. "Yes," I said, "potatoes, tomatoes, and peppers." "How about weeping widows?" Edward added, punning. "And mourning glories?" Francis said. "Both," I said, "and a grove of ghost gums."

In winter I spend more time in the house than I do in other seasons. Because I roam the landscape less, words surprise more than sights or sounds. In winter I read mail carefully. One Wednesday I received three letters. One of the letters announced a birth. The baby, the mother wrote, "Belonged to God" but had been "loaned" to the family. "No wonder Jesus tossed money changers out of the temple," I said. "They were competition." "At least," Vicki said, "those loan sharks didn't traffic in human flesh." In the second letter a man described the antics of some of the fictional characters who bumble through my essays. "Last week," the man recounted, "Hink Ruunt hosted a dove hunt outside Carthage. The fields were baited, and the hunt was a great success. The School for the Afflicted in Buffalo Valley was on holiday, and one of the boys from the school wandered out to the field and saw Hoben Donkin shoot a dove. "Hoben," the fellow said, "I don't mean to be inquisitive, but you're not thinking straight. An idiot could see the fall would have killed that bird. You wasted your shot." The same man, my correspondent continued, decided to walk to Lebanon, thirty miles away. Four days later, he returned to Carthage, foot-sore and exhausted. "If the world is as big the other way as it is from Carthage to Lebanon," he told loafers at the courthouse, "then it's a darn big thing."

While the stories caught the tone of my essays, the third letter captured the tenor of my days. "The semester is wearing me out," an academic friend wrote from Ohio. "Must be middle-age. Whatever reason, I'm damned tired of it all—students *and* colleagues." That afternoon I mailed a package at the post office. "Sam," Mark said as I walked in the door. "Has your older boy changed his name?" Francis reviews music for the high school newspaper. Instead of *Francis Pickering*, he signs articles *F. Ratcliffe Pickering*. "Francis is young enough to be different people," I said to Mark. "Not only does he surprise Vicki and me, but he surprises himself." "He's lucky," Mark said. "Yes," I answered, "some mornings before class, I dream of riding my bicycle over Spring Hill and vanishing into the distance, ringing my bell as I fade from sight." "Well," Mark said, "that's a nice fantasy. But you wouldn't get farther than Willimantic, and you'd have to telephone Vicki to retrieve you. Your legs couldn't take the strain of pumping back up Spring Hill."

Although I am too old to fashion a new identity or ride a bicycle for more than a mile or two, I put myself in the way of surprise. To escape being "tired of it all," the next day I wandered field and wood. Whenever I roam Mansfield, things startle me. Cedar waxwings foraged through hemlocks beside the Fenton River, the feathers on the birds' breasts yellow in the gray day. Near the beaver pond shelf fungus shingled the trunk of a red maple. While tops of the caps were brown and velvety, the gills were orange and ruffled. In the Ogushwitz meadow goldenrod and Joe-Pye weed had dried into scythes that hooked my trousers. Late in the afternoon wind kicked through the meadow, and leaves pitched off the ridge and scattered like sparrows. An orange band three and a half inches wide circled a white oak near the sand pit. Nailed to the band and sealed in plastic was a baggage ticket. Printed on the ticket was "Purple Passion." Later, in the wetland beside the beaver pond I found a second ticket. Printed on this ticket was the name of a popular singer, Shania Twain. As I examined this second ticket, color spun off barberry. Tired leaves circled canes, resembling teeth on old saws, for a moment keen in the sunlight. In the distance a blue jay fluted, its call honing rust from the leaves. Along the cut for the power line a decapitated crow sank into the ground. "Did you have a good walk?" Vicki said when I returned home. "Terrific," I said, walking to the kitchen sink and looking through the window at birdfeeders outside. A red-breasted nuthatch pecked suet, the first red-breasted nuthatch I'd seen in Storrs. "Just terrific," I repeated, turning the faucet in order to wash my hands.

In winter I travel in hopes of being surprised out of weariness, both of mind and of body. Each January the National Foundation for Advancement in the Arts brings 125 high school seniors to Miami for a festival. Panels select students from eight disciplines: dance, instrumental music, jazz, voice, photography, visual arts, theater, and writing. In late November I flew to Miami to choose 20 participants in writing. Just leaving the house awakened observation. In the airport at Hartford two school girls sat on the floor in front of a window. Behind them the tarmac stretched flat like a tray cluttered with medical instruments, the fuselages of planes fat as stethoscopes, wings cutting the air like scalpels. One of the girls wore a black windbreaker. Stitched in yellow over the left side of the jacket were the words "Hyde Athletics." As I looked out the window at the planes, the girl in the jacket leaned toward her friend and said, "I'm hoping that grandpa dies." Not until landing in Miami did I hear more words. Instead of talking on planes, people read airport books, adventure novels bound in blue and red and written by Lawrence Block or Robert Ludlum.

I stayed in the Sheraton bordering Biscayne Bay. I got up early each morning and roamed the shelf of land owned by the hotel. Coconut palms and small live oaks grew along a sidewalk. One morning a mockingbird sat atop bougainvillea, scissoring his tail in a drizzle. A sign in the middle of the bay read "MANTEE ZONE. IDLE SPEED. NO WAKE." Most mornings a committee of boat-tailed grackles met on the sign and squabbled about right of way. A green heron perched on a stone looking south along the bay while a great blue heron stood in gravel near the shore, his long neck thin as a wire cheese slicer. One afternoon thirty buzzards rode the wind, thermals eventually flushing the birds beyond sight. Throughout days airplanes slid upward throbbing. Pile drivers rattled on Claughton Island, pounding supports deep into the bay for, a man said, "more cocaine condos."

Hotel grounds had been manicured and polished into hard, gleaming neatness. Across the sidewalk in the water, however, garbage snagged on rocks: beer bottles—Pabst, Budweiser, and Corona; half a dinner plate, a plume of brown leaching across it; seven white plastic bottle caps; a length of narrow wire curving between rocks like a parasite; four chipped Styrofoam cups; a float torn from a toilet; the innards of a television, brushes of wires jutting out styled; and an adhesive Band-Aid, three inches long and still wrapped, the phrase "Johnson & Johnson" stamped on the paper in red.

Actually, I spent more time sitting in the hotel than I did pacing the shoreline. People stirred through the lobby, beating hours into a batter marbled with colors and cultures. Fingernails glittered like marzipan. Jewelry covered layers of clothing like meringue topping. Little girls resembled butter creams, short skirts basted on them like icing. The mix was too rich for a taste nurtured on pound cake and decorated with understatement. I felt ethnic, Southern American British to get the crust right, and at times I wanted to return to Connecticut where I passed for liberal. At other times, however, I envied Francis. I longed to change my identity and to leap frolicking into the compote swirling alcoholic in front of me.

No matter the heat, identity does not melt off someone like me. Instead of wandering mentally, I roamed Miami. Several times I meandered up Second Avenue to a book fair held at Miami-Dade Community College. I walked slowly. Atop Bricknell Bridge I watched a girl fish the Miami River and gazed at cruise ships docked at the Port of Miami. A man tried to sell me a brass chain, swearing it was gold. "You have an accent," a woman said to me. "What country are you from?" When I turned myself around roaming streets, I asked a policeman for directions back to the Sheraton. "You hotel is that way," he said pointing south, adding, "You'll be all right so long as you don't go north." When I looked puzzled, he said, "people like you can't go that way." "That's right," a policewoman said. "You can go south, east, or west, but you can't go up there," she said, gesturing behind me.

At the fair I sauntered through booths selling books. I saw two writers whom I had met elsewhere, but they did not recognize me, so I didn't speak. A representative of the alumni association of the community college gave me a six-inch paper ruler, and I ate dinner on a terrace, paying five dollars for Thai noodles, a spring roll, and chicken and vegetables. I also drank a papaya royale, a four-dollar blend of papaya, strawberry, and banana. At the fair I attended talks and readings. A well-known essayist and humorist told sorry stories mocking old age. I would have done better, I told Josh when I returned to Connecticut, to have gone to a country sideshow and seen the Living Skeleton or Otis the Frog Boy. One evening I heard a Washington hostess, or "party matron," as the man sitting next to me dubbed her. The hostess had written a book containing suggestions on entertaining and descriptions of ritzy parties she attended. Famous names decorated the fabric of the woman's talk, people for whom I would not have dropped a stitch to meet.

Chatter about "the powerful" brings lumpy democratic words to my tongue. The talk, I complained to Josh, was a tale of caviar and seating arrangements, signifying nothing. "When the monkey can't reach ripe bananas, he says they are sour," Josh answered. "You're jealous. You'd give your eyeteeth to attend one of the woman's parties." "Don't," he warned, "become one of those middle-aged men who are not happy unless they are angry." Josh may be right. I have not attended a fancy "do" since I started teaching thirty years ago. In January, however, I return to Miami for Arts Week, at the end of which is the "Gala," a five-hundred-dollar-a-plate dinner held to benefit the foundation. The evening is a black-tie affair for all guests, except for folks who chose the 125 students. Not only can we "artists" wear suits, something essential in my case because the puppy who once wore my dinner jacket has aged into a pot-bellied, long-toothed mongrel, but we also attend free. I cannot wait to ask some gussied-up gent how much he paid to gatecrash. When he sniffs that he bought a five-hundred-dollar ticket, I'll exclaim, "Holy cow, you got fleeced! The guy at the door let me in for thirty-five dollars, plus tax."

Surprise frequents byways more than it does readings in large auditoriums. I spent much time at the fair in Children's Alley. One humid afternoon I listened to eleven little girls and one boy sing Christmas songs in Spanish. The girls held sugar canes and wore red stocking caps, each with a knobby white ball at the tip of the stocking. The children performed on an outdoor stage. Painted on the backdrop was a scene from *Don Quixote*. While three windmills stood stark against the Christmas horizon, a cottage with a thatch roof hunkered close to the stage, a mane of smoke twirling from its chimney. Below the windmills Don Quixote perched like a long-legged bird on Rosainte, while Sancho Panza chased a mule across a green field. What a surprise, I thought, to listen to "White Christmas" and not understand a word, the sun beating like an anvil and Sancho Panza dancing a jig through grass.

I left Miami a week ago, but since arriving home, days seem warm with surprise. On the flight back to Connecticut, the woman sitting next to me said, "I know you. You are Dave Barry the humorist. I saw you at the Miami Book Fair." "I expect you did," I said, opening Connie May Fowler's novel *Before Women Had Wings*. On Sunday Francis took two showers, one at ten in the morning and the other at nine in the evening. "Do you realize," I said, opening the bathroom door that night and speaking to Francis while he was in the shower, "that this is the second shower you have taken today?" "No," Francis said. "I only took one shower today. This is tomorrow's shower."

Dysfunctional

"This is a dysfunctional family," Edward said at dinner. The phrase "I'll dysfunctional you" rose to the gorge. Before I spoke, however, Vicki set a cranberry pie on the table, and my mood sweetened. *Dysfunctional*, though, is a popular word, an ingredient of countless thick paragraphs. Plucked from the sociological kitchen by the fast education industry, the word has drifted into common parlance, becoming adjectival monosodium glutamate, transforming crisp thought into heavy crust. Just that morning, Ben, a former student, wrote me. "College," he declared, "has been an incredible experience. I never realized how dysfunctional the world was until now." "Not dysfunctional," I thought, "but odd, brutal, and gloriously entertaining."

Arriving in the same mail as Ben's letter was a broadside advertising a book, *How God Sees Princess Diana*. "An Exciting Princess Diana Book For Your Religious Shelves," the volume examined the question, "Will Diana go to Heaven?" "Of all her social and charity work, the greatest thing Princess Diana ever did is move God to speak." Published in Pembroke, North Carolina, the book listed for $16.95. Five copies, however, cost only $38.00 including postage. "Discount," the broadside urged, "so the customer saves $5 and sell for 11.95, a 71% markup." The volume contained a miscellany of matters exploring the "Princess Diana Mystique." Readers, the flyer declared, "*will enjoy* a game built around words which were dear to Diana. *They can share* info boxes giving Q & A about

God and His laws on marriage, adultery and general relationships, all topics which so greatly ruled Diana's life. *They can remember Diana with clip art* of women and flowers that give a special flavor of remembrance."

Ben is young enough to be surprised by irrational and indecent behavior. He likes stories which have beginnings, middles, and, above all, clear endings. In contrast, I think endings contrived, the question marks and fragments of life being forced into periods and declarative sentences in order to create illusions of meaning. Last month in Carthage Loppie Groat urged Orpheeus Goforth to buy a feather bed. Aside from the ground, Orpheeus had never slept on anything other than corn shucks. Orpheeus was conservative, and he labeled people who rushed after change "mist-gulpers." Before he purchased the new bed, he put a chicken feather on a rock. Then he sat down. "I damn near wrecked my ass and gave myself the Savannah croup," he told Turlow Gutheridge. "If a single feather is that hard, imagine what a pile of them would feel like? I'd rather sleep in a gravel pit than on one of those fancy mattresses."

Age brings, if not contentment, at least the capacity to enjoy the bruised and the absurd, or from a narrative point of view, stories that go nowhere. This past summer Loppie Groat went to Wrightsville Beach, North Carolina. Loppie had never seen the ocean, and he filled a bottle half-full with salt water and brought it back to Carthage. On Googoo Hooberry's asking why he didn't fill the bottle completely, Loppie answered, "I was afraid that when the tide came in, it would blow the top off the bottle." Googoo was tired. Consequently, he acted badly and called Loppie a jackass, hurting his friend's feelings. "Loppie," Turlow Gutheridge said to him later, "don't let Googoo upset you. Many jackasses are nice people. Why, even an intelligent, upstanding person like you could be a jackass."

Change, as Loppie once put it, "stands still for no man." Despite Orpheeus's opinion, a person has to swallow a teaspoon of the new each year in order to remain functional. December makes parents aware of change. No matter the rituals—cutting the tree, bringing grandmother's ornaments down from the attic—parents cannot escape change. Children grow into edgy difference. No longer do Francis, Edward, and Eliza accompany Vicki and me to the annual Christmas sale at the Horse Barn. Instead of a stall of inexpensive presents, they want big gifts, costing bales of money. While Edward received Weider barbells, an EZ Crome Set weighing 160 pounds, and a leather Rawlings football, the gold-lettered "NCAA," ST-5 or soft-touch variety, Francis collected parts for his mountain bike: a new head set and Marzocchi Bomber, Z.3 light shocks, the 1998 model, and then two tires, both Continentals manufactured in Germany. Along with upgrading his bicycle, Francis improved his "on road" appearance, getting a pair of thin black Trek cycling trousers. For her part Eliza furnished a closet with clothes, turning herself into a traveler hoofing into the present from an antique land, receiving, among other items, bell bottom leggings, platform clogs with pallets for soles, and hangers of shirts, all needle-waisted and too small for a robust twelve year old.

In November, Edward tried out for the freshman basketball team at E. O. Smith High School. As a result basketball shoes almost ruined Christmas. The day after Thanksgiving, Vicki and the children and I went to Buckland Mall to shop for presents. While Vicki bought clothes for Francis and Eliza, Edward and I searched stores for "the right shoes." We started at eleven in the morning. At seven-thirty we ended in Bob's, having rummaged through Dick's, Foot Locker, Athlete's Foot, and Toe Jam, this last a store specializing in basketball shoes. After an hour in Bob's, Edward found a pair of shoes which, he said, "might do." At the cash register, however, he suddenly remembered that the coach wanted players to have similar shoes. "If I make the team, I'll have to buy different shoes," he said, "so I better not get these." Edward is inventive, and I knew the coach's statement fictional. Last year Edward rarely played in games at the Middle School. Competition for the team at the high school was more intense, and he did not want to appear at practice in new shoes, then get cut from the squad. "I'll buy the shoes," I said. "I will take them home, and you won't wear them until you make the team. If you don't make the team, I'll return the shoes." What seemed good sense to me struck Edward as dysfunctional. Three days later Edward made the team. The next morning Vicki drove to Buckland and spent four hours in shoe stores. Eventually she bought Edward a pair of Converse Chuck Taylor All-

Stars. "They'll do," Edward said, trying them on at home. "Are you sure they fit?" Vicki asked. "I'm sure," Edward answered. Three days later blisters covered his feet like galls maple leaves in spring. The following night Vicki took Edward to Evelyn's and Sports Stuff in the East Brook Mall. When Edward did not find shoes at the mall, she drove him to Nassiff's in Willimantic. Basketball shoes papered a wall. Nevertheless, no shoe appealed to Edward. "Damn it to hell!" Vicki said that night. "He can wear running shoes. I don't care if his toes rot off." The next Wednesday after practice I drove Edward back to Nassiff's. Not only had he made the team, but he was the second substitute off the bench. While Edward tried on shoes, I sat on the floor beneath a rack of cross-country skis. Within twenty minutes, Edward had a pair of Nikes. "Perfect," he said. "How did you get him to buy shoes?" Vicki asked later, irritation seasoning her voice like curry powder. "I understand workings of the adolescent mind," I said, "unlike some."

Happily a seam of continuance ran reassuringly through December. Early in the month I received the annual fund-raising letter from The Carts for Wienie Dogs Foundation, a charitable organization founded by a waggish friend in order to help crippled dachshunds. Ivadell Teeverbaugh Naslund, "Fundraising Secretary, Pro Tempore, TCFWDF," wrote this year's letter. In bold type at the top of the page appeared a statement by Clayton "Buzz" Carmody, the mayor of Colo, Iowa: "I wish you could have saw that little wienie dog. I was visiting the cart installation center when a volunteer brung him into the room, smiled, and laid him over in my arms so that I could stand him up on his new cart. The emotion I felt at the moment he raised his little paw in gratitude can't be told. And I get nauseated to my stomach when I think that this good work might stop because funds are low. *Don't let them little wienie dogs down!*"

The foundation offered "a special gift" to its "$50 contributors": Douglas Fir, the Talking Christmas Tree. Stapled to the upper left corner of the letter was a picture of Douglas. A red stocking cap with a snowball bouncing at the tip perched atop Douglas's branches. A third of the way down his trunk two eyes peered from behind a branch. When someone approached Douglas, the eyes lit and blinked. Below the eyes curved a red half-moon-shaped mouth.

"In addition," Naslund wrote, "this delightful little tree talks and sings. But that's not all. A local distributor has generously offered to customize Douglas exclusively for supporters of TCFWDF to perform 'O Little Carts for Wienie Dogs,' 'I Saw Mommy Kiss a Wienie Dog,' 'We Three Carts for Wienie Dogs Are,' and 'Let 'Em Roll, Let 'Em Roll, Let 'Em Roll.' He's sure to become a holiday tradition in your family, providing years of seasonal pleasure." I showed the letter to Edward. Closer to Ben's age than to mine, Edward thought the letter "dumb." "Why would anyone write such a thing?" he asked. I replied that joy and good will shone through sentences like strings of bulbs, but with thoughts only for barbells and basketball shoes, Edward did not understand.

In contrast to literary matters in which narrative lapses often resuscitate gasping stories, physical breakdowns rarely invigorate. In matters of health I struggle to keep my modifiers convention-ally placed and to prevent participles from dangling. At the end of November my sinuses became dysfunctional, and I doused them with amoxycillin, ceclor, and finally biaxin. In hopes of making my sinuses strong enough to resist clogging, I drenched my nose with steroids. Outside the body dysfunctional is the stuff of story. In-side, dysfunctional is disease. I am over fifty years old, and in De-cember, Dr. Dardick subjected my innards to a sigmoidoscopy, or some such word. After the examination, I put the exact term be-hind me. Indeed while the camera tacked though my entrails, un-accountably I recalled a time when I was five years old and wildly functional. Mother and Father went to a party on New Year's Eve, leaving me in the protection of an aged baby-sitter. A hour after leaving home, Mother received a telephone call from the sitter. She had locked herself in the bedroom. "He chased me through the house with a butcher knife, and if I leave the bedroom, he'll kill me," she shrieked. "He told me he was going to cut my throat and feed me to the ducks in Centennial Pond." "That damned old fool," Mother told Grandmother later. "She fell for one of Sammy's stories. When we got home, he was asleep on the living room sofa. There was a butcher knife on the table beside the sofa, but if the woman had told Sammy to put the knife down, he'd have done so. He's a good little boy and doesn't disobey." The woman did not baby-sit for Mother and Father again. "I wouldn't let a jackass like that in my house again for love or money," Mother said.

Albeit not dysfunctional, some people are plagued by sorry states of mind. Parked beside the curb outside Store 24 on Christmas Eve was a black two-door Dodge. Strapped to the front bumper was a Teddy bear. The bear wrote black mittens and socks and a green jacket with red checked cuffs. Pinned to the bear's chest was a laminated card. Printed in blue across the top of the card was "Hello, My Name Is." Under the words in black capital letters appeared "BAMBI KILLER." "The swaggerer who owns this car," I thought as I strolled behind the sedan, noting a Rhode Island license plate, "will do poorly in life, especially if he has to impress people like me." Not only do words create mood but they cloud perception. I had just left the Cup of Sun. The Alamode Rhetorical Style of Language used by a student had soured my cup of coffee. "I was, like, slow dancing with, like, a blond girl. All of sudden, she just, like, walks away from me. I'm like," a boy said, pausing at the end of the last phrase because he could not think of a word to describe his feelings. My thoughts, on the other hand, were clear. I fled the café, abandoning the student to the linguistically hopeless world of the flesh and like.

Even people who think in simple sentences can occasionally behave dysfunctionally. Two weeks ago I suffered a panic attack. The men's locker room in the gymnasium is so small that Josh calls it "homoerotic." In the shower two thin poles extend from floor to ceiling. Two-thirds the way up each pipe four silver nozzles jut downward. When a knob is turned, each nozzle sprays a mist of water. Resembling a fog low over a hollow, the mist does not drift more than eighteen inches from the pipe. As a result when two men shower around the same pipe, collegiality results. "People are so arsiturvy," Josh said last Sunday, "that I often discover that instead of scrubbing my dandilollie I'm washing the friskorum wagging on the lad beside me. Indeed, to forestall embarrassment and misunderstanding, I now address my shower companion before lathering, saying, 'cousin, we are so close that I might as well wash yours while I wash mine.'"

I prefer relatives farther removed from shower. One Wednesday a man wearing a jewelry store on his ears pranced into the locker room. Like me he was going swimming. Unlike me he wore a banana hammock, as the fashion editor of *Vogue* labels skimpy trunks. The right sort of people in New England, at least in my New England, buy hammocks from the L. L. Bean and Crate & Barrel catalogues, not from the vegetable counter or the fruit bin at Mr. Frederick's of Hollywood.

Swimming beside the wagtail did not appeal to me. Attached to the keys of locks are safety pins. Once a person hangs his clothes up and shuts his locker, he usually opens the pin and buckles it and the key to his bathing suit. Unaccountably I became convinced that the man had AIDS. I imagined him opening the pin in the pool, and after jabbing it through a vein, springing into my lane and ramming the pin deep in my back. Throughout the swim I watched the man nervously, and when he splashed into sight, I paddled to the far side of my lane and clung to the rope. Not only that, but instead of swimming my usual mile, I swam a mile and a half, staying in the pool long after the man left so that I would not have to shower alongside him.

Season may have been responsible for the whirligig of fear. December bewitches. As the end of the year approaches, people evaluate their lives. Rarely do memories seem bullish. In retrospect life appears bearish. On the big groaning board failures outnumber successes. For children and adults Christmas is emblematic of the future, promising years of tinseled surprises to the former, reminding the latter of fallings, the mortality not simply of family and friends but also of talent and opportunity. "Hope," Turlow Gutheridge once said, "sets a good breakfast but a poor supper." For many people not Hope but Despair waits the Christmas table. Early in December Fred wrote from Ohio. The wife of Jimmy, a mutual friend, "had suffered some sort of breakdown." That afternoon I called Jimmy. His secretary answered the telephone and explained that he was out of state, adding, "He'll be sorry to have missed you." "Oh, well," I said, "wish him Merry Christmas from me, and by the way, how is Tina doing?" The secretary paused before she answered. "We hope," the woman said, "that she is now getting the treatment she needs." And what might that be, I thought after putting the phone down, the shock of an electric spring or doses of the capacity to dream?

In the mail next afternoon I received a postcard from Pickering, England. Four snapshots appeared on the front of the card. Bucolic and restful, the pictures depicted a slow, sentimental time. A canal curved like a silver elbow behind a red mill. Under a blue sky ruins of a castle stretched like a table setting across a green hill. A bicycle leaned against a rack outside the post office; in the distance a woman walked a dog along the street, chimney pipes tilting red over her head. In the last snapshot a couple stood outside the Forest & Vale Hotel. Two stories tall, the hotel was cozy and welcoming, its front door open, a mitten of greenery warm around it. Written in black ink on the other side of the card was "What a lovely village! I miss you." The card was not signed, but I recognized the handwriting despite not having seen it in twenty-two years.

I was pondering the card when Josh appeared. "Merry Christmas," I said. "Christmas, yes, but merry, no," Josh answered. The day before Josh had driven his daughter to a basketball game at the high school. In the parking lot he met Alice, mother of one of his daughter's teammates. "The season has driven me wacky," she said to him, "and I must tell you something." "Fred," she continued, referring to her husband, "is a fine man, and I'm almost happy. But during all those years you and I served on the hospital board, I used to look at you across the room and dream of what I missed. Isn't life peculiar?" "It sure is," Josh said, strangling the temptation to reply that the only thing that warmed his hours at the hospital were thoughts of her. "December makes people dysfunctional," Josh said.

After Alice left, Josh walked across the street to the Cup of Sun to "get a bran muffin and muse." He did not muse long. "Josh, I need advice," a woman said, approaching his table. "I was married for eleven years. Then I got divorced, and for the past thirteen years, a man and I have lived together. In October he moved out, saying he needed to mine the gems of his character. What he found was fool's gold. Last week he begged me to take him back. I refused, telling him that I was through with zirconium." "Anyway, Josh," she continued, "you are a man about town. Do you know any decent available diamonds?" Dislocations of season spun dizzying through the day. For years Josh has raised money for an orphanage. In the mail at his house was a check from a donor. The check was large. Accompanying it, however, was a stormy note. "I don't know what ails me," the man wrote, "but as I age I often think the best nursery for unwanted children is the bottom of the river."

Early next morning I walked across campus. The new chemistry building loured over the North Eagleville Road. Four stories high with thirteen gray chimneys resembling massive exhaust pipes rising from the roof and with its walls plastered with black brick, the building blocks the sun, turning noon to dusk, dusk to midnight, and blowing vital darkness into the phrase *dismal science*. The architect's favorite book, Josh said, was Charles Dickens's novel *Hard Times*. Before designing the building, the man studied Coketown, the book's industrial slum. "I realize that the building appears severely workful," an administrator said, "but the innards are functional." Often heard at universities, *functional* is used by bore constrictors, people who never have ideas they don't take seriously. Also popular in administrative halls, Josh tells, me is *accountability*. Unfortunately the word doesn't apply to ballet, theater, art, reading, raising a family, or eggnog on Christmas Eve. "The word strips away everything that really counts in life," Josh said, "leaving people with the illusion of being functional, making them smug and creating a dangerously dysfunctional state of mind. To folks deceived by rote and definition, truly functional people will always appear ditherers."

Josh thinks clearly, and sometimes I agree with him. Nevertheless no matter how well a farmer fences a pasture, or an argument, he'll lose a cow now and then. Still, dithering keeps me afloat, even though pools occasionally swamp reason. Instead of ruining shining hours by improving them and myself, as the busy bees did in Isaac Watts's *Divine Songs*, I simply enjoy whimsical moments. "Skylarking, that's how you spend paragraphs," Josh said. "Not skylarking. That's British," I answered. "In our New England December, chickadeeing, titmousing, nuthatching, or just finching around would be better."

The chemistry building soon slipped from mind. Later that morning I wandered woods. At first the going was gloomy. Along the ridge behind the sheep barns white pines split into two huge limbs, making the trees resemble massive tuning forks. Storms often snapped one of the limbs, throwing it to the ground, where it buckled and splintered across boulders. The broken trees reminded me of people who suffered strokes, parts of their bodies green and vigorous, other parts shattered, muscles sinking into soil, flesh rotting like damp wood. In forests metaphors are short-lived. Six does hurried across a slope, tails flagging, looking like finials atop the corners of board-and-batten fences. Forty feet above the ground a raccoon stared from an eyelet in an oak. At the edge of woods tree sparrows clustered in brambles. The tracks of a vole sputtered between two grass hummocks. Near the second hummock the tracks stopped. A hawk had dropped on the vole. Talons ripped the icy crust into scratches while the primary feathers on the bird's left wing combed across snow, brushing flakes into parts and waves. As the temperature rose, ice on the Fenton River wheezed and coughed. Big rocks thrust up tonsured from the river bed, milky ice hanging around them in patches. I walked across the beaver pond. Scalloped-shaped frost crystals shingled alders and rushes. Flaring outward, the crystals tied petaled willow galls into silver-and-black carnations.

In the afternoon I roamed the cornfields behind the old police station and the broken land above the dump. Beyond the dump two red-tailed hawks sat in a white oak. Mourning doves rattled from shelter as I walked the ridge. Maleberry grew at the edge of the swamp, red buds snuggling along twigs and the tops of seedpods split into five-pointed stars. On a lapel of earth hanging over a ditch, hop hornbeam grew twilly. Remnants of wild flowers embroidered a windy, snow-covered hill. From a distance the dried stalks looked like a frieze of Kate Greenaway characters: goldenrod curtseying; English plantain splayed out in napkins; asters sparkling and fresh as nursery schoolers; chicory, slats of a fence akimbo; parasols of Queen Ann's lace; and bull thistles empty as picnic hampers. At sunset gray birch along the ridge above the dump turned red. In a cornfield the sun skipped off snow, caught on stubble, splattering it yellow, before sinking and vanishing into dark furrows.

The next day university doings dropped from mind, and I was in Carthage for the annual Homegoing, not coming, parade. On the page the parade was longer than it would have been in life, covering nine paragraphs, the literary equivalent of two score city blocks. Proverbs Goforth led the parade, riding Jack, a white circus horse owned by Ben Meadows. Wearing a scarlet sacerdotal robe complete with breast plate borrowed from the high priest of the Carthage chapter of the Royal Arch Masons, a fez knocked from the head of a convivial Shriner during an evening's revelry at Enos Mayfield's Inn, and blowing a cow's horn and carrying a white cardboard shield, a Machabei cross painted on the front in purple, Proverbs represented the King of Kings and the Lord of Lords. Behind him followed a cart containing three buzzards, drawn by Jeddry, Loppie Groat's mule. Feeding on the body of a stillborn Jersey calf, donated to the parade by Big Mama Timmons, owner of the Butterburg Dairy, the buzzards were tied to railings running around the cart. Netted from chapter nine of the Book of Revelation, the birds represented the fowls "that flew in the midst of heaven" and fed upon "the flesh of mighty men." For its part the dead calf stood for the King's vanquished foes, albeit members of the Church of the Chastening Rod insisted upon calling the calf "the hairy leg of Satan."

Honking at Jeddry's heels was Morris Hamper driving a black Cadillac convertible. Perched high on the headrest above the back seat was Turlow Gutheridge, recently elected mayor of Carthage. On the seat beneath Turlow were four wicker baskets, each containing a bushel of kittens. Sponsored by the Lions Club, Turlow represented Daniel in the Lion's Den. As the parade wound through Carthage, Turlow gave the kittens to children lined along the sidewalk. "Seventy-two kittens," he said later, "and only one mishap." The accident occurred when little Chrissy Dodd dropped an orange kitten. Before anyone could scoop the kitten up, it scampered under the wheels of the Cadillac and was flattened. "Its head exploded just like a honeydew melon," Googoo said. "You could have heard the pop in South Carthage."

The only other mishap occurred on the Herndon Ice Company's float, Jesus Walking on Water. Workers at the company shaved blocks of ice and laid a pond out in the back of a flatbed wagon, for the safety of Jesus surrounding the pond with bales of hay. The best ice-skater in Carthage and editor of the *Courier,* the weekly newspaper, Levi Crowell portrayed Jesus. Before the parade began,

Levi salchowed over to Enos Mayfield's Inn and purchased a bottle of tonic, or as he told Chloris, his wife, "Mary Garden Perfume," in order to keep frostbite from nipping his toes. The perfume protected Levi from both frostbite and restraint. Two-thirds the way through the parade the perfume caused a stink, however. Just outside Haskins Funeral Home, Levi tripped on his robes while attempting a camel and, flipping heels over head, whacked his forehead on the ice, knocking himself unconscious. Dr. Sollows having decided that Levi had to remain flat while being moved, Slubey Garts opened the funeral home and spectators laid Levi in a Blue Pearl coffin. After wrapping him in a shroud for warmth, they carried him to the hospital. Levi, Slubey said, made a lovely corpse, adding that he was looking forward to the time when he could really serve Levi. "Though I hope that blessed dawn," he said, "is warmer than today. Funerals don't draw crowds on cold days." The sight of a horde of pallbearers rushing Levi through Carthage disturbed Chloris considerably, not so much, however, as learning later that Levi only suffered a concussion. "Chloris has long said she looks better in black that in any other color," Hoben Donkin told the crowd at Ankerrow's Café, "and her greatest regret in life is that Carthage is so small she don't get to wear black more often."

Behind Turlow followed a wagon containing Mayleen Smoots in trousers and playing her harp, representing David. Marching after David was the high school band, dressed in yellow caftans borrowed from Shriners belonging to the Zebulon Temple in Lebanon. Among crowds along Main Street the most popular music in the parade was that supplied by the choir of "First and Only Baptist." The choir sang old-fashioned, sentimental songs, among others, "Put My Little Baby Shoes Away," "I Went to Church Like an Honest Girl Should," and "When the Mountain Laurel Blooms Again."

Religion being corporate in Middle Tennessee, the parade was long. Knockley's Brass Foundry in Crossville sponsored Hiram of Tyre, Elias Gunny the blacksmith riding in a wagon and pretending to pound brass into pillars, the sides of the wagon being decorated with plaster of Paris pomegranates painted gold. Moody and Sankey, the coal merchants, sponsored Job on the pile of ashes. Risden Moore hunkered over a mound of cinders eight feet tall.

Every time a breeze blew, ashes swirled, and Risden, Hoben said, "choked like a catfish on a sandbank." On the float underwritten by Elam's Haberdashery, Bunberry Blodgett appeared as Joseph in the coat of many colors, wearing a sunny blue-and-white haspel jacket. Behind Bunberry stood two mannequins, Adam and Eve in formal dress after the fall, Adam attired as a Scotsman, wearing a kilt, the MacClaren plaid in honor of the McClarin family in Carthage and Eve in a boa and a green cocktail dress, sequins snaking over it, outlining magnolia leaves.

King's Barber Shop sponsored Delilah Trimming Samson's Hair. Wearing a long red wig and holding garden shears, Clevanna Farquarhson stood behind a barber's chair and pretended to give Belial Snethen a haircut. Because a childhood fever left him bald as the round end of a broom, Belial, onlookers agreed, made an especially fine Danite. Barstow's Ceiling Fans in Gallatin sponsored the Fiery Furnace, "Anti-Boilant for Home and Office. With a Barstow Fan You'll Never Overheat." Inside a circle of smudge pots stood Shadrach, Meshach, and Abednego, the parts being played by Ashael Otis, Gideon Palmer, and Matthew Lanktree, all wearing gas masks loaned by the Veterans of Foreign Wars. Occasionally a fourth figure flitted through the smoke, Mr. Billy Timmons's light-footed portrayal of the Son of God being easily recognizable.

One float even came from Nashville. The Vanderbilt Medical School sent an ambulance and two residents to mime Lazarus rising from the dead. Bags of intravenous liquid filled with colored water, Christmas tree lights blinking around them, lined the inside of the ambulance. While one of the residents lay on a pallet, dressed in boots and overalls, a pitchfork by his side, the other resident playing Jesus the Physician, shook a bag of golden water over the "patient's" head. Once the bag was empty, the driver of the ambulance blew his siren, and the patient sat upright and asked for a cigarette, saying loudly, "I can't resist Smith County burley." White canvases resembling shades rolled down both sides of the ambulance. Printed on the canvases was "MIRACLES HAPPEN EVERY DAY AT VANDY. GO COMMODORES. HOLD THAT LIFELINE."

Sponsored by the Male and Female Select School, the last float was educational. Quintus Tyler stood in front of six children sitting at desks. In his right hand Quintus held a ruler tipped with a silver star which he pointed at a blackboard. Written on the blackboard was "MENE, MENE, TEKEL, UPHARSIN." Near the end of the parade Billie Dinwidder handed Quintus a Roman candle. After lighting the candle, Quintus aimed above the blackboard, balls of fire shooting over the wagon "as signs signifying the destruction of Babylon."

Despite the benevolent, indeed scholarly, intentions of the parade, the most popular float was Bathsheba Bathing, sponsored by the Toodle Ranch on Highway 70. A wrangler at the ranch, Betty Lou Gamphasante, posed as Bathsheba. Betty Lou stretched out in a hot tub shaped like a policeman's cap. She wrapped a thick terry cloth towel around her legs, binding it together at her waist. She also wore a veil and on her head a cowboy hat, a white rose stuck in the band. In her left hand she held a louver sponge. Her right hand she waved at the crowd. Like Bathsheba when she flourished as the apple in David's eye, Betty Lou was naked from waist to veil. Because of the veil and hat, she was not easy to recognize, however, only being identified when Hopp Watrous noticed the tattoo "Viva La Amish" curving beneath her left "globe." "She got that on a spread in Pennsylvania," Hopp explained, adding that "Amish Catholics had impressed Betty Lou profoundly." "She's also got a tattoo of a horse-drawn carriage," Hopp said, "but it's mushed, and you can't see it now. She's a little ashamed of it, and the first time I was a dude at the ranch she didn't want to show it to me. But I told her, 'You can't conceal a tattoo from God, so why hide it from man?' That did the trick. She's got a way of moving so the horse gallops and the carriage, praise King Jesus, bounces up and down just like it was traveling on a dirt road back in the country."

Just as I finished describing Betty Lou, Edward came into the study and, standing behind me, read over my shoulder. "Daddy," he said, "none of this makes sense. What will readers think?" "Honey," I said, "my essays are so dysfunctional that pages always make sense. If you listen carefully to my pencil, you just might hear the choir from "First and Only Baptist" singing "Sucking Cider Through a Straw" or "Silver-Haired Daddy of Mine."

A Little Fling

"It was fun, nothing important," Ellen recounted, "just a little fling." How nice, I thought, to enjoy lightness of being and not be pulled down by words weighty as barbells: love, meaning, commitment. Of course essays are also little flings, consisting of only a few leaves, not the novel's tree of pages. Similarly, good conversation depends on fleeting, well-turned phrases that sparkle and for a moment make one forget significance. "If you swim the bayou," Josh said recently, "don't tease the alligator." Last Sunday in the Cup of Sun two religious fundamentalists had a heated discussion. "Why go to the law," one man said, balling his fist, "when the court is in Hell?" Instead of the crackle of proverbs, some bright sentences shine with personality. "Whenever people start riding fast on horses and shooting guns, I switch the channel," Ellen said on Monday. Not for nothing were old gravestones rounded across the top, making them resemble tongues jutting out of the earth. Not only can the tongue bury its possessor, but it can so destroy reputation that a person becomes the remarks he made. Josh says things I won't permit myself to think. Of a university trustee, Josh said recently, "He's the kind of man who would give even sodomy a bad name."

People who read my books occasionally write and describe the doings of my characters, "things they might not tell you about," a man from Tennessee explained in January. Clevanna Farquarhson and Vester McBee, the man wrote, went to Nashville to shop after Christmas. They exhausted themselves at Harvey's and Cain-Sloan's. When they returned to the Andrew Jackson Hotel, they collapsed in the lobby, sprawling out in big, red chairs, packages scattered about their feet, too tired to take the elevator to their room. After sitting for thirty-five minutes, Clevanna finally spoke. "I've got to get up. My rear end's done gone to sleep on me." "I thought it might have done," Vester responded. "I heard it snore three or four times."

Only a gastroenterologist could dig food for thought out of that tale. The truth, though, is that most thoughts are flings and don't bear thinking about. Ideas bubble into consciousness, shine for a moment, then explode into nothing. Not good, but bad example teaches lessons, Josh told me yesterday. "Good example bores, and people ignore it," he said. "In contrast bad example startles and impresses itself upon the mind, terrifying and teaching people to behave." "Think about it," Josh said, when I looked puzzled.

"I will," I said, and did not, my attention being diverted by the bowl of a pipe a reader sent me. Hand carved, the bowl was a small boot. While the pipe stem stuck into the toe, the uppers flapped open, resembling a funnel, the lace having been pulled from the eyes. As I sat at my desk pondering shoehorning socks of tobacco into the bowl—Havana seed, Sumatra, and Maryland and Connecticut broad-leaf, even a last or two of Tube Rose Snuff—Vicki handed me a box of Godiva chocolate. The candy was a Christmas present. "You are entitled to two pieces," she said. I put the pipe bowl on a shelf and promptly forgot about it. Not only are flings themselves short-lived, but people susceptible to flings have such a capacity to appreciate diverse things that they skip from one interest to another.

I ate only one bonbon, a Pyramid, a shirt of coconut cream inside a chocolate dinner jacket. Atop the first layer of candy in the box lay a broadside folded into sixths. On the broadside appeared pictures of Godiva candies, forty-six different candies, each followed by a name and a short description. Words seduce me quicker than sugar, and instead of munching, I read, mulling the sound, not the taste, of Daisy, Lion of Belgium, Almond Butter Dome, Feather, Starfish, Open Oyster, and Fabiola.

In Marzipan did Kubla Khan
A stately Scallop Shell decree:

Where Topaz, the Chocolate Mousse ran
Though Paola measureless to man
Down to a Praline Cascadē,

I said, adding, "The rhythmic ingredients need a shake of the old
Hazelnut before they'll be completely Cordial, not to mention
Carré Au Croquant." "Sure," Vicki said, picking up the box.
The next morning was cold and windy. I walked around Mirror Lake. Ice shuttered over the surface, spreading out from banks
like an eyelid closing. A dark pupil of water remained open, Canada
geese stirring through it like motes. An older man stood near the
causeway. When I sauntered past, he said, "The wind blows just
so." As he spoke, he moved his right hand up and down. Unlike
the words, which were controlled, even neat, the man's arm
trembled. Instead of capturing the movement of air, the hand quivered into ellipsis then dropped abruptly to the man's haunch.
"What should a person make of such things—the wind, the hand,
the words?" I thought as I approached the cottonwood at the end
of the lake. Answering would have inflated the scene with significance. Instead of an amble, my walk would have become a jour-
ney, and so wiping my palm across the rough bark of the cottonwood, I left the moment slack.

Success often depends upon puffing doings into meaning and
out of truth. Because my son Francis did well on the PSATs, a sort
of preliminary college entrance examination taken by juniors in
high school, a foundation invited him to apply for a summer fellowship, six weeks spent at Kenyon or Cornell discussing identity.
Applicants were instructed to write a series of short essays, one "on
a conflict you have faced and attempted to resolve," another evaluating a book "read outside of class." Francis is an amiable boy who
slips seamless in and through diverse groups, avoiding conflict.
Consequently I sought Josh's advice. Josh has no patience for the
sentimentality the application seemed to elicit. "Francis should
write," Josh said, "that for years a blond boy bullied me. This fall,
however, I took a course in conflict resolution. The class made all
the difference and taught me how to resolve quarrels. For a final
project at the end of term I borrowed an iron bar from shop and

hammered the bully's wrists through his elbows into his shoulder blades. Not only did I get an A+ for the course, but no one has bothered me since. In fact swarms of sissies admire me, and namby-pambies dog my every footstep."

Josh's ideas are provocative. Still, he can be too philosophical for the page. After saying that Francis would ponder his suggestions, I asked if he had any thoughts about evaluating a book. Francis has recently read Patricia Cornwell's thrillers, and Josh suggested that he describe Cornwell's heroine Kay Scarpetta, a medical examiner intrigued by all sorts of butchery. "Daddy told me to read *Moby-Dick* then pretend to be enthusiastic about it," Josh said, shaping Francis's essay, "but I think mammals with humpbacks who float in water and sing songs are for the *oiseaux*, so I shook my iron bar in his face and told him to 'kiss my blubber.' I'm writing about what I like."

Words, not deeds, compose my flings. In truth, accomplishment which appears inspired usually depends upon discipline. People who accomplish things lead monotonous lives. Although my paragraphs often celebrate spontaneity, routine buckles me to pad and pencil. Six days a week I swim a mile in the university pool. No matter how I vary the counting, going from top to bottom or starting in the middle and spreading out toward both ends at the same time, a mile is always seventy-two lengths. Four days a week I roam field and wood, jotting down notes. From a walk I often harvest a single observation. Yesterday I found shards of clay pigeons, Remington Blue Rocks, *218* stamped in the middle of some, *302* in the center of others. When bound together by grammar, observations transform walks into fabrics quick with color and event. Last week in the Ogushwitz meadow a red-shouldered hawk fell through a drizzle onto a vole. The hawk carried the vole into a small beech. Later the bird fluffed itself into a reddish butterball, the tree's caramel leaves twisting sweet about its wings. Three bluebirds tumbled out of a bar of sunlight and rained over corn stubble. Catkins on gray birch shredded into seed, each seed resembling a minute orange butterfly. A rug of juniper hairy-cap moss covered a damp slope. While leaves of the moss rolled inward and upward into red lances, spore cases crumbled, the lids having fallen off, exposing bald membranes, the teeth around rims silver clippers.

To break patterns of observation I travel, the trips flings, furnishing sentences for essays. In January I spent five days in Miami as judge on a writing panel sponsored by the National Foundation for Advancement in the Arts. Along with two score judges the foundation brought 125 high school seniors to Miami, winners of awards in eight categories. At dinner the first night I met students selected for their writing. Rebekah smiled like a sonnet. She was immediately likable, all lines of her personality rounded couplets, none trailing off into angular Alexandrines. "Mr. Pickering," she said, "do you know a writer named Fred Church?" Freddy was an old friend. In his mid-sixties, he is a distinguished and lively poet. "Mr. Church read his poetry at my school," Rebekah continued giggling. "I think he was a little tight because afterward he pinched me on the ass." "Freddy," I said, "is renown for good taste." The last evening in Florida judges and students were guests at a formal dinner. Champagne swept across the hours in creeks. I tried to leap gulches without getting damp, but, alas, I slipped and tumbled into a backwater. "Rebekah," I said at midnight, "if I give you a friendly little tweak on the bottom, the next time you see Mr. Church, you can ask him, 'do you know Sam Pickering? I met him in Miami. He got a little tiddly and. . . .'"

At least that is what I might have said after the dinner. For me flings occur more in imagination than fact. What really happened in Miami was that I spent long hours in a meeting room at the Sheraton Hotel on Biscayne Bay. The rug in the room smacked of a fruity, extravagant Florida I didn't see. Across the shag bromeliads blossomed orange and blue. Purple ferns waved. Green flames leaped from bird of paradise while red and black flowed across philodendron in an acrylic sunset. Often I stared out the window. Beyond the panes Florida was pastel. In a breeze leaves of royal palms shook like cowlicks. Caspian terns soared above the Miami River, their orange bills cutting the air like scissors. During a break I watched brown pelicans. Until they spotted fish the birds hovered above the bay like erasers poised above paper. Suddenly, though, they dropped their feet, for a moment stuttering and paddling the air. Then they pushed their wings back, and sharpening their bodies, fell, rotating their heads just before smacking the water.

One afternoon I walked South Beach. The water was green, and freighters glided along the horizon. Stranded amid tangles of weed and shells, Portuguese men of war trembled like small, leaky balloons. A flock of laughing gulls stretched across the beach. Ocean Drive resembled a shuffleboard, the art deco buildings clumped together like disks, blue and white, and sometimes yellow. Muscular men and women in shorts skated sidewalks, Walkmans clamped to their ears. Sea grape grew behind the sand. Trunks of the trees spiraled and bulged muscular, color staining bark: gray, yellow, white, and sometimes blue. Big as saucers several leaves had fallen and turned red and yellow.

One morning I walked north from the hotel through Bayfront Park to Bayside Marketplace. In the park chameleons skittered between ropes of figs while blossoms on a bauhinia broke and slipped silently to the ground. Green had drained from margins of the leaves, turning edges into dry crust. Much of the park was blighted. Alcoholics lay on the grass, thinning into stems. Pods of bottles rooted behind blocks of coral, the most common species being a malt liquor, Olde English 800, the quart "Wide-Mouth" variety. Shops at the Marketplace were the ordinary grafts of commerce: Brookstone, GAP, The Limited, B. Dalton, Warner Brothers, Foot Locker, Kids Foot Locker, Lady Foot Locker, and Accessories of Benetton. Female boat-tailed grackles perched on railings, swatches of yellow and green streaking their breasts like whistles. Big-bellied men smoked cigars, and everybody wore pagers.

The next day I explored Coconut Grove. On Mary Street I read a sign outside an orange building surrounded by an iron fence. "Parking For Premiere Center For Cosmetic Surgery," the sign said. "For Access Please Pull Up & Honk Horn." For a second I thought about "beeping" raucously. But I didn't. I have aged beyond the illusion that improvement improves. As I stood on the sidewalk, I wondered how doctors at the center removed warts. In Middle Tennessee Madame Exodius sold snails as wart removers. The snails cost three cents apiece. "Starve the snail two weeks so it will be hungry," Madame Exodius wrote on prescriptions. "Before applying a snail to a wart, paint the wart green. The snail will believe the wart a leaf. Snails are especially fond of rugosa roses, and if you spot the green with red, treatment will be doubly effective."

In December an agent urged me to write a novel about Carthage. I declined, explaining that a novel required sustained effort and adding that I visited Carthage for fun, not work. The first trip occurred ten books ago. Because I went for a quick narrative fling, I handled inhabitants carelessly. Shortly after Slubey Garts appeared, I killed him. A book later, however, I exhumed him. He popped into life like the memory of an old girlfriend, the difference being that instead of rummaging the past in search of tender recollection this time I created a past in the present. After I am dead, Slubey will live on my pages. "Readers like him, and maybe Daddy," Eliza said, "he'll bring you back from the grave just like you resuscitated him."

That cheery thought aside, however, on the flight back from Miami to Hartford, I stopped in Carthage. Last June Slubey opened the Victoryland nursing home. The home was shaped like a cross. The lower leg of the cross contained the lobby and office. Rooms for "dear ones" filled the upper three legs, or rungs of Jacob's Ladder, as Slubey called them, to the left the first rung for comparatively healthy patients, to the right the second rung, and at the top of the cross the third and last rung, from which Proverbs Goforth said, folks could hear angel wings rustling. A portico extended over the front door. Painted on it was Mt. Pisgah. The door itself consisted of double doors, scarlet waves splashed over them so that when the door opened "the Red Sea" parted. Lush with hostas, ginger, rubber plants, and three cages of turquoise parakeets, the lobby represented Eden. While nurses dressed in the customary white robes, they also wore gold slippers. Instead of physical therapy, patients signed up for Old or New Testament therapy. Patients who participated in New Testament therapy were inevitably calm. In contrast, Old Testament therapy often provoked physical exertion. While I was in Carthage, Sawyer Blodgett and Delmus Weymouth got into a fistfight after arguing over whether or not the angel who slaughtered a "hundred and fourscore and five thousand" Assyrians in Sennacherib's camp was actually the black plague.

Victoryland was not simply a warehouse for Children of Eve robbed of their blooms. Patients ran a bakery called Manna from Heaven. They baked loaves of whole wheat and sourdough bread. Their specialty, however, was cinnamon buns. "The miracle of the loaves and the buns," Slubey said. In a corner of the lobby stood a small coffee house, and people came from all over Carthage to buy buns and sip coffee, in the process providing patients with visitors. Dr. Sollows treated patients in the home. When Dr. Sollows was busy, Jacob Fagenbaum stood in for him. Born Jewish, Dr. Jacob, as patients called him, had become a member of the Church of Christ. Very ill patients, those ready for robes in the angel band, often requested that Dr. Jacob minister to them, always asking that he wear a yarmulke, explaining that the cap made the Holy Land seem close.

Religious themes were woven through the fabric of Victoryland. Not locks, but seals were on doors to rooms, seven trumpets radiating out from each seal. From the spokes of wheelchairs the Star of Bethlehem glittered. Rooms themselves were painted sky blue, and a rainbow sliced across each eastern wall. Headboards were white and heart-shaped, the lobes rising above the bed like cumulus clouds. Although electric, table lamps sat on bases curving like gravy boats, resembling the lamps carried by the five wise virgins. Instead of a chest of drawers to hold clothes, each room contained a "Christ of Drawers," heads of the apostles being carved down the two front legs, six on the left leg, and five on the right, Judas being excluded. Atop the third rung of rooms were the Enoch and Elijah chambers, held in readiness for dear ones soon to walk with God. Along the wall of the latter room a fiery chariot drawn by spotted horses fell out of a whirlwind. A bearded figure in a white robe stood in the chariot, his arms reaching toward the patient's bed. In the former room Enoch sat on an ivory throne, one hand resting on the head of his son Methuselah, the other stretching across the wall toward the patient.

Between Charlotte, North Carolina, and Richmond, Virginia, I described Victoryland to the man sitting beside me in the plane. He was a Baptist preacher. "Good Lord," he said. "The home sounds wonderful. How did you think of it?" "The idea came to me while I was having a little fling," I said. "Would you be interested in building a prototype?" the man asked. "Not really," I answered, suddenly thinking about Googoo Hooberry. Last August while Googoo was picking blackberries, he was surprised by a bear. Googoo escaped by running across a frozen pond. "It was practically a miracle Googoo escaped," Hoben Donkin said later. "It was," Loppie Groat agreed, adding, "not only does Googoo not believe in ghosts, he's not even frightened of them."

Killing the Bear

"I'm planning to buy a tractor," Ben Meadows told Googoo Hooberry in Ankerrow's Café. "I'll pay for it in fall with takings from tobacco I planted." Always careful with money, Googoo stroked his chin and stared out the window before replying. "Don't sell the hide before you kill the bear," Googoo said, turning toward Ben. The clearer the prose, the more cautionary the advice. The lumber used to frame good living is inevitably declarative, the end girders periods, blocking out disruptive questions. "If an antidote for poison isn't in the medicine cabinet, don't stick your hand in a copperhead's mouth," Googoo once warned Hoben Donkin. On pages supporting instructive bearing walls copperheads don't coil so venomously as they do on ledges. According to an old Turkish tale snakes themselves are loath to strike, and Hoben could have crammed his fist down a copperhead's gullet without being bitten. Like man, the snake has received much cautionary advice, and the Turkish story described the end of a snake which lost a portion of its tail every time it struck. "Eventually," the story recounted, "the serpent shrank to a head no bigger than a stone." Unable to crawl into shade, the head baked in the sun until it dried into ash and wind scattered it across rock and sand.

Instructive stories often urge controlling appetite at the expense of starving the imagination. Mules were once fertile. According to the *Legend of Abgar* a mule was present when Jesus was born. The night after the birth was chilly, and Mary covered her baby with straw. Returning to the manger after pulling sleds loaded with stones, the mule was hungry and without thinking chewed the straw blanket off Jesus. As a result Jesus became chilled and the next morning ran a high fever. The mule's behavior angered the Lord. He decided that a creature with so little discipline was dangerous, and He dispatched an angel to Bethlehem, ordering him to sterilize the mule.

Often people are so frightened of erring that they don't live, not simply burying talents as did the "unprofitable servant" in Matthew but destroying them outright. In his *Visions,* Saint Mechthild described a young nun with eyes "blacker than the tents of Kedar." The eyes captivated a prince. He fell in love with the girl and begged her to leave the nunnery and marry him. The prince was handsome, and for a moment the proposal tempted the girl. But, alas, she mastered desire. Grabbing a spoon, she pried the eyes from her face and dropped them "like eggs" into a silver chalice. She then gave the chalice to a servant, bidding him hand it to the prince and say, "Behold the eyes for which you lust. They are thine. Now leave me in peace and come not again between me and my God."

"Eight and a half men out of ten are women," Josh said after I described Googoo's advice to Ben Meadows. "Most folks won't strike the ground until after the snake has disappeared." "The foot that walks picks up thorns," Josh continued, getting into aphoristic stride. "The only people who don't feel pain are dead, those in graves and those without. A man learns to live with thorns. So many stick in a living person's feet that the bottoms seem wooden soles." When in doubt, Josh suggests acting, though his own actions consist more of words than deeds. "If you don't own a horse," he once told me, "ride the cow."

Josh thinks people who act boldly can skin bears and shape lives. Although Dink Barlam was the wealthiest man in Red Boiling Springs, he'd once been poor. One Sunday years ago, Turlow Gutheridge told the crowd at Ankerrow's, Dink skipped church and went fishing. On his first three casts he caught a tire, a fire shovel, and the mangle from a washing machine. On the fourth cast, however, he hooked a whiskey jug. Hoping that the jug might contain a drop of nectar, he pried the stopper loose. Immediately a dark cloud boiled from the mouth of the jug. After staggering along the shore, the cloud pulled itself into a genie. Decades earlier the genie had escaped from a sideshow and going on a toot had dived into the jar in hopes of lapping up a saucer of butane. Successful in the search, the genie took a nap in the bottom of the jug. While the genie was dreaming of Baghdad and the court of Haroun al-Raschid, a boy found the jug and, after cramming a stopper into the mouth, pitched the jug into the river so he'd have a target for rocks. Unfortunately the jug was ironstone and sank before the boy could skip a single stone across the water.

The genie appreciated Dink's rescuing him. After he sobered up and got rid of his headache, he told Dink that he would grant him a single wish. Dink was silent for several minutes. He and his wife Bryte Jewel were childless, and he knew Bryte Jewel wanted a baby. On the other hand his mother had gone blind two years earlier, and Dink realized that she'd expect him to ask for the return of her sight. For his part Dink wanted wealth. "Tell you what," Dink finally said when the genie began to waver like an afternoon shadow, "I wish that my mother might see her grandson drinking milk out of a golden cup."

Even if a person retires from the world, things will happen to him. According to another tale in the *Legend of Abgar,* mistletoe was once a tree. On Pilate's sentencing Christ to death, however, Roman soldiers felled the mistletoe. Afterward they used the wood to make the cross on which Christ was crucified. Because the tree loved Jesus, the wood wept sap while He died. Seeing the cross weeping, God pitied the tree and sent Peter to gather twigs lopped off by the Romans, instructing him to toss them into the branches of other trees where they could grow green and unfettered high above the axe. God then blessed the sap on the cross, transforming the tears into white berries and emblems of love. "At Christmas," God told Peter, "men and women will embrace under mistletoe and their lives will be fertile."

No matter how rigorously a person heeds cautionary advice, chance always hovers near, threatening to disrupt calm. Two years ago in St. Louis high water drove a hunchback from his favorite begging station above the river. For a day he accompanied a blind man in Union Station. At dusk the hunchback divided the day's gain into two piles. Casually the blind man ran his hand over the coins. "Divide them again," he said. "You have taken more than your share." The man's tone angered the hunchback, and shouting "You're not blind," he leaped on the blind man and rubbed his face into the dirt. Spores in the dirt got in the blind man's eyes and dissolved, in the process restoring his sight. Even before shouting "Eureka," the blind man studied the hunchback and said, "You're uglier than a toad." The remark invigorated the hunchback, and he attacked his companion again. Because his opponent could see, however, the hunchback fared poorly. The blind man flipped the hunchback over and straddled the lump on his back. Although the hunchback bucked and twisted, the blind man rode the lump, shouting like a cowboy. Eventually the lump collapsed, in the process straightening the hunchback's spine and changing him into a tall, handsome man. "Nobody will believe that tale," Eliza said after I read it to her. "No matter," I said, "much as hunger leaps the fence and picks the lock, so when story demands, my pencil writes both French and English."

Despite libraries of books urging people to escape the chaos of getting and spending, isolating one's self from commerce is impossible. Ben Meadows didn't heed Googoo's advice and bought a tractor. Keeping payments up will be difficult. Last week storms pounded Smith County. Rivets of hail smashed tobacco, splintering stalks and punching leaves to ground.

No matter how tightly a person clasps his nickels, commerce will try to loosen his grasp. Three days ago I received an advertisement over electronic mail. "Have you EVER dreamed about being able to grow your own quality 'GRASS' PRIVATELY?" the advertisement asked. If my answer was yes, then Linda Sue, whose spelling was weedy, would "discretely ship" me "a 2 oz. supply of PRIME seed from Jamaica" in "a plain wrapped package." Payment sent to her post office box, Linda Sue instructed, had to be either "CASH or MONEY ORDER." She did "NOT ACCEPT CHECKS." For a moment curiosity tempted me to order a package. I knew Linda Sue would mail seed, not, of course, from the *Cannabis sativa* or neckweed suggested by the advertisement, but some variety of *Poa* or *Panicum,* false redtop or old witch grass. "That won't bother the fools who answer the advertisement, Daddy," Francis said. "They are so spaced they will toke up anything: fescue, bulrush, worn pajamas. It doesn't matter so long as it burns." Association seeds barren moments. Suddenly I remembered a chat with a biology teacher. The man once taught in Ashford but last year accepted early retirement in order to write a textbook which, he said, "will beam new light into botanical greenhouses." "God created woman and her foals herbivores," the man cited as an example of what he wanted "to share." Unlike other grazers, woman and her foals possessed hands, and instead of cropping grass with teeth, used fingers to tear plants out of the ground, leaf and root. Because of their intemperate eating habits, woman and her foals stripped grass from a vast acreage, turning savannas into desolate plains. Famine resulted. To survive, woman and her foals killed and ate fellow creatures, necessity, the teacher declared, "turning them carnivorous and damning their descendants to the perversity of claw and blood."

Letters are quirts to the mind. Early in February Horace Newell wrote me, saying he visited Sawyer Blodgett in the Victoryland nursing home in Carthage. Age had made Sawyer philosophical. "Good evening, Sawyer," Horace said when he met Sawyer. "How're you getting on? Are you well?" "How do you think I'm doing?" Sawyer answered. "If a person lives long enough, he'll see sorrow. Life is fleeting." "Oh, shucks, Sawyer," Horace answered. "You'll live to be a hundred." "Woe is me," Sawyer moaned. "My father lived a hundred and thirteen years. Now you are telling me I won't see my grandchildren's grandchildren." Horace's letter sodded barren thought, so much so that if life did not resemble a graveyard, at least mortality bumped across my vision. After reading the letter, I went to the university pool. Standing on the deck above the water, I recognized people without seeing faces. As aged whales can be identified by barnacles icing their backs, so I identified friends by crusts of moles embroidering their hides and by fronds of hair twisting over their gills like kelp.

Although I agree with Josh in believing caution smothers vitality, I realize restraint often serves people well. Indeed, I strap clogs on the children's feet in hopes of protecting them from thorns. In

January Francis got his driver's license. Vicki's mother owns an 1965 MG automobile. For years the car has sat in her garage. After Francis passed the driver's test, she gave him the car, saying he could repair it for his senior project in high school. Besides resembling a four-wheeled bathtub, the car lacked seat belts, a rollbar, and airbags. After pondering the gift for an hour, I refused to let Francis accept it. "The car is a death trap," I told Vicki. "I haven't wrapped myself around Francis like a vine for sixteen years only to have a car tear him from me and squash him on asphalt like a grape." "Don't the proverbs you have been saying recently mean anything to you?" Vicki asked, adding, "Those maxims which urge people to seize opportunity and toss caution aside?" "They were only words," I said, "verbal jive for a page, palace bricks for an outhouse. Francis is my baby, and so long as I steer, the inhabitants of this house will remain in the slow lane. Proverbs sound good. But in family affairs sayings are as useful as umbrellas are to ducks."

For the sake of argument, and for my son, I misspoke. Words do influence passing hours. Because I write, words bump me off sandy shoulders and onto highways pocked with thought. The first week in February I spoke at a writers' conference in Hartford. After my talk I visited discussion groups. In one group a young woman read a poem. When she finished, the room was quiet for eleven seconds. Then a man across the table from the woman spread his arms, curving them out and around like the lip of a big basket, leaned forward, and said, "I give you my silence." For a moment I was tempted to fill the silence, but then I mastered my tongue. Later, after a man said, "I just look at things and wonder how they could be done better," I responded in cautious, literary character, saying, "I look at things and wonder why they were ever done."

Age brings not only discretion but also the disinclination to do anything. Absolute calm, however, leaves pages blank, so occasionally I travel in hopes, if not of killing bears, of so grooming thought that I can forge paragraphs. At the end of January I went to Sewanee for a poetry festival. I flew from Providence to Nashville, booking the flight on the Internet. I spent half a day mustering the gumption to approach the keyboard. The process was so different from telephoning a travel agent that at times it seemed like thrusting a fist of cash down a snake's throat. I worried that if I pressed the wrong command my money would vanish, and I did not know how to find the antidote button. Only after checking in at T. H. Green Airport was I certain that I'd booked the flight correctly. Because I was nervous I arrived at the airport an hour and forty-five minutes before the plane departed. For a while I watched pigeons skip through the air outside the terminal. Someone left the sports section of the *Providence Journal* on the seat of a chair. Sprawled across the top of the first page was "Head to Head." I didn't read farther. A schoolgirl managed a cart owned by "Gourmet to Go." Painted between "to" and "Go" on the front of the cart was a yellow airplane with five black diamonds for windows. A "big" cup of coffee cost a dollar and fifty cents. For five dollars I could buy a lunch consisting of potato chips, fruit salad, and a smoked turkey sandwich, this last containing a slab of Jack cheese. When not pouring coffee or selling sandwiches, the girl sat on the floor reading. I asked her what she was reading. "The poems of Emily Dickinson," she said. "They are wonderful." My friend Pat Hoy met me in Nashville, and together we waited for Neal Bowers, a poet who lives in Iowa. I made a sign, and when Neal's flight landed, I stood at the ramp and held the sign in front of my chest. "Professor Neal Bowels," the sign read. "Oh, shit," Neal said when he saw the sign. "Exactly," I said.

Atop a spur of the Cumberland Plateau, the Sewanee campus consists of ten thousand acres, much unspoiled forest. Between readings I roamed woods, first wandering Shakerag Hollow then at Morgan's Steep ambling down a ravine to Bridal Veil Falls, spending time exploring entrances to several caves: Kirby, Peebles, Wriggle, and Stream-Bed. A cap of sandstone rests atop the plateau. Beneath the cap limestone extends downward like a forehead. Behind a skin of foliage water pulses, forming veins and arteries. Over the years cracks have wrinkled through the sandstone. Water seeps into the cracks and freezes, sometimes breaking rock into beefy slabs, tumbling them down the plateau, smashing shrub and tree into butcher's blocks. At Morgan's Steep water sounded like a street-corner band: falls, brooms sweeping back and forth; creeks rubbing over washboards of stones; and from the edge of the plateau, the metallic clap and shake of utensils shimming in a kitchen drain, streams breaking and slapping rocks.

Near the top of Morgan's Steep bedded sandstone resembled bricks, and beneath overhangs angular unconformities pitched upward, forming paths. Trees stood like lamps atop stones, the trunks tall shafts and the stones bases. Massive roots coiled over rocks then resembling cords dug backward, plugging trees into the wall of the plateau. Kinglets zithered through branches, and winter wrens trilled through brush, their songs unwinding like old-fashioned doorbells. The ground was damp, and I slipped down the slope pushing leaves aside, those from chestnut oaks resembling fire shovels and digging into topsoil, those from sycamores, three times as large as my right hand, clutching the ground and not moving. While bark on ashes split into diamonds that on tulip trees gapped, almost as if furrows had been wedged open. In order not to miss the poetry readings I hurried through woods and ignored most of bluff and ravine. I paused at Bridal Veil Falls, however. Water gushed from the earth near the lip of a sinkhole, and after sliding out into pools slipped down mossy rocks silky with green. At the bottom of the sink the water drained into a pit and vanished. Ferns seeped through cracks in the limestone. While leaflets of southern maidenhair sprayed out like pressed green tears, those of cliffbrake jutted abruptly, their stems forcing them into formal purple elegance.

The day after returning to Storrs I roamed the university. In woods leaves clumped frozen to the ground. Instead of slipping sideways when I stepped upon them, the leaves collapsed, crunching and splintering. Rarely lumbered, trees at Sewanee rushed upward breaking against the sky like water racing through a spillway. In contrast, woods in Storrs appeared tame, saplings swimming tentatively across hillsides in schools. Still, I paused often. A barred owl dropped out of a white pine, its face flat against the wind. Hickory nuts lay beneath a spruce. A flying squirrel had chewed holes through the nuts, two holes to a nut. The holes were not perfect circles, being slightly wider than tall, the width of each hole half an inch, and the height three-eighths of an inch. Ice stripped a limb from a hemlock and hung it over the Fenton River. Needles had fallen from the limb reducing twigs to combs. A swarm of cones clung to twigs, their scales spreading, making them appear startled, almost as if they had been brushed off the surface of the water. On bark lichens bloomed, most blue and green *Parmelias*. I recognized dotted-shield lichen, pycnidia scattered over the surface in dark heaps, looking as if they'd rolled through coal dust. For the first time I noticed white-streaked lichen. Until rubbed, the lichen was brown. When I scraped a finger across the surface of a lichen, white poured out, much as water slipping from the sink at Bridal Veil.

On a trip something always pricks the mind. I slept six miles from Sewanee at the Monteagle Bed and Breakfast. Monteagle is small, and I wondered who patronized the bed and breakfast. "Sewanee visitors," Bob, the owner, said. "But," he added, "a surprising number of people stay here for funerals, and these folks sometimes remain in Monteagle for three or four days, even a week." One of the people frequenting my books is the Reverend Slubey Garts, an entrepreneurial Christian. In my last essay Slubey opened the Victoryland nursing home. On my return to Storrs, construction started on the Good-Bye Gate Bed and Breakfast, a pillow of nightly fire, as Proverbs Goforth put it, providing manna for relatives of "musicians promoted from earth's orchestra pit to the Rock of Ages band."

On a table in the entrance hall sat a silver bowl full of "koshered apples, rinsed and blessed by Slubey," Proverbs explained, "so good Christians could chew them in clear conscience and not worry about being stung by venomous bacteria." Beside the bowl was a tray of Amen Cakes. Cut into small squares, the sweets were sponge cakes, though when an especially prominent Carthaginian died Clevanna Farquarhson baked angel food cake. Each square contained a piece of hard candy. The candies were minute figurines depicting animals present at the birth of Christ: lime sheep, grape cows, cherry goats, and lemon chickens. While the rowboat representing Noah's ark tasted pineapple, a minute thrush was ginger. In hopes of easing Christ's pain, a thrush sang to Christ while He hung from the cross. Although singing exhausted the thrush, the bird did not stop until the moment of Christ's death. Before the crucifixion the thrush's voice was hoarse. Afterward God blessed the bird, so changing its voice that "it flowed like water through a golden lyre." Among the candies when Slubey opened the bed and breakfast was a liquorice coffin, its lid swinging to the side, to show, Proverbs explained, that a dear one had moved to the palace above. Despite this explanation the coffin upset mourners, and Slubey banished it from the cakes.

In rooms on the floor beside each bed lay a rush mat. Cut into the middle of the mat was a cross, and instead of placing shoes side by side, people put them on the mat at right angles along the cross. Atop bedposts were the heads of saints, all with mouths open in song. Slubey liked wood. Carved into oak above the mantle in the sitting room were a hatchet and a rose, symbolizing, Proverbs explained, the chopping away of dead branches and the emergence of blooming new growth, or as Slubey himself said, the felling of the body and the blossoming of the soul. By the fireplace an iron cat sat facing the flames. For a cat to sit with her back to the fire was a sign of rain. Nothing dampening the enthusiasm of mourners more than a drizzle, Slubey turned the cat toward the hearth in hope of guaranteeing good funereal weather.

Down the hall from the sitting room was a study. Stacked on a table were newspapers, the dailies, the *Nashville Banner* and the *Tennessean,* then the weekly *Carthage Courier.* The only book in the room was a Bible. When asked why the bookshelves were empty, Proverbs said, "Stars don't disappear if almanacs are lost." Despite the absence of books the room was cluttered. For years parishioners had left votive offerings in Slubey's Tabernacle of Love. Slubey stored the offerings in the broom closet at the church. When a donor inquired about the whereabouts of an item, Slubey dug it out of the closet and kept on display in his office for a week. When the Good-Bye Gate swung open, Slubey placed the offerings in the study, so that donors could see them at their convenience. Among the offerings was a jar of marbles, most agates, given by people who recovered from eye ailments. A fountain of crutches erupted from an umbrella stand. Leaning against them was a crutch with a shoe nailed to the bottom, a scuffed Johnston and Murphy wingtip. Sketched on a two by four was a farm, at one end of which a blue barn burst into yellow flames. Several offerings were carvings.

While a snake struck at a bare foot on one carving, on another a horse bolted, pulling a wagon behind it, the driver tumbling backward, his stovepipe hat flying off in the wind. Displaying the offerings at the Good-Bye Gate started controversy. After viewing them, Malachi Ramus, minister at the Church of the Chastening Rod, said that Slubey had kidnapped God and carried Him to Rome. "I'm not saying that people who sleep in that house are sheltering under the wing of Satan," Malachi said. "But at Judgment Day they will see feathers with horned cats' heads at the tips, snakes coiling around them, the horns so hot the serpents have let down their black feet." Malachi's remarks angered Proverbs Goforth. "The Devil is a busy bishop in Malachi's diocese," Proverbs told the crowd at Ankerrow's Café. "Malachi has gone through life without learning to observe anything except the Sabbath."

Not all folks who entered the Gate lived straight and narrow lives. When the Burrman visited Carthage, he boarded at the bed and breakfast. The Burrman sold Snsnoi Galvanic Drops, a patent medicine. People called him the Burrman because he wore a flannel suit decorated with dried burdock. The suit covered the Burrman's neck and head, even his shoes. In spring the Burrman stuck redbud blossoms on his head, in fall sprays of goldenrod. The drops themselves, he claimed, chased Pain's daughter, Death, from the kitchen table and "killing molygrubs and polygrubs, put to rout rantantorius diseases." A teaspoon a day kept away the fever demons, Shaker, Burner, and Freezer. Once, he recounted, he visited a house and found three people stretched out on cooling boards, "two dead and one lifeless." A woman had just brushed the corpses' teeth. "But," the Burrman claimed, "I unbound their jaws and poured a bottle of Galvanic Drops down their throats. Before you could empty a chamber pot, they jumped off the boards, joined hands, and sang, "Row, Row, Row Your Boat" followed by "The Preacher Got Drunk" and "The Battle Hymn of the Republic."

"Good grief," Vicki said after I described the Burrman. "You've drifted far from shucking bears." "No," I said, "I've just pounded the hunchback a bit. My conclusion will not appeal to people suckled on commonsensical prose, but still, the last paragraph is in sight." In January, I continued, getting the tale between my teeth, Hoben Donkin met Floyd Gaugh outside Read's Drugstore in Carthage. "Floyd," Hoben said, "I haven't seen you for the longest time. How've you been?" "Not so well," Floyd answered. "Last summer I disturbed a bear eating blackberries." "Oh, my Lord," Hoben said. "What happened?" "The bear chased me," Floyd said. "Although I ran as fast as I could, he caught me, and before I had a chance to introduce myself, he killed me and ate me." "That's the worst thing I've ever heard," Hoben said. "I'm so sorry." "Well, thank you," Floyd answered. "It wasn't pleasant, but I learned a lot from the experience, and if I weren't dead, I could put it to good use." "I bet you could. You're just the man for it. Nobody could do better. I'm really sorry you died," Hoben said somberly. "Thanks for that, too. I appreciate your sympathy and concern," Floyd said. "Jesus," Vicki exclaimed when I described the ending. "You've reached the bottom of the barrel now." "Not quite," I said, "there are bushels of young bears to peel."

Hear No Evil

I've aged, and my ears have stretched. Although the lobes sway when I walk and on wintry days brush snow off my shoulders, I hear less. Recently George the dog has begun to whine silently. Students have become docile. No longer do questions ripple the smooth surface of my lectures. When I write "Born To Teach" on the blackboard, the chicks don't cluck. After I rattle the platitudes on which conventions roost, one or two students shift in their chairs, rustling coats and pencils, but never do they peep. At home the telephone does not ring for me. Weeks pass without a single salesman, politician, or educator trying to bilk me out of money and common sense. The less I hear, however, the more comfortable life becomes. Complaint loses verbs, nouns, and bite. In the quiet conscience dozes, and I have become amiable, quick to stir nonsensical placebos into conversations acidic with zeal.

Not the deaf, but ardent, respectable people with good hearing drive others to suicide. Just last week Obed Eells cornered Loppie Groat in Barrow's grocery. Loppie enjoyed dancing, and almost every party in Smith County included Loppie's Chicken in the Bread on the dance menu. In contrast, Obed called dancing "weaving the shroud." "When the devil has nothing to do, he lights his pipe and dances," Obed began, then told Loppie a stem-winding tale describing the fate of "Good Friday dancers." "My gall like to have bursted before Obed finished," Loppie told Turlow Gutheridge later, adding that Obed "don't have enough heft to appreciate life." Four years ago, according to Obed, a swarm of Catholics in Polk County held a dance on Good Friday. The Devil's grandmother was the caller, and the World and the Flesh served punch. Once people started dancing, they couldn't stop. People danced so vigorously that their feet wore off, and their legs were ground into stumps. After dancing wrung all the water from their bodies, people began to sweat blood. "They were spinning so fast, their legs were so short, and the blood so red, folks looked like apples," Obed said. "At least they looked like apples until chunks of their chests and bellies broke off." Eventually nothing remained except skulls, eyes blue with terror staring from behind bones and hair frizzy across the tops like grass growing on graves. Finally the skulls shattered and vanished, and the hair fell to the ground, "covering the floor like parings around a barber's chair." "No corpses," Obed warned, "to receive friends at the funeral home."

Because conversation now depends upon guess rather than sound, I stay in the house more than before. As a result life is easy. Only by visiting neighbors can a person discover what's happening at home. Not only does becoming a homebody prevent gossip from tainting hours, but it also shuts the door to stories like those told by Obed. No longer am I privy to tedious accounts which hurl mind into the darkness of boredom, tales about somebody's horse's hoof's horseshoe having been lost or found.

Instead of being discommoded by talk, I sit at my desk and compose conversations. Not quick or witty, the conversations suit the failing ear. Easiest to understand are soliloquies. Last month near Carthage a terrapin pulled himself out of a ditch and started across a dirt road. Crossing the road took the terrapin a week. Just as he pushed into grass on the far shoulder, a huge oak tree thumped down behind the terrapin, kicking dust over his carapace and obliterating his trail across the road. After wheezing and snorting for forty seconds, the terrapin lowered the front lobe of his plastron and, sticking his head out, spat, then looked around. "Great God Almighty," the terrapin said, after seeing the oak not more than a tail's length from the tip of his shell, "Mammy was right. It pays to be lively."

Vicki's hearing is better than mine. Not only that, she is younger than I am. Consequently my literary conversation offends her youthful, impetuous ear. One night at dinner after I described the travels of Mr. Terrapin, she sat speechless for a moment. Then she pushed her chair away from the table and standing, said, "You might meet a snail, but you'll never catch one." On my pages one foolish story leads to two or three others. Vicki usually isn't patient enough to lend an ear to numbers two and three. Her absence does not upset me, however. Loss of hearing excludes criticism and neatens days.

Since I can't hear what people think, I don't shape stories to fit their notions. In Carthage the Pankeys were, as Turlow put it, a "twisty mouth family." While the faces of Everlena and Sister Sue Pankey twisted to the left, those of Pappy Farrell and Big Billy Pankey twisted so far to the right that the openings for their mouths seemed tracheotomies drilled under ears instead of beneath chins. In contrast to those of the rest of the family, the mouth of Jefferson Davis, the youngest of the Pankeys was normal. Moreover, unlike his family, Jefferson Davis was bright. After graduating from the Male and Female Select School in Carthage, he attended Austin Peay College in Clarksville in hopes of becoming an elocution teacher. At the end of Jefferson Davis's first semester, the Pankeys had a homecoming party for their son. Everlena set the big pot in the little pot, even putting candles on the table. At the end of the meal Everlena turned to her husband and said, "Pappy, would you blow the candles out?" Pappy leaned forward and blew vigorously. Instead, though, of streaming forward over the candles, air billowed out of his mouth to the right. "Mammy, you better try," he said, getting red in the face. Everlena had no more success than Farrell, her breath shooting out to the left. Eventually she asked Big Billy to blow the candles out. Next Sister Sue tried. Finally the family turned to Little J. D., as they sometimes called Jefferson Davis, and asked him to blow out the candles. Little J. D. sat up in his chair and with one breath extinguished the flames. "What a blessed thing it is to have learning," Pappy said, beaming at Mammy.

A real blessing it is to inhabit a world so silent that one hears only voices rich with story. A hundred years ago Carthage was not the sophisticated county seat it later became. Although people didn't believe in ghosts, occasionally a "haunta" virus infected Main Street. One evening after an afternoon's drinking Woody Ankerrow's great-uncle

Silvanus bet Proverbs Goforth's grandfather Gethsemane three dollars that he wouldn't spend a night in the old slave cabin at the foot of Battery Hill.

Although the cabin had been abandoned for three decades, some evenings lights flickered behind windows. Despite the lights' coinciding with nights the Masons dedicated to high mystical doings, people whispered white nothings about ghosts. Gethsemane took a Bible and a quart of spirits with him to the cabin, dipping more often into the "holy water" than the holy book. At ten o'clock a ghost carrying a bloody axe fell out of the chimney. The ghost started toward Gethsemane but then stopped and, sitting on the floor, said, "I'm going to wait until Emmitt comes." At eleven a second ghost tumbled out of the chimney, in his hands a pitchfork with a hand impaled on the tongs. "What shall we do with him?" the second ghost said, pointing toward Gethsemane. "Wait till Emmitt comes," the first ghost answered, whereupon the second ghost joined him on the floor. At midnight a third ghost strode out of the fireplace, a mound of eyeballs in his hands, ligaments hanging like Jell-O over his forearms. "What shall we do with him," the ghost said, nodding toward Gethsemane. When the other two ghosts said, "Wait till Emmitt comes," Gethsemane shut his Bible, drained the spirits, and stood. "Well, gentlemen," he said, "I'm certainly glad to have made your acquaintance this evening, and I have found the conversation edifying, not to mention stimulating. But when Mr. Emmitt comes, you can tell him that I've done been here and have done went."

Occasionally worldly doings break my quiet. Last week Baby Lane wrote an editorial for the *Carthage Courier* in which she pondered cavortings in the Oval Office. Shortly after she graduated from Wellesley, Baby married Elmo Tee Lane, known familiarly as Booger. Baby has been married for twenty years, and she didn't have much sympathy for complaints about the president's "unwanted familiarities." "Have these whiners ever been married to a man?" she asked. "When you buy meat, you get bones. White house, green house, blue house, orange house—mornings, evenings, afternoons, marriage is one familiarity after another. No married woman in Smith County cleans house when her husband is home. Just a glimpse of me bending over to mop the floor inspires Booger to gaiety. A happily married woman cannot prepare a meal without experiencing culinarius interruptus. Last Sunday after church I was rolling chicken in the dough tray when Booger crept up and pinched my drumsticks." "Good old Booger," Baby wrote, "he's sweet and sometimes sour, and he won't leave me alone for half an hour." "Ladies," Baby concluded, "if a cow's a good milker, a body can stand being kicked. Of course if you want life skimmed and pasteurized, you best hand the bucket over to a robust country gal and devote your days, and nights, to education, or some other airy-fairy political knickknack."

I have reached the fragile sparrow time of life. Nothing lasts long. The person whom I hear singing in the morning is liable to be in a hawk's belly by evening. Because I'd like to chirp a bit longer, I keep abreast of medical news. Last week on public radio an evolutionary biologist from Princeton described a new theory explaining the origin of disease. Animals, the scientist argued, created diseases in order to protect themselves against man. While adult humans killed and ate large animals, small male humans tortured and trampled little animals. "It doesn't take high intelligence to realize that big animals benefit from plagues of eating disorders and little animals from rashes of shin splints or ingrown toenails." "Once laboratories determine the animals which created specific diseases," the man continued, "then science can find, if not cures, ways of containing the ailments. In the future drug companies will market cages of anti-animalotics—cats, for instance, to prevent epidemics created by mice, dogs to isolate then eradicate sicknesses nurtured by cats. The possibilities are endless and exciting."

Medical talk sets the bells of mortality chiming. To escape the noise I went for a walk. Snow started falling while I was in the Ogushwitz meadow. Although March was half over, the snow was the first of the new year. Almost as if atoning for an earlier miserliness, winter coined snow, shaking bags of dime and quarter-sized flakes over hill and field. In the meadow empty milkweed pods dangled like quotation marks, making the snow seem temporary, the flakes out of season and ironical. For a moment canes of brambles glowed like welts. Then they vanished as if healed by soft white salve. Along ridges white pines seined the air, catching flakes like boys, the limbs arms, the needles fingers quick with white. I walked under hemlocks leaning over the Fenton River and listened to the juggle of water. In the low woods a pileated woodpecker shuttered his head back and forth, watching me from behind a tall tree. As the bird's head popped into sight, red and black snapped through the quilt of snow like stitches. Under the lip of a hill deer huddled on the ground like loaves of bread. On my approach the deer slid down the slope, leaving bare patches behind. The patches tapered slightly at one end almost as if loaves had been pulled out of an oven prematurely and scraped off a baking pan. Stuffed under a boulder atop a ridge was a blue blanket. A rainbow of white letters spelling "WINDHAM TECH" curved across the center of the blanket. Beneath the rainbow were two capital letters, *W* and *T,* the *T* a step below the *W.* Standing atop the *T* was a muscular chipmunk, the school's mascot.

That night the moon was full, and yellow melted through clouds like butter. Before breakfast the next morning I walked around a cornfield. Two killdeers stood on a manure pile. In woods a redbellied woodpecker clung to the side of a black birch, and a brown tree creeper cinched itself tight to a hickory, flattening against the bark like a belt buckle. I did not walk long. Sunlight sprayed over the cornfield and bounced off the snow in an abrasive glare. Moreover, later that morning Eliza played Comte de Guiche in the Middle School's production of *Cyrano de Bergerac.* Some things are worth hearing. Vicki and I attended both performances of *Cyrano* and sat on the first row each time. Tall and slender, Eliza made an elegant count. She wore white knee-britches and a shiny ruffled white shirt. Yellow bunting splashed down her right shoulder, and an orange garter circled her left calf. A black cape lined with purple swung off her back, a snow of fleurs-de-lis blowing gold across it. On her head perched a black straw hat, suitable for both the stage and races at Saratoga. Not only were Eliza's feet larger than those of the other female cast members, but they were also bigger than those of their mothers. As a result she wore men's black lace boots, footwear that seemed to combine combat with Christopher Street.

I heard every word of the play. Late winter is drama season in

Storrs. Two nights running I watched Francis dance in the high school production of *Guys and Dolls*. Essayists create their own characters as well as those of the people who strut their pages. At *Cyrano* I realized that for the sake of paragraphs I had posed as deafer than I actually was. When the count referred to his uncle the cardinal and said, "He is himself a dramatist; let him rewrite a few lines here and there, and he'll approve the rest," I pondered changing the title of my essay to "Hearing Everything." The next morning at the university I eavesdropped. A girl sitting on the floor at the end of a hall said to a friend, "He's all right. He's not anybody I'd date, but he's all right." That afternoon Edward walked the dogs. "Daddy," he said on returning home, "at the baseball field I heard a remark you can use." Edward had watched the university team practice. During a lull the right fielder turned to the center fielder and said, "I just can't stop thinking about how nice my cleats are and how ugly yours are."

Eavesdropping is strenuous. Rarely does one snag words as entertaining as those fungoed around the outfield. The girl's statement about courtship being typical of the genre, I quit eavesdropping almost before I began. Akin to conversations overheard are conversations read. Not only is lifting paragraphs from letters light work, but the labor appeals to the sedentary, contemplative, if not hard-of-hearing, me. Early in March Jack wrote from Ohio. His latest book, an edition of letters, had recently been published. A kind woman having given him several of the letters, he had intended, he wrote, "to refer to her as 'a gallant and spirited old lady.'" Unfortunately when the book was printed "the 'd' of lady was omitted." "No matter," my friend Ellen said. "The misprint is a better compliment. I'd be thrilled if someone called me 'a gallant and spirited old lay' when I was eighty."

Two days later I received a packet from a friend in Iowa. I know nothing about her hearing, but she and I share an age and minds that gallop to imaginary conversations. Some eighty characters wander her head, among others, Lumley Camop, Thelma Mae Biggles, Louis B. Charging Bear, Hondra Handoyo, Ismail G. Y. Chamdani, Panucah Gruber, Tony Tarbox, Leon Wuebker, Ti-Baby Stanky, Bobo Horness, and Hobbs Cowboy Lee. For a decade her characters have written me, all spelling my last name *Pickelring*. Supposedly the packet was sent by Merle T. Oderman, "Head Operative" of the Oderman Detective Agency located at "9½ S. East St. NW (Behind the Laundrymat)" in Sibley, Iowa, "Witness Relocation and Fill Dirt Obtainment Our Specialties." On this occasion Merle wrote at the behest of Starlene Zwanger. Mrs. Zwanger thought I might have heard from her husband the Reverend Russell Zwanger, who disappeared in Kansas City while in the company of Neeoscaleeta Pemberton, the founder of The Carts for Wienie Dogs Foundation, a charity established to aid crippled dachshunds.

Included in the packet was a flyer, Merle explained, "found in a beautyatrician shop" in Ames. "This is the work," Merle wrote, "of Zwanger since these were tacked up in several locations at Sibley six months before he disappeared and were traced to him." Handwritten, the flyer was photocopied on white paper, eight and a half inches wide and fourteen inches long. Printed at the top of the paper in capital letters was the phrase "CHRISTIAN FRIEND WANTED." At the bottom of the page Zwanger listed a post office box at the Welch Avenue Station in Ames. Running down the left margin of the flyer was a sketch of Christ on the cross. On the right margin Roman soldiers diced for Christ's clothes. Written in cursive under both pictures was "I wonder why?" In the center of the flyer Zwanger wrote, "My Good Gracious Lord, Jesus Christ, my Savior, You told us to make our prayers known to others, so then here I go my Lord: 'Dear Jesus Christ please send me an obedient fundamentalist, republican woman to help me study the Bible together. One who is not in the flesh, that does not shave her arms or arm pits Lord, and who likes to take long walks.' Thank you Lord Jesus, my Savior, for giving me this blessed revelation of yours today. And thank you Lord for making me a human being instead of a BIBLE, otherwise I would not have been able to write your revelation down on paper. Amen."

Although the whereabouts of the good reverend was a mystery to me, his flyer jangled association, bringing the "gospelling" activities of Cousin Leafy Snavely to mind. Leafy was tall and thin and vanilla to the bone. He was so skinny, Turlow said, that he had to stand up twice to make a shadow. The knobs on the outside of his wrists were big as Brussel sprouts, and his hair was red, this last condition resulting from, Turlow said, drinking moonshine then sleeping outside in cold weather, the temperature trapping sugar from the drink in his hair. "Anthocyanin," Turlow explained when the crowd at Ankerrow's Café looked puzzled. "That's the pigment that turns leaves red in autumn."

Bounding across Leafy's forehead was a scar shaped like a raccoon. Leafy claimed that one night a lizard with a human hand stood on fence rail and beaned him with a rock. "It's more likely," Turlow said, "that Leafy was scratched by a bottle of wildcat whiskey." Before becoming a cousin and a minister, Leafy tried several occupations. None took. For a while he was a dowser or, as he advertised himself, Professor of Rhabdomancy. He said he could find "water, oil, arrowheads, skull farms, anything just so long as blue cloth don't cover it." Business was flush until Hink Ruunt decided to irrigate his back pasture and hired Leafy to find water. The night before Leafy was supposed to divine Hink discovered him burying small squares of blue denim in the pasture.

Next Leafy sold sweetened pigtails. After buying a bushel of tails at the slaughterhouse, he cured them in sugar then soaked them in buckets of Kool-Aid, lime, cherry, and strawberry being the most successful flavors. Fit for gnawing or sucking, the tails were popular for a season. Leafy was feckless, however, and didn't cure his final batch of tails carefully. At the summer band concert Farrell Pankey chewed into a raw tail. Instead of lemon oozing out of the hide, a lump of skippers wriggled into Farrell's mouth. Farrell didn't want to disrupt the music so he tried to swallow the maggots. Unfortunately one of the worms gnawed his epiglottis, and Farrell coughed. Clevanna Farquarhson was sitting on Farrell's right. "And," Googoo Hooberry recounted, "Farrell sprayed skippers all over the left side of Clevanna's head. A worm was impaled on one of Clevanna's false eyelashes. Another rolled down her chin and flipping backwards dropped down the front of her dress. Two crawled into her ear, and before she could scrap them out with a paper clip scurried behind a mole and dug in. The rest of the worms burrowed into her hair just like rabbits scampering into a briar patch." To rid herself of the skippers, Clevanna had her hair fumigated and her ear washed out, this last procedure, Googoo said, being "a thorough colonic irrigation."

Having failed in everything else, Leafy decided to preach. The Lord moving in wondrous ways, as the Reverend Zwanger knows, Leafy was successful. A two-seeder Sanctificationist, he preached that God sowed two kinds of seed over the earth. People who sprang from good seed were destined to be saved, while those who came from bad seed were bound for Hell, and nothing they said or did could "erase the printing on their tickets."

Although this dark doctrine scared the bejesus into a few people, song had more to do with Leafy's success. "Singing," Leafy said, "builds bridges to heaven." Leafy knew more old songs than practically anyone in Smith County. He began church with songs, no matter that many were not religious, old favorites like "Behind the Parlor Door," "My Horses Ain't Hungry," and "Go and Tell Aunt Patsy." Turlow once heard Leafy preach at Chestnut Mound. "First, he sang," Turlow recounted,

> I wouldn't marry a poor gal,
> I'll tell you why:
> She'd blow her nose on a cornbread crust
> And call it pumpkin pie.

Next Leafy sang,

> You ride the old gray mare
> And I'll ride the mulie.
> You go round by the new-cut road
> And I'll go home with Julie.

Leafy was also sheriff of the Jesus posse. "Marshall of the whole gang," Turlow said. Late at night "when the bowels of the congregation moved with desire for Salvation," Leafy turned out the lights and leaping from behind the pulpit, shouted, "Where's Jesus?" After a while someone always shouted, "He's over here." Whooping and moaning, the congregation rushed toward the cry. Eventually someone else yelled, "He ain't here," whereupon another person was bound to scream, "He's over yonder." Within a short time the posse was galloping in a divine slather. One night when Googoo walked past the church as the posse was bouncing heaven for leather, he heard a man sing out, "Come on Blue. Come on Blue. There's a possum in heaven for me and you."

Leafy had a brother, Sycamore, known around Carthage as No Tongue because he was garrulous. A garage mechanic, No Tongue was unfortunate in love, in great part because of the language he used. "When the towel thinks itself a tablecloth," Vester McBee said referring to No Tongue, "there's no bearing with it." Last December No Tongue conceived a passion for Clevanna Farquarhson. "Have you any objection to my parking my chair on the shoulder alongside your curb and revolving the tire of my conversation around the axle of your understanding?" he asked Clevanna at the annual Hoot Owl dinner. "Many top-of-the-line ladies have booted horns at me, but never have I left the single lane of bachelorhood to follow their tail lights. But when you skidded in front of my windshield, my heart accelerated, my clutch popped, and my crankcase commenced to dripping molasses." The still pig gets the swill, as the old saying puts it. While No Tongue simonized his prose, Clevanna motored off with Loppie Groat. Or to put things another way, the man who is deaf in one ear and can't hear out of the other often enjoys life more than other folks, no matter that their conversation has dual carburetors and runs on overdrive.

Numbering

Before age reduced my energy and decreased my linear functions, I was an ardent counter. I counted steps, hickory nuts in the yard, and automobile advertisements in magazines. I kept track of states in which I'd been kissed. I enjoyed multiplication, and if quizzed about romantic matters, cited an imaginary product. "True love," Josh said, "is rarer than an amicable number." Two hundred and twenty and 284 are amicable numbers. While the divisors of 220— 1, 2, 4, 5, 10, 11, 20, 22, 44, 55, and 110—add up to 284, the divisors of 284—1, 2, 4, 71, 142—total 220, "a marriage blessed," Josh said, "by Newton, Euclid, and Pythagoras." Although my mathematical aptitude for affection has sunk to a low denominator, occasionally after pondering an irrational number, I imagine adding Idaho and Delaware to my list. The probability of increasing the geographical range of such friendly experiences will, however, remain theoretical. Still, once a counter, always a counter. Yesterday afternoon I interviewed candidates for a teaching post at an elementary school. During a thirty-one minute period an applicant said *definitely* sixty-eight times.

In February I read Simon Singh's book *Fermat's Enigma*. A mathematician, Pierre de Fermat lived in the seventeenth century. For three hundred years mathematicians tried to prove "Fermat's Last Theorem": when n is greater than 2, there are no whole number solutions for the equation $X^n + Y^n = Z^n$. Four years ago a professor at Princeton proved the theorem. Instead of solving problems, however, counters toy with them. As familiar essayists often delight more in verbal play than meaning, so counters don't care if their doings do not amount to much. In Singh's book palaver about numbers interested me more than discussion of proofs. Many of my friends, I concluded, resembled excessive numbers. As the sum of the divisors of an excessive number is greater than the number itself (the divisors of 24—1, 2, 3, 4, 6, 8, 12—total 36), so my friends' virtues—loyalty, honesty, and integrity—added up to more than what appeared to be the whole of their characters. Similarly, public figures often seemed defective numbers, their divisors adding up to less than the number itself, those of 35, for example, being 1, 5, and 7, totaling 13.

"So instead of labeling someone a skunk, a counter would call him a 10 or a 27," Vicki said, "the specific number determining the impact of the insult." "Yes," I said, "since the divisors of 10—1, 2, and 5—add up to 8, only 2 short of the number itself, calling someone a 27 would be a much greater insult, the number's divisors, 1, 3, and 9, totaling only 13, the gap between 27 and 13 being 14." "Do you think a person will understand if you call him a 33?" Vicki said. "I speck not, as the fly said after sipping paregoric," I replied, adding affectionately, "My sweet little perfect number." "I refuse to be typed as a 6 or a 28," Vicki said, leaving the room. Perfect numbers are, incidentally, numbers whose divisors add up the number itself—1, 2, and 3 adding up to 6; and 1, 2, 4, 7, and 14 equaling 28.

Although I shuffle numbers about like pieces lifted from an absurd Scrabble game, colleges take numbers seriously, basing admission, in great part, upon class rank, scores on the Scholastic Aptitude Test, and figures on parents' bank statements. The first Saturday in March Francis and I went to Woodstock, where he took the verbal and mathematical aptitude tests. Because Francis is easily led into byways of thought, I drove. While he took the examination, I ate breakfast in Pomfret, a feta and broccoli omelet at Bob's Bread and Breakfast, costing $3.95. In Pomfret, gas cost $1.11, four cents cheaper, I noted, than in Storrs. After breakfast I wandered the graveyard beside the First Congregational Church in Woodstock. Mica flickered, animating markers, and lichens blossomed in green and yellow boutonnieres. A wetland of carved willows draped atop many stones, their limbs shading urns. I read inscriptions. Under the influence of mathematics, I imposed pattern upon the reading, grouping stones in orderly threes. After deciphering engraving on a tombstone carved in the eighteenth century, I next read stones from the nineteenth and twentieth centuries, respectively.

Temperance Williams died at twenty-one in 1795. "Adding Lusture to amiable character," the epitaph stated, "by sustaining her last illness with Christian resignation." Nancy Taber died in 1836 at fifty-seven. "Ye mourning friends weep not for me," her epitaph urged. "From toil, from pain, from sin, I'm free. / I sleep in death, but hope to rise, / To brighter joys beyond the skies." In 1927 Herbert Wolcott Brown died, the carving on his tombstone declaring,

> I strove with none, for none was worth my strife.
> Nature I loved; and next to nature, art.
> I warmed both hands before the fire of life:
> It sinks and I am ready to depart.

Graveyards are rich with the figures of story. "Mrs. Bathshua," the relict of Captain Hezekiah Bugbee, died in 1833 at eighty, the captain having died four years earlier, also at age eighty. Next to their markers stood a double stone, the left half marking the grave of Mehitable Bugbee, who died August 30, 1778, in the "5th year of her age." Beside Mehitable lay her brother Walter. In the "3rd year of his age," Walter also died on August 30, 1778. What happened to the children on that August day? Did fever slay them or did the Bugbees' house burn? Beside the markers of Samuel and Eleanor Palmer, who died in 1887 and 1889, respectively, stood the stones of five children, one of the stones a triple marker. While Rosalinda Healy died at twenty-four in 1869 and Lousia Viola at twenty-two in 1868, Hezekiah Bailey, Oriana Sigourney, and Mary Grundy died in Worcester, Massachusetts, within six days of each other in March 1845. Just short of eight, Oriana was the oldest. Mary had turned two, and Hezekiah, four. Only one of the Palmer children appeared to have outlived her parents. Born in 1839, Ellen survived the terrible week in 1845 that slaughtered three of her siblings, eventually becoming the wife of the Reverend Benjamin Dean. Perhaps marrying a minister taught Ellen resignation. Still, as I looked at the markers tilting across the hillside like stubble, I doubted Ellen's parents forgave the First Cause the cruel reaping. "Daddy, I did well," Francis said after the test. Counting myself fortunate to see my red-haired boy, I didn't answer for a moment. "Aren't you pleased?" Francis said. "Yes, honey," I answered, "but the test doesn't matter. Education has lost direction and become a defective number." "What?" Francis said. "Nothing," I said, taking his hand. "Let's get a sandwich at the Vanilla Bean." Numbers divert. By playing with them, one can avoid truths which reduce lives to epitaphs and hearts to stone. For happy moments counters inhabit fictions in which children recover from fevers and in which solutions lurk but an addition away. At the university I teach children's literature, another comforting fiction. Rarely are the books I assign occasions for warning, in contrast to inscriptions on many tombs in Woodstock. "Reader!" a carving harangued, "be wise, remember judgment and prepare to die."

In class I eschew somber wisdom for play. Luck more than learning determines lives. That thought aside, however, the Monday after Francis's test, the class read Kenneth Grahame's *Wind in the Willows,* an account of the doings of four buddies, Mole, Rat, Toad, and Badger. Under the denominator of numbers, I surveyed the class, asking students to name their favorite animal. Twelve students chose Mole; five, Rat; four, Badger; and eight, Toad, albeit two students referred to Toad as Frog. "I like Mole best because he treasures all the beautiful things," Melissa wrote. Suddenly tombstones toppled out of mind. Students liked Mole's "youthful innocence" and "sweet shyness." He was "kind and thoughtful and always helped his friends." "I like Mole best," John explained, "because everything he sees he likes." "I can relate well to him," Amy wrote. "He is well dressed, proper and remembers his manners most of the time." For an older student Mole's escaping his burrow and having an adventure was appealing. "From the beginning of the story I wished that I, too, had been able to live for the moment rather than worrying so much about school work."

Students who liked big, silent Badger often resembled him. "The other animals in this book," a girl who sat alone in the back right-hand corner of the room explained, "are too nosy." "Okay," a gruff boy declared, "I'm a little behind in the reading, but so far I like the Badger because he seems like a grumpy old man. I think that's kind of funny." A girl who giggled uncontrollably but who wrote splendid examinations preferred Badger "because he was an example of how not to judge an animal by its fur." In contrast to Badger's "quiet dependability," Toad's supporters admired his "whims," "flights of fancy," and capacity "to become passionate about new things." "He's scatter-brained, forgetful, and fickle, and I like that," Becky wrote. "The frog gets what he wants even if it means being punished. But he always seems to get out of the punishment by fooling someone. Bravo!" Jessica cheered. "I like Toad," Matthew explained, "because he wants to travel all over. I like this because I love to travel and wish I could do so more often. I guess I'm living vicariously through Toad." Almost all the students who liked Rat mentioned his "caring dearly for his friends." "I absolutely adore Water Rat," a girl wrote. "He is intelligent, nice, charming, and takes good care of his friends. He is always forgiving and understanding. I love the Water Rat!"

Counters are not original. Once I plot a cheery line, I follow it repeatedly. The next week students read Jean Webster's *Daddy Long-Legs*. In the book an eccentric philanthropist paid for the education of Judy, an orphan, in the process saving her from drudgery and getting himself a wife. All Judy knew about her benefactor was that he had long legs. Consequently when she wrote him, she addressed him as "Daddy Long-Legs." In class I asked students to transform Daddy into another insect. The swarm was diverse: eight butterflies, four lightning bugs, three house flies, two centipedes, and five bees, two of this last being bumble, another two queens, the queens, as one boy put it, "not gender specific." Among other creatures selected were a cockroach, an ant, a moth, a mosquito, and a "stick insect." "After leaving the cocoon of his secret identity," Aimé wrote, "Daddy became a beautiful creature." "I would make him a firefly," Ariella said, "because a firefly stays hidden until it helps people by lighting the dark. Also fireflies are fragile and don't cause harm." At the end of the paragraph Ariella drew a firefly, hot dog-shaped with buns for wings and a dark glob of mustard at its end. "I just have no artistic ability when it comes to insects," she explained. While Jeffrey changed Daddy into a fly because Judy "got only a fleeting glance of him," Meredith made him a weevil "because a weevil has a long mouth, and Daddy doesn't talk unless he has something important to say." On the page Meredith sketched a weevil. The insect resembled a squat bottle, the neck of the bottle, the weevil's snout, the body of the bottle, the weevil's "multiple cavities," as Meredith labeled them. Because Daddy "was hidden from Judy and stayed in the shadows," Mark turned him into a cockroach. For a similar reason Karen made him a tick. Since Daddy was "steadfast and hard-working," Tyrone transformed him into an ant. By scampering across the surfaces of ponds and creeks, water striders do the impossible, Vanessa wrote, adding, "Daddy does the same. He sends an orphan to school to get educated and there she learns about books and love." According to Katie, Daddy should have been a doodle or pill bug. "Doodle bugs roll into balls when you pick them up. In the same way Daddy seems scared to be found out, and he rolls into hiding." In contrast to Katie who thought Daddy shy, Chris thought him bold. "I would make him a tarantula indigenous to Central America because these tarantulas look scary as hell but are not venomous and would not hurt a human. The Central American part is made up, but I saw a documentary on tarantulas, and I think they were from C. America. I'm not sure."

As I read the last paragraph, Eliza walked into the study and stared over my shoulder. "Spiders are not insects. They are arachnids," she said. "The answer is not precise." "Precision is a small matter," I said. "*Tarantula* is good enough for English class." On my pages addition, subtraction, multiplication, and division are the fuzzy matter of words. Frequently story depends upon simple addition. After Googoo Hooberry said he did not believe in ghosts, Loppie Groat dared him to spend a night in the slave cabin at the foot Battery Hill. Words spit into the air fall on speakers' heads, and to save face Googoo slept in the cabin. Until eleven o'clock all was peaceful. Googoo smoked his pipe and recited the thousand and one names of Christ. Earlier that night, however, Proverbs Goforth attended a church supper in Maggart. Coming home late after four desserts, Proverbs took the short cut over Battery Hill, following a path that wound past the cabin. Just as he rounded the corner of the cabin, he stepped on a branch. The branch snapped and startled Googoo. "Who dat?" Googoo exclaimed, fear making him turn the *th* of *that* into *d*. When Googoo spoke, Proverbs jumped, then answered trembling, "Who dat, who says, 'who dat'?" "Who dat, who says, 'who dat, who says, who dat'?" Googoo replied, leaping out the back window or else the *dat*s would still be accumulating. For the purpose of story low math is preferable to high. This spring Lowry Barrow received a shipment of navel oranges. Seeing them in the store, Googoo picked up two, and after slowly rolling them over in his hands, turned to Lowry and said, "These sure are mighty handsome oranges, Lowry. It wouldn't take many of them to make a dozen."

Often linked to increases in wealth or good spirits, addition generally causes positive thoughts—not always, of course, as Slubey Garts once warned in a sermon, "God gives, but He won't tote." In contrast subtraction is more often than not associated with negative thoughts. Harkness Blodgett was a miser. Each December buying a present for his little boy, Donny, gave him diverticulitis. One year, though, Harkness concocted a medicinal ruse. On Christmas Eve, he removed his shotgun from the gun rack and, climbing on top of the outhouse, fired both barrels into the air at once. Then he ran into the house shouting, "Donny, something terrible has happened. Santa Claus committed suicide just before sliding down the chimney, and that means you won't be getting a present this year." Some people are born subtractors and spend their lives reducing life's gifts to fractions of their original worth. This spring Francis asked Martha to the Junior Prom. An A student who played the lead in the school production of *Guys and Dolls,* Martha suffered from sinus infections. The morning of the prom she felt ill and didn't go to school. She did not miss much. Students attending the prom were allowed to leave school at eleven o'clock. After calculus class, Francis came home and napped. At three-thirty the telephone rang, and a girl asked to speak to Francis. "He's asleep," I said. "Do you want me to wake him?" "Yes," a small voice said. The vice-principal had just called Martha, informing her that because she'd been absent that morning she could not attend the prom. When the vice-principal phoned, no one was at Martha's house to stand up for her. Her parents were divorced, and her mother worked in Worcester to support Martha and her two brothers. "Teachers exist to better children's lives," I lectured the district superintendent then a member of the school board. "Only cruel people enforce rules that bruise fragile youngsters." In talking to the superintendent, I multiplied all the variables. "And you know, of course, that sixteen- and seventeen-year-old girls periodically suffer from feminine ailments, something I would prefer not talking about in detail now." "No, no, neither would I," the superintendent answered hastily. Ten minutes before Francis arrived at Martha's house to take her to the prom and while I sat outside the dance hall to ensure the couple was admitted, the vice-principal called Martha again. "I have talked to your teachers," the vice-principal said. "They tell me you are a good student, and I have decided to let you attend the dance." "Not just anal, doubly anal," Vicki said.

On the page the line between subtraction and division is often unclear. While subtraction smacks of petulance and meanness, division produces an acidic quotient. Last year when Phares Brubaker died, his wife Angelica had him cremated. Phares's will did not please Angelica. When Slubey Garts brought the urn containing Phares's ashes to the house, Angelica was sitting at the kitchen table drinking bourbon. "Ashes?" Angelica exclaimed, pouring herself another shot. "I don't give a damn about ashes. Where are the drippings?" While division reduces, literary multiplication exaggerates. The Turbletons lived beyond Dugget near Guess Creek. Only rarely did a member of the family wander far from the creek bed. Recently Ligon Turbleton went to Carthage to buy seed. "Since you are going down to town," Axseph his mother said, "would you try to find out when Sunday will be?"

That particular story depends upon understated exaggeration, the sort of verbal equivalent of a quadratic equation with both pluses and minuses. Other statements, although logical, don't seem reasonable. "To be honest," Monroe Dowd told Judge Rutherford, "I'd rather lie than tell the truth." Not surprisingly such statements are frequently heard in courtrooms. "Judge Rutherford," Googoo Hooberry said recently, referring to Monroe's aptitude for frying other people's chickens, "it's my opinion that anyone who is bad enough to steal is no respecter of property."

Not only have numbers been on my mind, but they have also preoccupied characters in Carthage. "Quite a congruence, isn't it," I said to Vicki at dinner. She did not reply. Two weeks ago Malachi Ramus send a patriotic letter to the *Carthage Courier*, urging schools to teach "the Southern American Christian numbers, one through ten." Schools ought not, he wrote, teach "those foreign Roman Catholic numerals." Irrational notions stick to Malachi's brain like bean leaves to palms. "How many pounds of birdseed do you suppose the Pope buys each year to feed his College of Cardinals?" he asked Turlow Gutheridge. "About as many," Turlow said, "as Carthaginians buy to feed their University of Chickens."

Counters enjoy things that don't add up but which paradoxically brighten hours. Last week my friend Sam had a sigmoidoscopy. The day before he bought two Fleet's enemas at Storrs Drug. After Sam paid, the girl dropped the enemas into a paper bag, stapled the top shut, and handing the bag to Sam said, "have a nice afternoon." Early the next morning Pam took Sophy her Airedale for a walk. The morning was warm, and the stroll made Sophy thirsty. Sophy's water bowl being empty, as soon as Pam returned home, she set the bowl on the edge of the sink. Instead, though, of turning the faucet on, Pam reached to her right, and picking up the coffee pot, filled Sophy's bowl with fresh-brewed Chock Full O' Nuts. Spring may have been responsible for Pam's mistake. While fall subtracts from life, spring adds. Instead of calculating and conserving, people act spontaneously. At ninety-five Richard's father "doesn't usually make sense." "Last week," Richard wrote me, "Father astonished us." "I have something wonderful to tell you," he said, facing Richard's ninety-year-old mother. "What?" she asked. "I love you," he said. "In June," Richard continued, "my parents celebrate their sixty-ninth wedding anniversary, and this was the first time Father said, 'I love you.'"

Francis scored 1550 on the SATs. The semester ended early in May, and I turned my grades in to the registrar. Three months earlier knowledge that twenty-six was the only known number sandwiched between a cube and a square (5^2 and 3^3) intrigued me. Not now; I'm done with numbers for a while. This week I wandered Mansfield. A marsh hawk sledded down Horsebarn Hill riding a wind shear. A bluebird sunned itself atop a fence post, and a turkey chattered at the edge of the woods. A Hereford bull dozed under an ash, looking like an shelf of granite, red moss blanketing all of him except his head, a white outcrop, the moss peeled back by winter storms. While pigeons hovered unkempt about silos, knots of starlings tangled loosely down the slope below the sheep barn. On the top of Ski-Tow Hill, the aroma of black cherry was pasty, spires of flowers reaching out from trees like fingers fat with dough. Along the cut for the power line the fragrance of hay-scented ferns rose yeasty from the ground. Autumn olive soothed the broken land above the power station like a murmur, the fragrance at first white and sterile but then becoming bruised and clotted as blossoms yellowed. Above a sandy road poplars shimmered in a pale drizzle. Woods themselves were yellow and chartreuse, new leaves not yet having pulled dark from the soil. In dells skunk cabbage frayed into liver spots, but Jack-in-the-pulpit and red trillium blossomed. On Clintonia buds swelled red and so heavy that stems bent like scythes. A dryad's saddle clung to a fallen log. Orange, fan-shaped, and shingled with flecks, the mushroom measured seven inches from saddlebag to saddlebag and six and a half inches from the edge of the saddle to the horn.

On dry slopes Canada lily and dwarf ginseng gleamed, violets often spotting the mealy ground between them, purple, white, and yellow. I said the names of flowers aloud, rolling them about, savoring season: Quaker ladies, golden Alexanders, gay wings, pussytoes, Solomon's seal, field penny cress, and wild strawberry. The names sounded as familiar as poetry memorized in school, and I sat on a log in the Ogushwitz meadow and stared at winter cress until yellow slipped from the small horns and wavered over grass in a musical haze. As the temperature climbed, color melted from flowers staining the air. From pink azalea fragrance fell along curved stamens then rolled above the beaver pond where it hung in a cloud. Shrubs bloomed at the edge of the meadow beside the Fenton River: hawthorn; Morrow honeysuckle, bumblebees twitching through flowers; and wild raisin, the leaf stems rudders stabilizing blooms top-heavy with buttery stamens. Tiger swallowtails bobbed across the meadow while spring azures puddled the road, their wings tapping a ragtime of blue. Two black racers curled under a board. When I swung my hand in front of them, they laced back and forth, their mouths open and red. The snakes lunged at me several times. The strikes were short, none extending longer than eight inches. In April ring-necked snakes lurked under rocks beside the gravel pit. I turned over several rocks, but I found only crickets then a single bombardier beetle. The beetle's head was red, and the surface of the hard front wings folded above his abdomen was luminously blue. "What a treat," I thought as I put the rock back.

In woods observation simply exists. It is neither excessive nor defective. The skull of a rabbit bleached behind the beaver pond. A dead raccoon lay beside a rock, flies shrill around it. In nearby grass a thread-waisted wasp stung the green caterpillar of a skipper. Wrapped about a twig on a white oak sapling were four wool sower galls. Orange blotches rose perky from the white fibers of the galls, turning their surfaces lumpy. As I studied the galls, a pair of chickadees flew into a shagbark hickory, and the male fed the female. Birds bundled through the woods in pairs, orioles noisy atop Ski-Tow Hill, and in the damp, thrushes, their songs blue ribbons. Catbirds chattered in scrub hanging over the Fenton, and kingbirds tumbled above the beaver pond, the tips of their tails whitewashed. A hummingbird pulled fluff from a willow, and in the fork of an alder a yellow warbler built a nest shaped like a silver christening cup. While red-winged blackbirds paddled across the meadow, red and yellow splashing loudly, a lone sandpiper picked a quiet way along the edge of the beaver pond. That night Eliza asked me to explain Pythagorean triples. "A Pythagorean triple is three whole numbers that fit the equation $x^2 + y^2 = z^2$. For example $5^2 + 12^2 = 13^2$ (25 + 144 = 169)." "What's the name of the brown bird whose call sounds like 'seet,'" Eliza asked next. "A cowbird," I said. "There is a lot to know in the world, Daddy," Eliza said. "There sure is," I said, "a lot to enjoy."

The Traveled World

The last Saturday in May Francis drove me to Hanover, New Hampshire, and we looked at Dartmouth College. Thirty years ago I taught at Dartmouth. Not much had changed. In the middle of the green, men and women in Bermuda shorts practiced fly-fishing. Students were blond, and if not six feet two or three inches tall, looked like quick, muscular soccer players, "cookie-cutter kids," Francis said, "baked by prep schools." To vary the day I took Francis to the basement of Baker Library to show him the famous, and hideous, Orozco murals. As we strode into the room, a middle-aged woman leapt up from a table and ran over. "Sam," she said. "Wendy," I said. The last time I saw Wendy was twenty-four years ago. She was headed for San Francisco in a Volkswagen bus, not flowers in her hair, but big yellow sunflowers with purple centers painted on the doors of the bus and a white Spitz named Miranda on the front seat beside her. "Sam," she said, reaching out to a blond boy standing beside her, "this is my son Bill. He is seventeen." "This is my son Francis," I said gesturing to the red-headed boy on my left. "He's seventeen, too." While our sons stood holding their chins in their palms, wondering what to make of their parents, Wendy took my hands and asked, "Has life been good?" "Yes," I said, "it's been great." "For me, too," she said. "It's been great. What a gift. What a glorious gift."

Wendy and I did not chat long. She was helping her son write a history paper, and Francis and I were roped to a schedule that included Williams and Amherst. Still, as we stood in the dank basement, the air dried and sweetened, the grapy fragrance of the locusts blooming along the interstate suddenly billowing honeyed and delicate through the room. "Who was that lady?" Francis asked as we stepped out of the library and started back across the green toward our car. "A girl, I know," I said. "She's not a girl, Daddy," Francis said. "She is your age." I almost told Francis that the Wendy I knew would always be young. But instead I talked about writing, explaining that for an essayist life was fresh and people blooming, no matter their ages.

The Monday after the trip was Memorial Day. The parade started at nine o'clock at Bassett's Bridge Road. Marchers strolled along Route 195 for three hundred yards then turned right into the cemetery in Mansfield Center. Each year marchers are the same: bands from the high and middle schools, both playing patriotic music, "Anchors Aweigh," "The Star-Spangled Banner," and "America, the Beautiful"; a pound of dogs, small dogs on leashes, the others, Labs, panting and drooling; volunteers from the South Eagleville Fire Department; antique cars crammed with children tossing hard candy and unshelled peanuts to onlookers; the high school Latin club shaking banners and spears and pulling a small two-wheeled chariot; and then a crowd of Cub and Brownie Scouts and recreational base and softball teams, the players ranging in age from six to twelve. Charles arrived at the parade late, and his little boy Jimmy stood on the shoulder of the road, kicking his right shoe through gravel until his team, "Mansfield Supply," appeared. Jimmy then darted onto the pavement, and sandwiching himself between two outfielders, skipped down the road. This year Eliza played French horn in the Middle School band, and she marched next to her friend David, wearing khaki trousers and a light blue shirt with "Mansfield Middle School" stitched above the left pocket in dark blue.

The parade ended under a sugar maple in the cemetery. The master of ceremonies was a member of the town council. He retired from the army two decades ago, and no one knew his rank. Still, he wore military fatigues. Each year he says the same thing, "When the Brownie Scouts start to nod, the speakers cut the words off." This May no one talked long. The town's representative in the state legislature read a message from the governor. The mayor mentioned "sacrifice" and "love of country." A Congregational minister said three prayers, and townsfolk recited the Pledge of Allegiance. Near the end of the ceremony a six-man honor guard fired a ragged three-round salute. Vicki and a simple boy collected the brass shell casings, Vicki, three, one for each of the French horn players in the Middle School band, the boy, the rest. The casings were two and a half inches tall and half an inch in diameter. Stamped on the bottom was "LC 75," the letters, Eliza guessed, standing for light carbine. People milled about after the parade, nibbling doughnuts and discussing schools and sick friends. Roger ambled over, leading Marty, his six-year-old daughter, by the hand and told a story. Euple Brainard, he recounted, was the laziest man in Ashford. Because Euple had borrowed harvesting tools for years but had rarely returned them, neighbors decided to bury him alive. They tossed him into the back of a pickup and were on their way to the graveyard when they met Toby Crocker, mayor of Ashford. Toby asked where they were taking Euple. When the men told him, he was shocked. "Look," he said, "I'm willing to give Euple some peas. They will keep him alive for a while, and he won't have to borrow from you." "Are the peas shelled?" Euple asked, half-raising himself on his left elbow. "No," Toby said. "You'll have to shell them yourself." "Well, then, boys, drive on," Euple commanded, slumping back in the truck. "This parade is the high point of the year," my friend Peter said later, his youngest son sitting on his shoulders, hands wrapped around Peter's head like blinders. "Yes, it is," I answered. "Nothing can match it."

The parade made place appealing. That afternoon I wandered the university farm. A knobby colt bounced across a pasture and nuzzled me when I leaned against the fence. Swallows looped around the beaver pond, not only barn and bank but northern rough swallows, too. Rain fell in midafternoon, and a female scarlet tanager foraged under brush at the edge of the pond. Along the Fenton River alternate leaf dogwood bloomed, the flat white clusters ragged with blossoms and buds, these last minute mallets, green staining their tops. A great crested flycatcher called from a dead tree, each cry spinning like a bicycle bell, all the tin melted out of the sound. "Did you have a good walk?" Eliza asked when I returned home. "Yes," I said, "I saw a great crested flycatcher in the Ogushwitz meadow, the first I've seen there in twenty years."

The Wednesday after Memorial Day I flew to Nashville to give the commencement address at Montgomery Bell Academy, a country day school I attended in the 1950s. Edward, my fifteen year old son, accompanied me. Nashville and graduation being more formal than Storrs and schooldays, I bought Edward a blazer at the Salvation Army store across from East Brook Mall. Originally sold by the "English Shop" in West Hartford, the blazer cost four dollars and fit Edward perfectly. On the flight from Providence to Nashville, I read some of *The Night Crew,* an airport best-seller written by John Sandford. After ninety-six pages, I laid the book aside and studied the wrapper on a package of Chee-tos, six sandwich crackers filled with "Golden Toast Cheese." On the front of the wrapper appeared an orange leopard with a black nose shaped like a heart. The leopard wore sunglasses and raised the pad on his left front paw, making the thumb's up sign. Baked by Frito-Lay, the crackers contained 240 calories, 130 of which were fat calories. If a gourmet had "Questions or Comments," the wrapper instructed him to call 1-800-352-4477, on weekdays between nine and four-thirty "Central Time."

Edward and I stayed in Belle Meade with Bill Weaver, my oldest friend. Recently a brood of thirteen-year cicadas hatched. When I walked near trees, cicadas exploded outward in gusts. At first the gusts were dark, but as the insects separated from each other, veins on their wings seined sunlight out of the air, creating haloes. "I can hardly go outdoors," a woman told me at the airport. "I imagine the bugs getting in my hair, and I go cold all over." Measuring one and a quarter inches, the cicadas had bulbous red eyes, and their wings seemed lacquered, the veins a bright but aged orange, the spaces between stained glass. When I was a boy, I spent summers in Virginia on Grandfather Ratcliffe's farm. Each summer I caught scores of cicadas. In Nashville I did the same. Edward caught them, too, calling them "flying fiddles" and handling them gently.

The first night we were in Nashville Bill took Edward and me to dinner at the Belle Meade Country Club. I ordered a brace of braised quail, "almost boneless" and gamy with liver, wild rice, and mushrooms. Alas, by meal's end the bones had molted, transforming the soft meat into hard humerus and sternum, making my stomach dance the giblets. I longed for a wishbone that would lift me from the table and deposit me far from coffee and dessert. On returning to Bill's house, I fluttered into the side yard and like a cowbird shoveled the quail out of the nest. The quail cost twenty-two dollars, and later Edward asked, "didn't you feel bad throwing up such an expensive dinner?" The next morning Edward and I went to Vandyland, where I drank a pick-me-up, not a feather of the bird that pecked me, but a double-chocolate soda. For fifty years I have drunk sodas at Vandyland and its predecessor, Candyland. Whenever I visit Nashville, I have a soda. After the soda I drove around Belle Meade. Many new houses were huge, "hide-and-seek houses," Edward labeled them, "places in which people could vanish and not be found by a pack of bloodhounds."

The man who wrote the movie *Dead Poets Society* attended MBA. Early that afternoon a statue commemorating the film was unveiled. The statue was sentimental. A student sat in a captain's chair, staring into space, an open book on his lap, inspiration glazing his eyes. To the student's left stood a teacher, slim and fresh with intellectual vigor, his right hand resting lightly on the boy's left shoulder. "Thank God, the two are clothed, and the teacher is only tickling the boy's shoulder," a man standing beside me said. "I feared the statue might smack of the intimate glory that was the Greek educational way. What a relief!" "Yes, what a relief," I echoed wanly, having just noticed the plaque beneath the statue. Engraved on the plaque were lines from Tennyson's poem "Ulysses":

> I am a part of all that I have met;
> Yet all experience is an arch wherethro'
> Gleams that untravell'd world, whose margin fades
> For ever and for ever when I move.

Yipes, I thought reading the plaque. In four hours I delivered the graduation address. In great part the talk was a pastiche of instructive maxims, urging students, for example, to broaden themselves in college so that in after years hours would rest lightly upon their shoulders. "If you ponder becoming a lawyer," I advised, "take courses in ecology and evolutionary biology. If you know you are going to be a chemist, study music and theater. Participate in life so you will have a rich life." Unfortunately I wandered beyond the platitudinous. Because motivational speakers inevitably urge students to set high goals so they "can achieve great things and make a difference," I reminded the graduating class that their real accomplishments would probably be domestic and immediate, not distant. To buttress my argument I also quoted "Ulysses." Instead of praising Ulysses, however, I celebrated his son Telemachus. "In Tennyson's poem 'Ulysses,'" I said, "the hero Ulysses tires of governing Ithaca in his old age. He remembers the great battles at Troy and his twenty years wandering the Mediterranean. And so turning the kingdom over to his son Telemachus, Ulysses leaves Ithaca. 'Come my friends,' he says to his old comrades, 'Tis not too late to seek a newer world. / Push off, and sitting well in order smite / The sounding furrows; for my purpose holds / To sail beyond the sunset, and the baths / Of all the western stars, until I die.'"

"When I was young and first taught poetry," I continued, "I thought Ulysses heroic, the type of person, who, as he put it, found it dull to pause, to make an end, not to shine in exciting use. Well, I have changed. I now think Ulysses a man who drowned, not seeking, as he phrased it, the Happy Isles, but who drowned in irresponsible selfishness. My hero is now Telemachus, remaining at home to govern, to mow grass, to take out garbage, to lend his strong arm to the weak—to a mother when she totters into old age, to a child weeping because of night terrors."

For children capable of imagining Happy Isles, roving Ulysses is admirable. I, though, have aged into being responsible Telemachus, and as I looked at the plaque, I knew I was too tired to draft another speech. "Edward," I said, "start the car when I stand. If you see me leap from the platform and come running, open the door." In my talk, of course, I said other things, most of which, however, revolved around appreciating the immediate. "The lessons you learn in college will sometimes come from class," I said,

> but most will not be what your teachers or parents expected. Oddly, I think the most valuable lesson I learned here at MBA was on the athletic field. I was the school's worst athlete. I could not catch or throw a ball. I could barely run. I

struck out seven straight times when I played baseball. My senior year the coach did not award me a letter. The captain of the team talked to him after the letter assembly, and I got my letter in physics class. From sports I learned that I was never going to be wonderful in anything. I learned to be satisfied with small matters, getting, for example, into a football game for three plays. I learned that real success and pleasure lay in appreciating ordinary doings. No one in this courtyard will change the world. You can, however, change your back yard and maybe your neighborhood.

The talk was personal, like my essays. "What the world calls achievement does not often produce genuine pleasure. In vain moments," I said, "I look at the books I have written, and I marvel. Looking at them is not pure enjoyment, however. Dissatisfaction nags at me, and I wonder why I have not written more and better. I wonder why Oprah has touted the books of my friends Wally Lamb and Kaye Gibbons and ignored my writing. The answer is that Wally and Kaye are better writers than I am. Someone will always be better than you. Realize this and learn to enjoy the everyday so you don't squander the bright ordinary hours."

In the talk I urged graduates to support their school. "In the years ahead," I said, "you won't remember MBA very well, but you will, at least once or twice, come back. You will walk around buildings and run your hands over bricks in hopes of awakening association so you will recall the boys with whom you played and studied. A scrubbed young student will approach and ask if he can help you. But he won't be able to imagine what you are looking for. As I glance around this courtyard, I see men whom I have not seen for years, but whose memories are dear to me and whom I love. Many of you will become benefactors of this school. In public you will say that you are benefactors because you believe in education. In private you will remember Jeffrey and Garth, Richard and MBA, and you will smile."

After the talk Edward and I ate dinner at Sportsman's Grill on Harding Road. Later I drove through Belle Meade one last time so Edward could see "lights shining from the big houses." Seeking a new anything at middle age is too dislocating to be attractive. Edward and I spent the night at the Shoney's Inn in Lebanon. Six years ago Vicki and I stayed in the same motel while driving from Houston to Storrs. The next morning Edward and I drove to Carthage. I told friends in Nashville that I was going to visit graveyards and talk to dead Pickerings. Three generations of Pickerings are buried in Carthage, and after placing a pot of chrysanthemums at the head of the family plot and sending Edward off to search for snakes, I talked to Mother and Father. I described the children's appearances, and I told them how fine the children were and how much I loved them. "They are almost as nice as you were," I said. I recounted Edward's success in school and in right field on the junior varsity baseball team this spring. I warned them that he had decided to go out for football next fall. The second week in June, I said, Eliza was going to History Day in Maryland. "She also took a test," I said, and won a medal as "Best Introductory Latin" student in Connecticut. Similarly Francis did well on the college entrance examinations and at the end of school was spending three weeks riding a mountain bike in Colorado and Utah. I broke the bank account to send him on the trip because crew had been disastrous. Last year Francis rowed in the first boat, and the coach told him he had the smoothest stroke in the eight. Unfortunately a new coach appeared this year, and Francis did not row a single race. In practice he rarely got to row, and if he rowed, he rowed in the girls' boat. "One afternoon," I said, "I came home early and found him in his room crying, the only time I have ever seen him cry." "So," I continued, "I'm sending him out west to sweat crew out of his hide in hopes he'll come home feeling good about himself." Although I missed Mommy and Daddy terribly, I did not talk long to them. They did not respond to my chatter. Moreover, I became teary. If Edward saw my tears, I knew he would be upset, and for him I wanted the trip to be "an arch wherethrough" gleamed happy, light experiences.

Before leaving Carthage, I stopped at Sanderson Funeral Home. Mr. Sanderson was a childhood friend of my uncle Coleman. Coleman died in the previous August, and I asked the director of the home to tell Mr. Sanderson about Coleman's death. Before I left the director gave me two cloth tote bags. Printed in a claret band across the middle of one side of the bag was "SANDERSON FUNERAL HOMES INC." Arranged in neat lines above and below the band like rows of tombstones were sixty-eight claret medallions an inch and a quarter in diameter, a white *S* and the date 1904 in the middle of each medallion. Curving like a halo over the top of each medallion was the phrase 'COMMITTED TO EXCELLENCE.' "The very slogan," my friend Josh said after I showed him the bags when I returned to Connecticut, "the university uses as a motto." "Since the funeral home was founded in 1904," Josh continued, "an educational grave robber must have stolen the phrase."

On that trip six years ago Vicki and I spent a night in Red Boiling Springs, an old resort town, twenty-three miles north of Carthage near the Kentucky border. Edward and I repeated the stay. The road from Carthage wound through small valleys, hills rising above them like cupcakes bristly with trees. On damp slopes shining sumac bloomed, and nodding thistles bent over fences like congregations dozing in church. Tobacco barns huddled against hills, their tin roofs rusty and their sides warped gray and weather-beaten. In panlike fields corn stood knee high. Tractors pulled carts across bottom land. Usually two people sat in a cart, one person to the right, the other to the left, both pushing small tobacco plants into the soil.

Edward and I stayed at the Thomas House, a restored hotel. The Thomas House perched on a knob above Salt Lick Creek. This spring Edward said he wanted to be either an entomologist or a herpetologist, and before dinner we explored the banks of the creek. Four northern water snakes lay ropy on a ledge, red saddles broad across their backs and yellow gleaming like bits under their lower jaws. Atop a rock a yellow-bellied water snake curled almost invisible on a cushion of dried grass. While robins foraged under maples, a phoebe bobbed on a telephone wire, and a kingfisher swooped and circled the creek. At dusk lightning bugs rolled over the knob. Small bats wagged overhead, and perfume from tangles of honeysuckle suddenly blew luscious along the slope. Under a board lurked a pedunculate ground beetle. When Edward held the beetle, it swiveled and hissed.

On a trip people ponder meals more than they do at home. For dinner at the Thomas House, Edward and I ate country ham, biscuits, mashed potatoes, creamed corn, and beans and bacon. For dessert we had strawberry pudding. On the bedside table in our room lay a book containing comments from previous guests. Salt in the ham made my heart drum. In hopes of muffling the beat I read the comments. "My wife and I thank you for allowing us to grace your home," a man from Selma, Alabama, wrote. "The stay has given us the opportunity to grow even closer together in the Lord." "After thirty years as husband and wife," a Californian declared, "we're still learning that the best things in life aren't things." "Everything was great until about twelve o'clock," a woman from Knoxville wrote, "then something in the wall began fluttering and chirping." The something was swallows. They made such a ruckus that I got up at five and walked the grounds, looking at trees. While tulips and oaks surrounded the Thomas House, down the east side of the knob grew pignut hickories, shaggy silver maples, and two persimmons, the bark on these last thick square blocks, gray across the tops of the blocks, but black in furrows.

During the trip Edward and I visited the Hermitage, the home of Andrew Jackson east of Nashville, then the battlefield at Chickamauga in north Georgia. In April tornadoes bounced through Middle Tennessee, toppling scores of trees at the Hermitage. As I walked across the lawn, I heard chain saws whining and smelled the smoky sawdust of red cedar. The day was so bright that historical fact bleached into mirage, and Edward and I spent more time wandering the scrub behind the spring house than we did in the mansion itself. Privet bloomed, and magnolia blossoms unfolded, the white on petals so pure it seemed distilled. In shade nuts on beeches were orange; in the sun they appeared green. Dirt daubers pasted nests to the sides of wooden buildings, the pipes looking like clusters of chopped roots. Snout butterflies whisked a path, and cicadas flurried through the day, their wings chattering.

Although hearts had been pounded into powder at Chickamauga, again the day was so bright that I didn't glimpse a shadow of the past. Near the spot where Polk attacked Thomas's Corps on the last day of battle, I caught a fence lizard, the first I'd caught in fifty years. Catching lizards was easy when I was a boy. Age has slowed me, however, and for a moment I thought the lizard would elude me as it dodged around and up the trunk of a small tree. Edward had never held a spiny lizard. "They are beautiful, aren't they, Daddy," he said before placing it on a nest of leaves. "Yes, they are lovely," I said, memories of my Virginia, the acrid taste of boxwood and the thunder billowing dark along the Pamunkey River in late afternoon, pushing Chickamauga out of mind.

One day, according to an old tale, two acquaintances walked along a dirt road. Suddenly they chanced upon a horse standing by a fence eating grass. "I could steal that horse and cut your throat," the first man said, "and no one would find out." "God would be my witness and avenge my death," the second man said. "We'll see what your God can do," the first man said, pulling a knife from his boot and stabbing his companion in the heart. Next spring a grapevine grew on the spot where the man died and wound around a fence post. A single bunch of gray and white grapes clung to the vine. Bees swarmed around the fence, preventing passersby from plucking fruit from the vine. One humid fall morning the grapes burst, and a flock of mockingbirds broke from them, all the birds singing, naming the murderer. The truth of story is rarely that of history, and although Edward and I studied two score monuments at Chickamauga, the inscriptions did not rattle like musketry through emotion. We walked across Dyer Field up the south slope of Snodgrass Hill to the South Carolina monument. Like mica flickering in the bed of a shallow green river, black-eyed Susans, purple clover, ox-eyed daisies, and Queen Anne's lace sparkled amid the grass. On the base of the monument a weary infantryman held a rifle and an artilleryman grasped a plunger ready to swab the barrel of a Napoleon. For a moment I glanced down the hill and imagined lines of gray and blue wavering in the heat. But then I stepped behind the obelisk. In the shade a middle-aged couple kissed. The man had a handlebar mustache. His belly swung over his trousers like roe, and he wore a creamy yellow shirt. The woman wore a bright pink blouse and khaki shorts, and varicose veins coiled down the side of the calf on her right leg.

Edward and I also spent two days roaming the Cumberland Plateau at Sewanee. Edward wanted to hear "the eloquence of the canebreak rattler" and see copperheads curled like pies on ledges. Alas, we saw only two snakes, a red-bellied snake half a shoelace in length and a black racer which slipped across our path, vanishing like a draft when a window is shut. Still, we saw scores of millipedes, all wedges and rammers. Brown and two inches long, the rammers seemed chains of metal rings. The insects' legs extended from the trunks of their bodies, resembling the legs of Victorian tables, curving like S's turned sideways. The wedges were dark brown with orange or yellow lines separating the segments of their bodies like washers. Instead of walking, wedges rolled forward as if surfing the crests of three waves. Early in the morning wood thrushes called from damp woods below Morgan's Steep. In the afternoon hawks shrieked and rode thermals above Proctor's Hall, a box-shaped stone tunnel.

Most spring flowers had swollen to seed. But at the sunny beginnings of trails American ipecac bloomed, and along humid paths spiderwort stamens hovered loose and yellow above purple webs of petals. Fire pinks twisted from cracks under sandstone overhangs and sprawled lazily along the ground, their stamens flaring like matches. While leaves of leafcup sliced hillsides jagged, pools of May apples filled dells, yellow rectangles splotching the umbrellas of leaves, the green fruits floating above the ground, bobbing in shallows. Greenbriar tangled tops of slopes while poison ivy and Virginia creeper knotted trees and boulders together. Redbud, sassafras, and tulip tree saplings sprouted in hedges. Above them fanned witch hazel and spice bush. For the first time I saw mountain hydrangea, the sterile outer flowers on clusters, three petaled, broken fans.

Above the undergrowth towered sycamores, buckeyes, and white oaks. During the rambles I noticed bark: jerky strings of black locust; gray trails melting down northern red oak; the red cork of large chestnut oaks; and the light gray bark of small tulip trees, blue strips drifting then spreading, dammed behind green mounds. When I rested, I noticed small things, circles of maidenhair ferns then fragile ferns spilling out of crevices. Under a ledge gray-and-white orb weavers hung webs, and a green salamander pressed itself against stone, gold patches glittering like nuggets along its back.

Days were hot. No matter what we saw and how we rested, walking exhausted us. Late the second afternoon we swam at Lake Cheston on the Sewanee campus. Afterward I drove to the Dairy Queen in Monteagle, seven miles away. I bought us each a medium-sized cone dipped in chocolate and costing $1.15. We ate the cones outside, sitting in plastic chairs at a green plastic table. Vanilla seeped in rivulets through the chocolate and running over our hands dripped onto the table. We watched the Monteagle policeman cruise back and forth waiting for speeders hurrying off the interstate. Above us stood a sign advertising the Dairy Queen. "Family Owned and Operated. Established in 1962 By Don and Phoebe Underhill," the sign said. "This is a glorious life," I said, biting off a hunk of chocolate. "You bet it is," Edward said, "what fun."

Profound

Ellen settled into a study on the fourth floor of Babbidge Library. After spreading books across a table and picking up a yellow pad, she heard a commotion. A work crew began removing the hall carpet, their voices bantering like starlings. As Ellen shifted a book, a young man appeared at the door to the room. "Ma'am," he said, thinking Ellen was packing, "you don't have to leave. We might be a little loud. But we're not going to be profound or anything. We'll be civil and all." "When I learned the crew was going to avoid profundity," Ellen said, "I knew the clatter would be enjoyable."

In contrast to Ellen, many of my acquaintances want profundity to be part of every hour. The prophet Ezekiel described "a wheel in the middle of a wheel," a vision appealing to people determined to see meaning spokey behind the quick roll of event. Studying the turning moment eventually dizzies and confuses, however. Often people are so nauseated by the complexity they fancy exists in life that they forswear observation and, becoming fundamentalists, embrace narrow, reassuring dogma. In truth Ezekiel was a nutter, or "a bit squirrely," as my friend Josh says. He saw sights no one has seen since, UBOs, Josh calls them, Unidentified Biblical Objet. Ezekiel, a Presbyterian mogul told me, "hauled sunshine and described the imaginary in hopes of dazzling the benighted." Although sunshine often reflects brightly from words, shadows lurk near the ends of sentences. "We are three identical twins," Elmon Haywood said recently, introducing his sisters

Kate and Duplikate to Turlow Gutheridge. That afternoon in Ankerrow's Café, Loppie Groat asked Googoo Hooberry why *III* appeared after the name of their friend John The Baptist Preaching In The Wilderness Tomkins. "It's easier to write 'John The Baptist Preaching In The Wilderness Tomkins, III' than 'John The Baptist Preaching In The Wilderness Tomkins, John The Baptist Preaching In The Wilderness Tomkins, John The Baptist Preaching In The Wilderness Tomkins,'" Googoo explained.

Such high seriousness aside, profundity does not determine the course of my days. This summer Vicki and I aren't going to the farm in Nova Scotia. Responsibility has not bound us to Storrs. A foundation has not dumped funds into my lap in hopes that I will produce the definitive study of "Walking and the Ecological Man." No, a toilet has sealed us to place. In July Bill will redo the bathroom, and Vicki insists on remaining at home to oversee not simply tub and vanity but also valve and faucet—lockernuts, retaining clips, escutcheons, and diverter assemblies.

I do not spend days plumbing thoughts that run too deep for tapping. Instead, ordinary events leak across hours, turning life weedy and green. Last Thursday the seventh-grade class at the Middle School picnicked at Bicentennial Pond. I sat atop a knoll and looked down at the pond. Behind me at the edge of the woods multiflora roses bloomed, some blossoms spilling over canes in white clusters, others stretching in rows flat as wallpaper. A family of Canada geese drifted along the shore of the pond, four goslings low in the water sandwiched between two adults. Down the slope and along the beach children frolicked, boys and girls rarely mixing, however. While a gang of awkward boys smacked a volleyball, a large group of athletic boys played touch football in the sand. Several cool girls, as Eliza calls them, tried to join the boys, sprinting giggling through the game. The boys ignored the intruders, and eventually the girls skipped loudly into the water and screeching, splashed each other. No cool girl wore a bathing suit. In contrast Eliza and her friends wore suits and swam, most imitating porpoises, diving under the water, their backs arching.

I stayed on the knoll two hours. At three-thirty I drove to the high school. In fall E. O. Smith fields its first football team. Baseball having just ended, spring practice was underway. I sat under a black birch near a rock students had painted blue and white. I recognized Edward. Instead of football cleats he wore baseball shoes. Hanging beneath his shoulder pads and jersey was the green end of a shirt he wore when he played recreational baseball in eighth grade. A sophomore next year, Edward is five feet eleven inches tall and weighs 130 pounds. He runs well and is an easy athlete, and the coach tried him at backup quarterback and first-team wide receiver and free safety. As I watched Edward crouch behind the center and shout "power left" and "power right," I recalled days when I played football. I was a poor athlete, and migrating from the bench onto the playing field took three years. I envied Edward's ability, and as I watched him lope effortlessly across the grass, I began to live vicariously, imagining myself succeeding at a sport. "What fun games will be in the fall," I murmured, then stopped. Invariably the children's failures cause me anxiety. This spring after Francis lost his seat in the school eight, I awoke several nights running, always sitting up, pondering how I could ease his disappointment. Rarely, however, had the possibility of a child's success awakened my imagination. The realization that I enjoyed watching Edward play football made me uncomfortable, and I slid off the rock and went home.

That evening Edward looked mottled, bruises welling over his arms and chest like mold through bread crust. "I love football, Daddy," he said. "I'm the only Latin student on the team," he said later, adding, "I'm also the only boy who plays the piano, but I'm keeping that secret." Bullying occurred at practice. Since Edward was a freshman and some older boys weighed twice as much as he did, I asked if players bullied him. "I've never been bullied," he said. "It is because I am taller that most players. Bullies don't pick on people they look up at."

If a person believes all he hears, he'll fish for birds and hunt for fish. "The link between football and adolescent hormones," Josh told me last week, "has long been established." Josh lies so much that if he were a pig farmer he'd have to hire someone to call his hogs. Still, at the end of spring practice, Edward asked me to buy him a hairbrush. For fifteen years Edward avoided brushing his hair. On formal occasions, he drizzled water over his right hand then combed his fingers across his forehead. I bought Edward an ACE Club Brush. Made from "100% Boar Bristles," the brush, the package stated, had been "designed for shorter length hair of all textures," "perfect," Josh said, "for a high school football player." Preening is for the young. In contrast to Edward I have aged beyond thinking about hair. "Or about anything having to do with appearance," Vicki said yesterday. "Guilty but drunk," I answered, continuing to scribble. Years ago maxims passed for profundity, instructive aphorisms such as "While the wise man walks, the fool runs"; "Flatter the world and dine on sweets"; and "Washing your own feet isn't slavery." Today slogans have replaced maxims. Although slogan and maxim are both tonguing, maxims bite. In contrast, slogans are usually toothless, and a reader has to gump through them. In March Francis took the college board examinations. Since April advertisements from colleges have almost burst the mailbox. Emblazoned across envelop and brochure are slogans. While the University of Delaware is a "Teaching University," the University of Rhode Island provides "Education for a Lifetime." Emory is a "Not-So-Hidden Treasure," and the University of Central Florida is "Florida's Educational Attraction." Neither Emory nor Central Florida merit a footnote on the educational sightseeing tour when compared to the Rose-Hulman Institute of Technology, the "Western World's Best Kept Secret," located in Terra Haute, Indiana, zip code 47803. At Washington University in St. Louis, "you" can "*Discover* and *Develop* Who You Are . . . Who You Want To Be!" In Philadelphia, St. Joseph's is dedicated to "Making A Good World Better." In Ohio, Oberlin urges students to "Learn. Make a difference." At the Rochester Institute of Technology, students receive "Tomorrow's education today." "Chart Your Own Course," the United States Merchant Marine Academy urges students. "World's best playground for MATH, SCIENCE, and engineering," declares a pamphlet from the California Institute of Technology. I think these last two slogans better than most others. What Francis thinks is a mystery. He hasn't read a brochure. "Pick out the colleges, Daddy," he said yesterday, putting on a helmet to go mountain biking, "and I'll apply."

On my bedside table is a brochure advertising holidays on St. Lucia. Three pink bands stretch like garters across the top of the cover. Stamped on the bands in white is "A Romantic Guide To The Most Beautiful Vacation In The Caribbean." Perched on a rock below the slogan are a man and a woman wearing bathing suits. Bermuda-shorts length, the man's trunks are blue. The woman's suit is yellow and has a skirt sewed to the waist. Behind the couple waves flutter over a green reef. Throughout the brochure palms sway lazily, and hibiscus ooze red and yellow. The sea is always blue; sands are white; and wines, golden. College brochures are similarly lush. Students smile and resemble waiters at Sandals and the Wyndham Bay Resort, holidays at this last "spa" being all-inclusive, unlike fees at colleges. Tilting across the front of Rutgers' brochure is a boy wearing a tie-dyed shirt. Blue and white ripple off his shoulders then churn into waves. Sunbursts explode down the sides of the shirt, breaking at surf's edge into coral reefs of color. At Rhode Island and Lake Forest students stroll beaches, threesomes wearing sweatshirts in contrast to scantily clad couples on St. Lucia. In all brochures students are busy playing, soccer being the preferred leisure activity in preference, say, to golf on St. Lucia. Much as resorts describe activities, schools list sports and clubs. While Vassar fields twenty-two intercollegiate teams, half for boys and half for girls, the Wyndham Bay offers tennis, "volleyball, snorkeling, scuba diving, kayaking, Sunfish sailing, windsurfing, and a fitness center."

"Picture Yourself in This Photo" declares the brochure from Mary Washington. Above the words three students stroll across a wooded hill, all underbrush swept away, white ashes almost palmy above, fifty yards behind them a red brick cabana, white columns supporting a portico, inviting and friendly as a complimentary drink. Not only could Francis picture himself in the brochure for New York University, buying yellow apples from a vendor at Union Park Square, but he could also imagine himself at American University glancing through leaves turning red and orange, seeing the Washington Monument split the sky, the Capitol a mushroom in the distance. For my part as I examined college brochures, I imagined myself at Ladera Resort, splashing in a "private pool," mountains to the right silver with dew, the ocean a thousand feet below bookishly blue.

Although colleges described intellectual doings, somewhere into the second hundred pamphlet, plants began to interest me more than faculty or books. Across the brochure sent by the University of Southern California coconut palms swept a pink sunset shaggy. At dusk at West Point a trellis of redbud leaves sliced black across a purple sky. While daffodils smiled at prospective students at Towson, lupines waved at Ohio Wesleyan. At Macalaster a circle of burning bush smoldered like a cookout at camp, and at Johns Hopkins saucer magnolias were frilly as postcards.

Rarely does profundity attract seventeen year olds. Even the University of Chicago, whose advertisements were more studious than those of other universities, sent a map of campus and city. Drawn and colored in exaggerated cartoon fashion, the map showed not only the locations of classrooms and dormitories but also restaurants and video stores. Soldier Field appeared in orange and blue; Comisky Park, in yellow; and the United Center, purple and red. "Carnival, crawfish boils, and café au lait," began a letter from Tulane, "the French Quarter, cool blues, and all that jazz." Later in the letter the director of admissions called Tulane "a world-class research university." "While New Orleans may be the Big Easy," he wrote, "Tulane University most definitely is not." Several schools began letters by mentioning seductive local attractions. "Dear Francis," the director of admissions at Miami wrote, "let's be honest. You may be considering attending a college in a wintry climate. And you might be distracted by the tropical beauty of Florida. If so, the University of Miami is not for you." "Why did the man mention climate if he thought it a distraction?" Edward asked. "An oily case," Eliza said, "of advertising sunshine then basting the paper with sunscreen and disclaiming responsibility for all burns."

Letters accompanying brochures were printed from the same glossy commercial rag. Most began with compliments, congratulating Francis on his "outstanding job," as Bowdoin put it, on either the PSATs or the SATs. "Your PSAT scores indicated exceptional ability," the letter from Williams said. "So Williams College—considered by many to be the best liberal arts college in the country—is a place you should know about." Colleges less well known struggled for recognition. Ohio Wesleyan handled comparative obscurity better than other schools. "Hello Stranger!" the dean of admissions began. "Introductions between strangers can be difficult, but we'd like to try. We are Ohio Wesleyan University, a distinguished national liberal arts college of 1,850 students and 122 dedicated faculty members. Founded in 1842, we are located in the charming town of Delaware just north of Columbus, the state capital and 16th largest city in the United States."

Some schools tried to startle children into attention. "The pressure, as Billy Joel said, is building," Quinnipiac College wrote. "Will all your plans work out? Will you have a career that is well paying and personally satisfying? Will you be prepared—in mind and heart—to enter the high-powered, high-tech 21st century?" That which covers you discovers you, be the *that* a comforter or a letter. "Dear Francis," the director of admissions at Duke opined, "I expect it was the name *Duke* that made you open the envelope." I showed the letter to Josh. "Oh, Duke! Shout Little Lula!" he exclaimed, paraphrasing the title of an old song, adding, "I'm cutting quite a figure, said the chorus girl as she sat on a pane of glass." "The man who owns a dog," Josh continued, "doesn't have to bark."

The letter from Harvard was studiously restrained. Instead of Francis, my son was Mr. Pickering. "We are writing," the letter began, "to offer our congratulations on your academic achievements and to encourage you to consider Harvard and Radcliffe as a possible college choice. Like many other colleges, we take advantage of the search services of the College Board and the American College Testing Program to identify students whose test scores and grades suggest that they may be good candidates for our college. We hope that as you sift through the piles of college mail you are no doubt receiving, you will take time to look closely at the special opportunities Harvard and Radcliffe have to offer. Under separate cover, we will be mailing you a packet of material, including an application."

On letterheads most schools listed toll-free numbers. Members of the Ivy League and several eastern colleges did not provide such numbers, implying their mailboxes overflowed with applications. "Your call is unimportant to us because," Josh declared, quoting God's statement to Moses in Exodus, "I AM THAT I AM." No telephone number of any sort appeared on Harvard's letter. Stamped in the upper right-hand corner of the letter from Yale was "i 1 0017861." The notation mystified me, so I called undergraduate admissions. Like several schools Yale had planted a telephone tree. Once a person climbed onto a limb, getting back to the trunk and reaching a human was impossible. I left a message in the nest of an admissions officer, asking her to return my call. The officer did not return the call, and the message addled. Perhaps that was for the better. Unbeknown to his family, Ray, one of Francis's friends, tried to arrange an interview in New Haven. Like me, Ray found himself dangling on a limb, so he left a message. A member of the admissions staff returned Ray's call. Ray was not at home, and his mother answered the phone. "The call irritated me," Ray's mother recounted. "The woman was the most arrogant jackass I've ever spoken too, so not knowing she was from Yale, I gave her the bird. About the time I realized the call was from admissions at Yale, the woman recognized I was mocking her. 'Who am I talking to?' the woman demanded. 'Ray's younger sister Beth,' I answered, not wanting to bugger the poor boy's chances completely."

Ours is an age of celebrity. Princeton, Harvard, and Yale are educational equivalents of GAP, Nike, and Tommy Hilfiger. Parents purchase schools for marquee, not educational, value. Most parents realize that twenty-year-old children are incapable of thought, not to mention learning. By the time students age into wisdom, they will have forgotten the particulars of school education. Will Francis apply to marquee schools? Yes. Despite my criticisms of academic matters, Francis's applications will wheedle and supplicate. As the old saying phrases it, "Behind dog, it is Dog. Before dog, it is Mister Dog."

Essayists meddle. I called admissions officers at several schools. Invariably undergraduates answered the telephone and attempted to answer questions. The students gushed. Thoughts about fees being prophylactic, I did not catch their enthusiasm and remained rational. "I know you are absolutely charming, but you sound like a baby," I said, "and since the subject of this call is $140,000, I'd like to speak to an adult." Students then routed my calls to recent graduates. Not only had the graduates not aged out of puppyhood, but they knew little about education. Insecure, they often seemed smug know-nothings, children who believed position made them important. Occasionally admissions staffs entertained me. "Other than this place," a woman at a small college in Massachusetts asked, "what schools is your son considering?" I mentioned MIT. "What a marvelous college," the officer said. She paused then added, "But wasn't that sad about the young man who died from alcoholic poisoning at a fraternity party there? Decades ago we banned fraternities. Such things don't happen here." Telephone calls to the Ivies often made me scratch. I asked an officer at an Ivy League school if she liked the university. She grunted then said, "I don't know. It's all right." "Would you send your child there?" I asked. "No," she said, "not my baby."

The butterfly once invited the lightning bug to a ball. The prospect of revels thrilled the bug. "Delighted, no end," he exclaimed, backing into a fan as he read the invitation. Efficiency delighted me and shortened conversations. The best admissions officers to whom I talked were at Cal Tech and Cornell. Women, both understood that tuition would push many parents into the poorhouse. "Universities compete with nursing homes for middle-class dollars," Josh said. "Schools pick pockets while parents still wear trousers, reducing their old age to barebones and johnnies."

Designer schools do not offer merit scholarships based upon academic potential. "We have six scholarships not based upon need," said the director of admissions at a small college in Pennsylvania. "Unfortunately your son is not eligible for four of them. Two go to residents of this county and two more to residents of the region. Still, your boy will be considered for the other two. Who knows? He might win one." "I know," I answered. "Thirteen percent of your students come from New England. A red-headed boy from a public school in Connecticut doesn't stand a chance." "Yes, he does," the director responded. "Bullshit!" I exclaimed. "One scholarship will go to a boy from Alaska, the other to a girl from Mississippi." For a moment the director was silent. Then he said, "This has been quite a frank conversation." "Your lot needs frank conversations," I said. "You are the parent from Hell," my friend Tom said when I described the chat to him.

On university campuses candor is not endangered but extinct. Occasionally a fossil of frankness surfaces and startles. This past spring I taught a course on American nature writers. Four days after the third and final examination and twenty-two days after the term paper was due, I received a packet from a girl. In the packet were the term paper and a letter. "I wonder what stale excuse she will foist off on me," I muttered, starting to read the letter. "I am in a predicament in that I missed the second exam and also some of the Friday discussion sessions," Suzanne wrote. "I read most of what was assigned and came to Monday and Wednesday classes. In these classes I took notes on the day's topic as well as wrote a little bit of my own on the side. I was involved in the class the only way I could have been this semester, considering that as a Senior, I seem to feel very strongly about my particular arrangement of priorities, school being lower than friends and 'quality time' and such, and I guess I lost track of things. I was a thoughtful participant when I participated. What I am asking here may be in your estimation too much. I am asking for a D minus, enough for the three credits." Suzanne got the D and the three credits. She should have asked for more. Her paper was excellent, and in comparison to the dead tone of the letters Francis received her wacky candor invigorated.

The workman in the library meant to say *profane*. The gods of the present being mercantile, I blasphemed in criticizing educational marketing. "Beware," Josh warned, "of alumni, bilked parents, wizards, haruspices, snake handlers, and congressmen sugaring bank accounts by distributing salt pork—all wearing hair and sweatshirts and ready to defend Anubis and Dartmouth, Amherst and Quitzalcoatl against infidels bearing truth." Because he does not have a child applying to college, Josh expresses things in words stronger than I think appropriate. Still, occasionally I like language meaty and underdone.

Rather than profane, many rough stories strike me as pleasantly silly. Instead of irritating, the stories entertain and balm-like soothe the abrasions of a day. After the conversation with the director of admissions in Pennsylvania, I felt testy. That afternoon I received a letter from Turlow Gutheridge in Carthage. Reading the letter returned calm of intellectual digestion. This spring rains were heavy in Smith County. When Hopp Watrous tried to cart a load of building stone to Maggart, the wagon slid through a wash into a ditch. Malachi Ramus, minister of the Church of the Chastening Rod, came upon Hopp after Hopp had unloaded the stones and was struggling to wedge the back axle out of the mud. Hopp, Turlow wrote, "had sweated considerably, and his language was intemperate." Upon seeing then hearing Hopp, Malachi stepped under an oak, took off his hat, mopped his brow, then holding his hat before his chest like pot of green peas, looked down into the ditch. "Brother," he said addressing Hopp, "do you know the name of the One who died for sinners like you?" "Damn it to hell!" Hopp exclaimed, leaning against the left wheel of the axle. "I've got no time for riddles now. Can't you see I'm stuck ass high in this frigging red clay?"

Rarely is Turlow penurious with story. Two days after the mishap on the Maggart Turnpike, Hopp, Turlow wrote, went fishing in the Cumberland River. He had just hooked the rib cage of a mule when a "huge blow-toad catfish" rose from the mud and opening his mouth swallowed Hopp, the mule cutlets, and the rowboat. Catfish are not picky eaters, dead mule and boat being particular delights. Hopp, however, was a dish of a different flavor. He stank so much and his clothes were so grimy that the catfish gagged and high-finning it to the bank threw up, pitching Hopp weeping into a willow. Immediately afterward the fish leapt into a drainage ditch and washed his mouth out with runoff from Hink Ruunt's cow pasture. "The gargling was so loud," Turlow recounted, "that Ben Meadows heard it four miles away." Thinking a thief was trying to start his new tractor, Ben grabbed a shotgun and, running out of his house, tripped over a root in the yard and fell to the ground. The gun slapped against the well cover and fired, killing Cornbread, Ben's favorite pig. "Oh, well," Turlow concluded, "a hog isn't good for much until it's dead."

Profundity, in story or without, isn't achieved easily. The picky person will never be profound. To reach profundity one has to munch life—catfish, rowboats, and red clay. He must appreciate, or at least sample both the tasty and the tasteless. Not only should he know that far from highways beside lonesome waters a country piano is a manure spreader, but he should also be able to hum tunes the spreader plays, old favorites like "I Have No Mother Now," "Turnip Greens," and "I Danced with a Gal with a Hole in Her Stocking."

After a person has lived a few years with himself, odd workings of his mind seem ordinary. No matter the subject I ponder when I pick up my pen, be the topic profound or profane, a preacher is sure to appear. In Maggart Malachi Ramus met the White Pilgrim, a "Postapocalyptinarian," and escorted him to Carthage, where he led a revival. The Pilgrim's head was shaped like a radish. He wore a white robe, white sandals, and a white steeple hat. "He wears the robe," Piety Goforth asserted, "because he's so bow-legged that the seat of his trousers drag the ground like a towel." In his right hand the Pilgrim carried a white radio. When he preached, he held the radio against the side of his head, listening, he testified, "to the Master's Voice broadcasting from the other shore." Often the Pilgrim related weather reports, "sin dark and stormy," he said, "but the bright day is coming and flood waters will abate." Occasionally preaching unplugged the cord of reason, and the Pilgrim praised sponsors, his favorites being Wildroot Cream Oil Hair Tonic, Decon Mice and Rat Killer, and White Rose Petroleum Jelly.

In my books Carthaginians have listened to many preachers, and the Pilgrim did not impress the cognoscenti. Googoo Hooberry called him gizzardless. Hoben Donkin said he was a hollow stump, and Loppie Groat declared that he grinned like a baked possum. "Don't be fooled. Hidden in many smiles are needles," Piety Goforth warned before telling an instructive story. One afternoon King Lion, Piety recounted, called a meeting of animals. All the creatures showed up, from the biggest to the smallest, from Mr. Shrew to Old Lady Elephant. The animals promised to suspend appetite and inclination and to behave at the gathering. Nevertheless, when Rabbit hopped in front of Hound, Hound gapped and saliva ran down his teeth. "You better muzzle that son of a bitch," Rabbit shouted. "He'll bite somebody directly."

Despite Piety's misgivings, the Pilgrim did not inspire the sanctified to misbehavior. Before leaving Carthage, the Pilgrim preached three sermons: "Cat in the Meal Tub," "Damn a Jersey

Bull," and "Watch that Snake." The title of the second sermon referred more to exhorting than to theme. "Our Savior," the Pilgrim shouted, "was born in Bethlehem then pierced with spears, nails, thorns, and horse shoes. Yet the wounds never gathered, smarted, nor festered. Praise God and Damn a Jersey Bull!" Later the Pilgrim declared, "You can't find a termite on a white man or see through a glass eye into a stone wall. Damn a Jersey Bull!" The Pilgrim condemned alcohol as the yeast starting most evils. "The righteous," he said, "only drink water that has had the Hell boiled out of it. Poor Little Polly stepped out and drank wine at the Midnight Inn. Nine months later she had her appendix removed and started giving milk. Damn a Jersey Bull!" In "Watch that Snake," the Pilgrim described a twelve-headed legless serpent that ran on ball bearings and devoured sinners "like a Cannibal Meteor eating a flock of sheep." Joints on the monster's body were reversed, its elbows appearing on the front of its arms instead of the backs. The creature had nails sharp as the beak of a pigeon hawk and didn't talk but whistled. Its breasts were under its arms, and its milk was black and thick as molasses. Its tongues looked like syringes. When jabbed into the dead, the tongues drew blood, making corpses scream, no matter they'd been buried for six months.

Collections not amounting to enough to detain the spirit, the Pilgrim left Carthage after the three sermons, explaining that the radio instructed him "to spread the fleece under the feet of the enslaved sons and daughters of Adam in Cookeville." For my part paragraphs had begun to swirl. To escape words I spent a morning wandering yard and campus. In the back yard chipmunks scurried down drain pipes, and gray squirrels bustled into black birches. A fledgling sparrow perched on a gutter and begged for food. A young grackle stood motionless on the birdfeeder and didn't fly until I was within arm's length. At the edge of the woods broad-leaved helloborine orchids grew amid pachysandra, seed heads immature and curtseying. Behind the speech building I surprised a fawn. Along streets littleleaf linden bloomed, blossoms hanging in pads, bees spraying about them, the creamy fragrance softening air dried and worn raw by fumes from automobiles.

Several trees bloomed to welcome summer. Four-and-a-half-inch flowers bristled out in brushes from Chinese chestnut, the perfume simultaneously musty and dry. Edges of the chestnut's leaves curved upward into gunnels, transforming leaves into canoes, floating lightly through sunlight. On Kousa dogwood petals bent stiffly backward, the fresh white discs eroding into spurs of green and brown. On copper beeches red spines curled frizzled over nuts. Blossoms on tulip trees had shrunk to sharp cones. I rubbed my hands over several cones then smelled my palms, the aroma magnolia, making me long to revisit the Virginia of my childhood. "Just once more," I said silently, "I'd like to sit on the front stoop at Cabin Hill and chew boxwood. I'd like to find a dead copperhead and stretch it across the doorway to Mother's room. I'd like to churn butter and eat Grandma's yellow cake." The hankering did not last long. Writers lose their actual lives. Pages force them to shape event into illusion. Truth vanishes, and only shaping remains. Died in Connecticut, returned to life in Virginia, I thought, suddenly distorting nostalgia into the literary.

Because I had not seen Stewartia until I moved to Storrs, flowers on the tree did not stoke a train heavy with association. Petals ruffled around the centers of flowers in white, elegant informality. Five ricks of stamens leaned over pistils, their anthers bready and orange, their filaments yellow. The fragrance of the flowers was slight as summer laughter. Many flowers had slipped from branches, and weeping into dirt around the trees made beauty appear fragile. When I returned home, a stack of mail sat on the kitchen table. Addressed to Francis, most pieces were letters from colleges. I didn't open any. After dinner rain fell. A gray tree frog clung to the spout of a plastic water can by side door. The frog's eyes were scarlet, slats of dark cracking the red like night creeping into a room through an open window.

Not Enough

In May the university awarded an honorary degree to Frank McCourt, author of *Angela's Ashes*. Before the big doings Vicki and I ate lunch with the McCourts at the home of the dean of arts and sciences. By meal's end I was slightly elevated, and I asked Mr. McCourt if I should shout anything when he received the degree. "Not enough," Mr. McCourt suggested. Graduation ritual is ornate and lengthy, and Mr. McCourt got his degree near the end of the ceremony. The tighter I get, the looser I behave. To pass time I visited with faculty, mostly ladies known to be candid, as my friend Josh puns, because "they are so sweet." For years I've admired a couple of Godivas from distant classrooms. Swept out from behind my desk by a flash flood of wine, I confessed admiration. The next morning I felt like covering my head not only with Angela's but with an entire incinerator of ashes. "Oh, Sam, don't spoil the poetry," Betsy said on my starting to apologize, "you were graduation's rhyme royal. What you said inspired me. Next year I'll sip lunch before the ceremony and prime myself for a stanza of confessional verse."

When Mr. McCourt stood for his degree, I was silent, not because discretion beamed hot responsibility down upon vulgarity and dried enthusiasm, but because I was pondering the phrase "not enough." Dissatisfaction invigorates and satisfies. Getting less than one thinks he deserves stirs resentment and keeps malcontents almost content. Wind, according to the old saying, does not overturn stones. How dull to be a stone, comfortable and forever sedate. For my part, I decided during graduation, I preferred to be wind, light and insubstantial, blowing through afternoons, riffling pattern then pages. "Better," Josh said later, twisting another aphorism into shape, "to be dust rather than broom." While dust swirls through houses, brooms stand at attention, confined to pantries. Coming out of closets only to work, brooms are condemned to drab, useful toil.

Of course, dust occasionally settles, and the person whose days dissatisfaction pocks can become melancholy in quiet, empty moments. The market for essays almost matches that of spectacles for blind bees. In these fast literary times I'm going no place slowly. So rarely does the telephone ring that I don't own an answering machine. In contemplative moments between paragraphs, I sometimes long to be startled. "Even the appearance of the rowboat of doom," I told Josh. "I'm tired of sitting on the pier waiting for a heart attack or whatever is going to kill me. Knowing would relieve anxious boredom."

Instead of transforming day into night, such dark moments only flicker like shadows across my life. Usually dissatisfaction brightens hours. Each time one of my books is published, childhood friends believe I earn a quarter of a million dollars. In 1997 royalties from ten books brought me $100.25, or .000401 of what friends assume I make on a book. One morning not long after receiving my royalties, a quarter vanished through a hole in my trousers. The loss prevented me from buying a second cup of coffee at the Cup of Sun, and I mentioned it to Josh. "That leaves you a hundred dollars royalty," he said. "That's not bad. Multiply the amount by twenty-five hundred, and you'll have a quarter of a million." "The multiplier alone would satisfy me," I said. "Think big. Francis starts college next fall. Colleges don't accept pennies. They extort dollars," Josh said, adding, "Look what your friend Wally has done."

Recently Oprah Winfrey chose Wally's new novel *I Know This Much Is True* for her book club, the second novel by Wally she has selected. The Sunday after I talked to Josh, the *Hartford Courant* reported that Wally sold movie rights to the new book for a fortune, adding parenthetically that by the following Wednesday 565,000 hardback copies of *I Know* would be in print, this at a time when his first novel was still among the best sellers, having sold over 3,000,000 copies in paperback. "The daily number," Roger said Monday morning, "is 244." "What?" I said. "That's the number of copies of Wally's new book the university store has sold so far," Roger explained. "But Suzy told me sales are just starting. I'll keep you informed." Two days later the number was 301. "Are you envious?" Roger asked. "Envious!" I exclaimed. "Hell, yes! If I tell you I'm not envious, I'm lying and not to be trusted. Envy hardly begins to describe what I feel. Still, all I covet is money. I don't want Wally's books, bicycle, laundry, decency, spirituality, neckties, or shoes. I want the money." "Well," Roger said, pausing for a moment, "at least you are honest." "Yep," I said, suddenly feeling on top of the world. "What do you call the mother-in-law of your sister's husband?" "I don't have a sister," Roger said, shaking his head. "Mother," I said, skipping away.

The next morning Vicki, Eliza, and I left Storrs to take Edward to camp in Maine. The trip was dull. Before closing the car door, Edward made me promise not to mention Wally's books. We spent the night in South Portland, at the Howard Johnson's Motel on Route 1, just off Exit 7 on the Maine Turnpike. After I checked in, the desk clerk handed me a complimentary copy of USA Today. While Vicki unpacked toothbrushes, I thumbed the paper. A list of best sellers appeared in the arts section. "Holy cow," I said aloud. "*I Know This Much Is True* is already six in the nation, and this list includes not just hardback fiction, but nonfiction and paperbacks as well." "And," I continued, "Wally's other novel is number twelve." "Daddy," Edward said reprovingly, "you promised."

We ate dinner at the Lobster Shack at Two Lights. I behaved. Not once did I mention writing. Instead I talked about waves, gulls, cormorants, and crustaceans. After dinner we wandered the gravely beach north of the shack, searching for sea jewels, bits of glass ground smooth and cloudy by the surf. Once our pockets bulged with treasure, I drove into Portland, and we roamed the chic, restored section above the harbor. Edward and Eliza got cups of ice cream at Ben & Jerry's, Edward, cookies and cream, and Eliza, chocolate. We then ambled along Middle Street until we came to Starbucks, where Vicki and I bought coffee and split a piece of carrot cake. Edward and Eliza sat at a table with us until Edward glanced at the counter. Three copies of *I Know* stood beside containers of milk, cream, half-and-half, and a reed basket stuffed with packets of nondairy creamer. Edward stared at the books, then stood and said, "I'm going to finish my ice cream outside." Edward leaned against the corner of the building and observed people. "Daddy," Edward said later when I joined him, "people here are different from people at home. In Storrs if you catch someone's eye, he looks away. Here people stare and look you up and down." "Chicken hawks riding inner thermals," I said. "They noticed you slumped against the building and began to circle. Now that the farmer has arrived with a shotgun, they'll wheel away. Let's go back to the motel. Tomorrow I want to get an early start, so you can pick out a good bed at Timanous."

I was a counselor at Timanous for five summers in the 1960s. Each June when I drop Edward at camp, I meet old friends, former campers and counselors, bringing their children to Timanous. "I'd love to return as a counselor just once more," Billy said. "But my law firm is thriving, and I can't get away." Success trapped Billy. When viewed from the perspective of my finances, the saying "gold is bold" appears wrong. Judging from bank statements I have read, gold imprisons more people that it frees, often making behavior timorous and conservative. On being asked about a man who had moved onto Beacon Hill after making a fortune banking in the Bahamas, Arthur Mocksberry was cautious. "I don't like to comment on neighbors. But insofar as Mr. Tyburn is concerned, I occasionally ponder after which I conclude that he'll prove to be a good deal like the sort of man I take him to be."

The person whose achievements are modest rarely achieves temperate worldly wisdom. Not constrained by position or convention, he sees and acts peculiarly. "He doesn't have to buy deodorant when he skins a skunk," Josh said. "And he skins it how and when he pleases." Last month in Ankerrow's Café, Loppie Groat described a box turtle he saw on the shoulder of the Maggart Turnpike. "When the turtle noticed me," Loppie said, "he pulled his head into his shell." One of the fellows attending the School for the Afflicted in Buffalo Valley listened to Loppie's account. The man had never seen a turtle, or at least had no memory of seeing one, and he was incredulous. "Pshaw," he said. "What's all this business about a head and a shell? All you seen was a hoppie toad hiding in a gourd."

The person whose doings neither gossip nor public opinion scrutinize can relax and enjoy silly tales, stories, Josh says, told by "animated carcasses that turn the cerebrum inside out and pauperize the intellect." "How," Hoben Donkin asked the lunch-time crowd, "can five eggs be divided among five people so that each person receives an egg and one egg remains in the dish?" Regulars at Ankerrow's prided themselves on their abilities to solve riddles. But even after Casper Higgerty fetched a slide rule and figured the multiplication tables up to nine times seven, the question remained unanswered. "The last person served," Hoben explained, "takes the dish with his egg in it."

To get enough requires endurance. Writing *I Know This Much Is True* took Wally six years. I lack endurance. In part I'm an essayist and not a novelist because essays are short matters of a month at the most. Just thinking about planning a novel, the end of which lies hidden behind years tall as mountains exhausts me. Moreover I'm allergic to calluses. When push comes to gainful shove, I amble softer, less-taxing landscapes. Whenever I am invited to a gathering in New York which might flush cash through my literary career, I decline the invitation, the prospect of a five-hour bus trip from Willimantic looming as an insurmountable ordeal.

This past year my oldest friend Bill Weaver attempted to endow a chair and then settle me comfortably atop the wicker at our undergraduate college Sewanee. Small schools are conservative beyond a layman's comprehension. Not only do such schools live by pattern, they live for pattern. During the last decade Bill founded four businesses and invigorated half a dozen charities in Nashville. Opposition to the chair surprised but did not deter him. To him what appeared bumps that money and time would level loomed sharp as ridges to me. "If we are firm," Bill said, "Sewanee will come round, even if I have to spin it myself." I lacked glue. "If people at Sewanee had been enthusiastic when you suggested my teaching there, I would have been eager to go. But they were not," I wrote, "so Bill, the day is done. Like Longfellow's poetic Arabs, we must fold our tents and silently steal away." "If you hadn't backed out, I could have managed matters," Bill said later. "I know," I said, "but the bruising would have been black, not blue or yellow."

Many things which constitute enough seem showy rather than substantial. High schools change real, breathing children into sandwich boards of honors, so they will appear to have more than enough achievements to gain admission to colleges, which, for their parts, panhandle, pasting brochures shimmering like Harlequin over cracks in faculties and facilities. "New sleeves get good dinners," Josh said, "no matter that the arms they cover are unwashed." Clothes, be they words or fabric, become truth and win the shiny things of this world. Alphonse Ludlum was ill tempered and so penurious, Proverbs Goforth said, that he'd steal pennies off a dead child's eyes. When Alphonse died this past winter, Proverbs said selfishness, not pneumonia, killed him. "Slubey Garts," Proverbs said, "promised him a free shroud, and Alphonse died just to get it."

Despite a reputation earned by years of unrepentant meanness, at the funeral mourners praised Alphonse, a few people even calling him "saintly." A tale spread by Alphonse's son Linnie caused the transformation. "After I laid father out and spread ashes and salt under the cooling boards," Linnie recounted, "the family knelt in prayer." "Big Pappy was so sanctified," Linnie continued, "that as soon as we said, 'Our Father,' he raised his right arm and pointing toward heaven repeated the rest of the Lord's Prayer with us. He whispered, and a body had to strain to catch the words. But his tongue was liberalized, and we could read the holy language on his lips. He's Jesus' new bride now, and I know he's having a fine honeymoon in Beulah."

Eaten food is soon forgotten, with the exception, of course, of spicy Indian dishes. Pages distort experience. If truth must be known, I've enjoyed more than enough in this life. Unfortunately, not only have the morsels I gnawed disappeared from mind but the menus themselves have slipped from memory. Two weeks ago my friend Ellen mentioned that when she was a child the Bond Bread man brought baked goods to her parents' house in Ware, Massachusetts. Suddenly I remembered the Bond Bread man driving the road to Cabin Hill, Grandfather's farm in Virginia. Every Friday, Grandma bought white, sugared doughnuts for me and the Thomases, my playmates. I hadn't thought about Bond Bread for forty years. If I've forgotten such a good, little thing, there is no telling how many big, untoward matters have vanished from recollection.

Things so clutter my days that the past has become the forgotten, mysterious stuff of tag sales. Last Thursday after morning coffee at the Cup of Sun, I sprayed Ortho ant killer on the foundation of the house. Next I mowed grass and clipped yews. Early in the afternoon I swam a mile at the university pool. At six o'clock I took Eliza and her friend Sarah to the pool and remained there two hours while they swam. Afterward I drove Sarah home. Then Eliza, Vicki, and I watched a movie, *American Werewolf in Paris*. Sometime during the day I wrote three pages. In midmorning I took George, the dog, to the veterinarian. A black knob was growing under George's ear. Although the knob didn't bother George, it worried Edward sick, so I instructed the vet to spade it out. The vet gave George laughing gas to deaden the digging, and I left George at the animal hospital, retrieving him just before driving Eliza and Sarah to the pool. "Blue Cross," Vicki said, "don't forget that." My insurance policy entitles each of the children to a yearly physical, and before Edward left for camp, the doctor examined him then pronounced him fit for summer's canoeing and fall's football. Blue Cross erred, however, and rejected payment for the physical. That morning, maybe between the grass and the yews, I harvested a bushel of forms from a file cabinet. Afterward I telephoned the insurance company and had the claim for Edward resubmitted.

Not earning royalties doesn't really bother me. The plebeian and the everyday are almost good enough. Last fall in order to build dormitories, bulldozers chewed the South Campus flat. Trucks dumped dirt from the excavation into the open field bordering the small wood behind my house. The dirt grew into a stony red mound, 20 to 30 feet high and 169 long paces in circumference. Winter was warm, and the mound oozed mud. In late spring a mist of weeds turned the mound green. The day after George's growth was removed, I studied the weeds growing on the mound.

On blue toadflax blossoms perched atop leggy stems like minute pelvises, the lower petals satiny and looking porous as bone. Quack and Italian rye grass grew in lumps; pineapple weed, in loose baskets; and carpetweed, in thick mats. Clinging to the side of the mound like new skin were hedge mustard; ragweed; white campion; yellow wood sorrel; plantain, both English and broad-leaved; horse nettle; and lambsquarters, aphids clustering near the tops of the plants, drying leaves so that they curled and blackened. Aphids themselves were food. I flipped a leaf over and counted five lady bug larvae underneath. Weeds congregated in family threesomes: white, red, and rabbit foot clover; then smartweed; lady's thumb, dark splotches staining the middles of leaves; and Pennsylvania smartweed in sheaves, purple and vital at nodes, the leaves nine inches long. Fruits on field pennycress resembled small fans. Seedpods of wild radish tasted like radishes themselves. While the pale flowers were flimsy, stalks of radish were virile, prickly with hairs that jabbed then broke off in my fingers. Here and there on the mound, mayweed bloomed in woody bouquets, spokes of white rays spinning around yellow hubs.

"You spent hours clambering over dirt?" Josh said later that day. "Don't mention 'not enough' to me again. Storrs will always furnish you with more than enough entertainment." The next morning at the Cup of Sun, Pam told a story about Jane, an acquaintance. The hinges of Jane's and her husband Charlie's marriage swung free and easy, no behavior ever causing husband or wife to shriek like a badly sprung screen door. One night in the '70s, Pam recounted, Jane and Charlie were having a drink in a neighborhood bar. Just as Jane lifted her glass off the table, a handsome, leathery biker walked into the building. "Lord, look at that," Jane said, putting her glass back down and staring. Charlie glanced at the biker then picking up his drink, turned to Jane and said, "Go for it." Occasionally the same expression can be heard in my house, most recently late Saturday. Near dusk I said to Vicki, "I think I'll dig compost now." "Go for it," she said, bending over the stove to push a strawberry-rhubarb pie into the oven.

Once a month I suffer through an embarrassing spasm of going for the jangling, if not the leather. Instead of coin and bill, though, I reap compost for essays. I have never been to the Caribbean, and early in June I decided to cart the family to St. Lucia and stay at Ladera, a resort built into a hillside a thousand feet above sea level. Because Camp Timanous ended August 13, and football practice began at the high school on the twenty-fourth, only an eyelet of time existed through which I could thread a holiday. My university salary covers daily living, and royalties, vacations. A hundred dollars would not pay for boarding the dogs for five days. Consequently, I telephoned Atlanta and the company that booked reservations for the resort.

I talked to Ryan, explaining that I did a bit of scribbling, asking if I "could barter a little on the cusp of hurricane season" by writing an article about Ladera for reduced room and board. "Pickering? I've heard of you. Aren't you the guy who wrote *The Hunt for Red October?*" Ryan said, then laughed riotously. I laughed, too, not quite so enthusiastically as Ryan, the sound, however, hiding my envy of yet another best seller. Threadbare suitors are poor catches, and to win fair prizes, they must pound themselves into soft, sweet affability. After the conversation ended, I wrote a letter to the booking agency, larding sentences with oratorical nosegays. Three days later the resort halved the rate for a villa with a private pool, shrinking it from $490 to $245 a day. "Sand, surf, snorkeling, Stuffed Crab Back Supreme, Creole Scallops Ladera, Cabbage Leaf Soup, Seafood Gazpacho," I shouted to Vicki, the last items being selections from the menu of Dasheene, the resort's starry restaurant. "Whoopee!" Eliza answered. "You're a magician, Daddy."

Unfortunately I had pulled only half the rabbit out of the hat. I celebrated before booking plane reservations. Alas, the high financial altitude of tickets reduced my plans to contrails. For a short time a ticket priced at $557 floated through the Internet. However, we had to fly on days kicked off the calendar by football. In any case the rate soon evaporated. On American Airlines we could fly from Hartford, each round-trip ticket costing $683 or $774, the fee depending on the day. The flight left Hartford at 6:40 in the morning. Because of a seven-hour-one-minute layover in Miami, the plane did not reach St. Lucia until 8:39 that night. If we flew from New York at 7:00 A.M. on August 14, we would arrive on St. Lucia at 12:40, in time for lunch. "The airport is at least four hours from here," Vicki said. "We'd never pack the kids into the car and make the flight." "We have already missed connections," I said. "The price for the five of us is $4,935." "What's the price for the next day?" Vicki asked. "Flying on the fifteenth would add $610 to the fee, the total being $5,545." For four days I telephoned discounters and roamed the Internet searching for better rates. On the fourth day the Hartford flight showed "NO AVAIL-ABILITY." A discounter said, "These tickets are as high as cat's teeth. Why don't you stay home and put a new roof on your house." On the fifth day I contacted an airline magazine in the forlorn hope of swapping essays for tickets. I did not succeed. The woman to whom I talked was so tough she could munch frozen possum, spit out the fur, then order a platter of roadside rabbit. The sixth day I told Ryan the family wouldn't be going to St. Lucia. On the seventh day I moped through the morning. At lunch Vicki said, "Being a high-flyer for a week at least passed the time. But now you are grounded. What are you going to do?"

The word *grounded* brought me back to the good-enough black earth. Years ago I planted daffodils in the dell between our house and Mrs. Carter's. In hopes that leaves would strengthen the bulbs for winter I didn't mow the dell after the daffodils blew this spring. As a result the dell grew weedy. "A wild garden," I suddenly thought and walked outside. While self-heal, yarrow, Deptford pink, and enchanter's nightshade bloomed, seeds on doll's eyes swelled, slowly shoving green out and absorbing white. I recognized the leaves of wood asters, goldenrod, and horse balm. Daisy fleabane seemed as delicate as scrimshank. On forsythia ants milked herds of purple aphids. A billbug bored into a bundle of buds on an aster, his nubby body curving, gray drifting milky across his back, making him resemble a bird dropping. A tiger swallowtail shimmed through bars of light, and a mosquito pranced the air and dropping atop the disk of a black-eyed Susan sipped nectar. At the edge of the dell beaked hazelnut leaned into the sun. Fruits swung sideways, the nuts bulbous, below them long tails curving languidly, lounging on leaves. I strolled back to the house. As I stood on the stoop, I noticed a finch nesting in the clematis by the back door. "Hey," Vicki said, seeing me outside the kitchen and holding the newspaper in her hand, "Wally's book is now number one on the *New York Times* list. How does that make you feel?" "Good," I said. "Pretty damn good."

A Goer

Gideon Palmer's mule Tecumseh was stubborn. "And I said *go*," Gideon recounted this past June in Ankerrow's Café, "and Tecumseh wouldn't go, so I said *go* again, and still he would not go. I said *go* a third time, and he wouldn't go. Then I said to myself, 'not even the devil could make this mule go. Tecumseh is just not what folks call a goer.'" Gideon himself was not fleet of thought. According to Turlow Gutheridge, Gideon once asked Clevanna Farquarhson about her family. "I've heard," Gideon said to Clevanna, "that your ancestry is interesting. I knew your mother Bertha, but I never met your grandmother. Did she have children?"

"Damn it!" Vicki exclaimed when I introduced her to Gideon. "You've been rocking in the shade long enough. This is an action age. Write a mystery that will pay Francis's college tuition." Doings on the computer provoked Vicki's impatience. Amazon ranks books on the basis of sales. That morning my friend Wally's novel stood first on the list. Alas, no collection of my essays made the top ten best sellers. *Trespassing,* for example, rang through the cash register at 873,720, and *Let It Ride* at 962,783. Ranked at 258,466, *The Blue Caterpillar* sold better than any of my books. "All right," I said to Vicki, "I'll write a thriller about a serial killer who likes flowers. I'll call the book *Flower Child.* After each murder the killer will cram flowers into the orifices of his victims' bodies." "Even into their nasties?" Vicki said. "Especially there," Eliza interrupted. "That stuff really sells."

I didn't get beyond title and a blossom or two, sweet William and

gall of the earth, as I recall. Eliza clipped my sinister bouquet, informing me that in the future she and her friend Sarah were to be addressed
as Fred and Mickey. "Fred from Sarah's middle name Winifred," Eliza
explained, "and Mickey from McClarin, my middle name." "Okay,
Mickey," I said, Eliza's remark burying thoughts of cash under the
potting soil of family living. Despite occasional hankerings, I'm not
a goer. Not ambition but habit determines my days. After lunch I
donned work clothes and spent four hours in the basement of the
university library digging through the *Knickerbocker Magazine* in hopes
of unearthing stories.

The *Knickerbocker* was published in the nineteenth century, and
its leaves had dried. When I left the library, I looked as if I'd shoveled
compost. In a notebook, though, I carted off a bag of fictional bulbs.
After burying them and shaking bony nouns and verbs over them,
the bulbs sprouted and budded in Carthage. Religious tales filled a
border, several runners bright with the wanderings of Malachi Ramus,
minister at the Church of the Chastening Rod. This past March
Malachi roamed hills north of Carthage in hopes of "dousing spring
onions with God's pomegranate oil." Outside Dugget Aunt Huldah
sat on the Spooners' porch drinking iced tea. "My good woman,"
Malachi said, his voice toothy and gleaming, "do you have the gospel
here?" "No, praise Jesus, we haven't got it, but down to Lebanon it's
raging something fierce," Aunt Huldah answered. "It's carried off a
passel of folks, including a Methodist deacon, his new young wife,
their baby, and a flock of Nubian goats, every one of the goats and
the wife prime milkers. Every night before bed I read the scriptures
and pray for those poor unfortunates."

At the Hargreaves, the next house along the ridge, Malachi didn't
fare better. When he asked Shearjashub Hargreave, "Do you love the
Lord?" the old man rolled his tongue forward, tamped a wad of snuff
down behind his lower lip like a dentist filling a cavity, then said, "I
ain't got nothing agin him." Thinking true faith might thrive in low
coves, Malachi descended from the high moral ground. In Bug
Swamp, he stopped at the Thomases and asked to see a Bible. Barzillai
Thomas walked around the side of the house. Two minutes later he
returned holding three pages. "I declare this is all we have," Barzillai
said. "I didn't know we were so near out. But you're welcome to them.

Maybe they'll come in handy on your travels. Don't worry none about my family. I'll pick up another testament or two the next time I buy meal in Carthage." Because Barzillai was friendly, Malachi began a sermon, declaring, "Don't put your trust in princes." He got no further. "Princes?" Barzillai interrupted. "Not many of them come way out here. Not that they wouldn't be welcome. Folks in these coves are tolerant. Who or what a fellow marries is his business. Anyway, mostly what we see around here are salesmen peddling ear trumpets and hominy mortars."

"Lordy," Vicki exclaimed, "those stories are shrouds. They'll smother the few readers you have." My mind works by association. When I heard *shroud*, I forced two more bulbs. At the annual dinner of the Cookeville Chamber of Commerce, Maury Stonebridge sat next to Sam Horn, owner of Infant Samuel's Funeral Home. "Is business brisk?" Maury asked Sam over fruit cocktail. "Mournfully so," Sam replied. "Scarlet fever has been prevalent among children hereabouts. The demand for three and four footers is so great that I've been obliged to hire another sawyer part time." On returning to Carthage, Malachi learned that Shemlek Carroll had died. The morning after the funeral Malachi visited the grieving widow Ester. He intended, as Turlow Gutheridge put it, to strum the Harp of Zion and spraying Shemlek's relic with the Balm of a Thousand Flowers turn "the dusk of her gloom into the dawn of happiness." Ester met Malachi at the front door, a bucket of water sloshing in her right hand, a damp mop in her left. "Parson," she said, "it's good of you to call, and I'd like to pass time with you, but as you can see I'm cleaning house." "But what about our dear brother Shemlek?" Malachi said. "Parson," Ester said, shutting the door and scrubbing the conversation away, "I've never been one to cry over spilled milk."

Instead of a mystery, Josh suggested I write a self-help manual. "If you haven't got anything to say," he advised, "write it well and people will think they are reading something important. Think of the book as head cheese. Press all the indigestible sentences you've ever butchered into paragraphs: cheeks, snouts, feet, tongues, underlips, and, most importantly, subcutaneous cysts of advice." "How about this?" I said, remembering a statement I unearthed in the library. "It is better to have a little too much than a little too little because it is harder to raise a little too little up to a little too much than it is to pull a little too much down to a little too little." Josh thought the advice a mite too simple. "Richly caparisoned words," he said, "buckled to a ghost of meaning delude people into believing pages gallop."

That evening I swam in the university pool. Pasted on a wall near the entrance of the gymnasium was a paragraph describing the recreation department's "mission." "We are committed," the department testified, "to offering safe and quality programs, facilities, and services to the University of Connecticut in order to foster personal growth. We do this by promoting healthy lifestyle choices in an environment that values, embraces, and enriches individual differences in which customer satisfaction is the priority." "Did we leave anything out?" a boy behind a desk said, noticing my copying the statement. "Not much," I said, "the paragraph contains everything except elephant milk." "What?" the boy said. "Never mind," I answered.

Scribbled on a scrap of paper at home was an even more inclusive paragraph:

> When I was not expecting it, Sorrow visited me. I wasn't looking for Misfortune, but it came unannounced. It didn't ring the bell, knock on the door, or slide down the chimney. It just appeared suddenly without my seeing, hearing, or feeling it approach. Grief overtook me. Calamities and Afflictions weighed heavily upon me. Troubles bowed me down to the ground, pushing my head, feet, and stomach into the grass. Sadness pressed ponderously upon my body, mind, and spirit. Then was I taught the value of earthly matters. Then did I learn the emptiness of sublunary objects. Then was stamped indelibly upon my soul and in print never to be erased or obliterated or blotted out the insubstantiality, the vanity, and the evanescence of all things worldly and terrestrial.

People who have no principles are usually decent and congenial.

Alas, sometimes ambition infects them, and they sicken into goers. Soon afterward principles spot them like chicken pox. Ultimately they so narrow living that they lose all aspects of the breathing self except selfishness. Getting up in the world transforms life into a lie, forcing reaction into platitudinous pretense. "I have aged beyond pretending," Josh said last week. "I have reached that time of life in which a person takes more pride in what he doesn't know than what he knows." Of course pretense is so woven through the fabric of days that avoiding lying is impossible. For the sake of college applications, schools teach children to distort whim into achievement. For their parts, instead of telling the truth and announcing that they provide day care for post-adolescents, bush colleges make claims as extravagant as faith doctors: that they can train flies to dot *i*'s, or, more astonishingly, influence the minds and morals of teenagers.

When thoughts of worldly matters provoke ambition, I seize a pen and proscribe a cure-all, most recently Myrilla's Medicated Sweet Potato Pudding, a nostrum sold door to door in Carthage by Captain Goliath, a peddler, who, Turlow said, had so much hair he looked like a walking haystack. "Throw away your Scuppernong Biscuits, Turkey Rhubarb, Hygeian Vegetable Pills, Brazilian Syrup, and Mrs. Jarvis's Cold Candy," the captain commanded. When stripped of its earthy vest, the sweet potato, the captain asserted, became a heavenly, rose-colored physician capable of straightening bow-legs, curing tetter and scald head, restoring spring to the thighs of aging bullfrogs, removing spots and cellulite from carpets, and shucking "pedal maize" from tired feet, leaving toes smooth as corn silk. "Mothers," he declared, "if you dose children every evening, the bowels of the rising generation will sing your praises." In just a week the pudding stripped botrytis blight from the blossoms of Fanny Flowerpetal. Not only that, but six weeks later she was a blooming bride dressed in white, all spots vanished. "When Goneness empties the breast and the heart is a wilderness of owls," the captain said, "feast on Myrilla's pudding, and soon you will smell the summer rose and the tufted turnip."

Occasionally contemporary doings interest me, and I write about them. Rarely, though, do the remarks boost my literary career. Last week on public access television, a local veterinarian appeared on a cooking show. As soon as the program ended, I wrote the man. "Dear Chef Branson," Abner W. Clopton, Ph.D., began, "last night my wife Rhapsodia and I seen you on the television cooking chicken bosoms. The very sight made the low end of my bottom pucker, if you know what I mean. When I was a baby, there won't nothing my adenoids liked seeing better than chicken titties fried in shortening and bacon grease. But I am not writing you about birds—roosters or hens, or capons like what you see strutting around this town on two drumsticks."

No, it's the jelly that sticks to my giblets. You said you made shelves of jellies, raspberry, garlic, pineapple, and Rhapsodia says road apple, but her hearing ain't what it used to be, and I reckon she misunderstood. Be that as it may, do you make petroleum jelly? If so, I'd like to purchase a gross. For years Rhapsodia and I have been spreading White Rose Petroleum Jelly on our cornbread, so to speak. Well, dinner is on the table, and I have to go. We are having dumplings cooked in pot likker, not caramelized like you because we ain't quite so fancy pants. You'd love Rhapsodia's dumplings. They've been known to play "The Star Spangled Banner" on folks' tonsils. Before I go, I want to ask about the rumor. Is it true that you sell animal parts to the butcher at the A&P, or is it the Safeway or Big Y?—I gets the meat counters all mixed up. You will be glad to know I've told neighbors the only animal organs you probably sell are livers and intestines for sausage, nothing like anal sacks for coming out parties or shoulders and rumps for hamburgers and front yard grills. God bless you, and God bless America, the Beautiful.

On the page past determines present. For years my thought has circled the essay like a jogger a track. Every time I sprint off toward thrillers or self-help books I fall off the page and sprain my writing hand. For a decade I have struggled to escape being identified with John Keating, the teacher in the movie *Dead Poets Society*. Alas, no matter my verbal leaps, the film clings to me. The last week in June I received a postcard from Seoul, Korea. On the front of the card was a painting depicting a lion. While the lion's eyebrows resembled sawfly caterpillars circling the edge of a leaf, the animal's tongue lolled out of its mouth, red lumps dangling from each side like galls. The lion was unique. Unfortunately the paragraph on the back of the card was familiar. "How do you do Mr. Pickering?" my correspondent began. "A few days ago I came to know that Mr. John Kitting in the movie Dead Poets Society is an actual person. He is living and teaching in Connecticut. The information is quite old, but I am hoping that he still does. Also, I am hoping that it is you. Please write back to me whether you are him or not. It is very important to me." That afternoon I wrote a two-page letter, explaining the nature of fiction and my slim connection to the character. When I finished writing, I shrugged and, picking up a yellow pad, started an essay.

A goer probably wouldn't have answered the card. Focusing on matters that improve one's corporate lot pinches existence. "What time in the afternoon, do you eat breakfast?" Eliza asked Francis on Tuesday. "Is he still married to the same person he married when he left Penny or has he left that person and married another person?" I heard a woman say in the Cup of Sun yesterday. Three weeks ago on Friday Vicki's mother's heart stopped. Because Vicki's mother was in the doctor's office, technicians jump-started her heart. Still, the heart did not purr, and that night a doctor told Vicki her mother would die. "Let's pack the kids in the car and head for Princeton," I suggested at dinner. "No," Vicki said, "I've scheduled a tag sale tomorrow. Family is family, but business—well, that's business. I'll drive to Princeton after the sale." That night after dinner we watched a movie, *Romy and Michele's High School Reunion,* a comedy, its heroines airheads, one unemployed, the other a cashier in an automobile repair shop. At eight the next morning the sale began. Vicki did not make much, $103.59, enough, though, to pay for the trip to Princeton. Even better I disposed of two mattresses from the attic. I put a sign atop the mattresses, reading, "FREE—TWO FOR THE PRICE OF ONE." The sign confused a Korean woman. Only after Vicki explained that the mattresses cost nothing did the woman haul them away. Vicki spent Saturday night in her mother's home in Princeton. At five-thirty Sunday morning the telephone rang. "Come and get me," her mother whispered into the phone. "I've been kidnapped, and I'm imprisoned in Kingston." Vicki's mother refused to believe she was in a hospital. "You're in league with them," she said, hanging up the telephone. "I'm calling the FBI."

Or at least that's the way I recall matters. I doctor recollection as much as I squeeze corn oil into the crankcases of old tales. Instead of sterilizing and tidying, I shake event out of order and cleanliness. "Sam," Josh said, "I admire you greatly. You have such a high regard for the truth that you don't waste it on ordinary occasions." Still, how nice it is to enjoy events almost as they happened instead of having to batter them into the presentable. As the old rhyme put it, "Things as the are! / Vive la Bizarre!"

Goers rush through hours bowing, fetching, and planning better lives. In so doing they miss place. Literally and literarily I am stationary. Instead of traveling to change my lot, I sit at my desk and visit Carthage, the characters I created eight books ago more interesting to me than anyone who could jab spurs into my essays and send them cantering up a list of best sellers. The Sunday Vicki spent in Princeton, I attended the Tabernacle of Love. Slubey Garts dressed his sentences in parsonic livery and was in shining potable form, as Proverbs Goforth phrased it, adding, "That Slubey was the only preacher in Smith County who could pour the Almighty into a cedar bucket." Slubey began his sermon poetically, describing the vestibule of bliss outside the sapphire gates of heaven. "Stand on the banks of deliverance," he said, "and see the pearly fishes frolic in the evening sunlight. Listen to the honeyed songs of the anointed warbling through the amaranthine glens, Carmel's green palms swaying above, casting glassy shadows."

An influenza of wine-bibbing having recently spread through Carthage, Slubey soon stomped into the wine barrel, crushing grapes under words. The previous Monday a stranger appeared in Enos Mayfield's Inn in South Carthage. Explaining that he was wandering the wilderness and sleeping in tents of tribulation until he reached Canaan, the man handed out woodcuts depicting the Good Samaritan binding the wounds of the traveler beaten by thieves. After distributing the woodcut, the man asked for food and drink. "Fix him a ham sandwich and give him what he wants to drink," Enos instructed Tyrrell, his son who worked in the kitchen. "Would you make me a lemonade?" the man asked the boy. Tyrrell squeezed a lemon and poured the juice into a glass. After spooning in sugar, Tyrrell was about to fill the glass with water when the man stopped him. "Wait, child," the man said. "What's in that bottle by your right hand?" "Rum, sir," Tyrrell answered. "That goes well in lemonade," the man said. "Pour in half a glass of that." After Tyrrell put the rum down, the man said, "Child, what is in that bottle by your left hand?" On Tyrrell's saying bourbon, the man said, "Top the glass off with that. Save the water for another poor wandering Christian." The man then raised the glass and swallowed half the liquid. "You are a little tike," the man said, brushing his tongue across his upper lip like a damp mop, "but you make a great lemonade." During the evening Tyrrell freshened the man's glass several times. At midnight the man addressed Enos, calling him the Provider. "I was dead on the road to Jericho, and you bathed my wounds with wine. In recompense I'll sing the true faith." Albeit hoarse, the man had a fine baritone voice. His songs, however, smacked more of hops than they did hope.

The most popular song was the old favorite, "The Long-Leg'd Flamingo."

> Oh! tell me have you ever seen a long-leg'd flamingo?
> Oh! tell me have you ever seen in the water him go?
> Oh! yes, at Bowling Green I've seen a long-leg'd flamingo,
> Oh! yes, at Bowling Green I've seen in the water him go.

Carousers so enjoyed the song that they serenaded South Carthage, the concert ending only when Sheriff Baugham appeared, nightcap on head and pitchfork in hand.

The festival, as Enos dubbed the celebration, influenced Slubey's sermon. "Every grape," he declared, "contains a devil, and not a soft-shelled Episcopal devil who paints his tail sky-blue, sells mansions in Hell, and grazes on caviar at the Belle Meade Country Club in Nashville." "The biblical etymology of *devil*," he continued, "starts with *il*, ill with drink, then slides to *vil*, vile with lust, then falls to pure *evil*, murder and Sabbath-breaking, culminating in brimstone and the Grand Duke of Pandemonium. Spelled backward *live* is *evil*. Whiskey poisons the soul and makes men live backassward. When Isom

Legg carves 'Gone to Glory' on your tombstone, live so that he puts a period, not a question mark after *Glory*."

Getting people to go, as Proverbs Goforth put it, the whole hog for Christ was hot, salty work. Religion, Slubey said, resembled marriage. It was easy to begin but hard to continue. Every spring, he recounted, the Cumberland River flooded. Water swept logs and slabs of brush out of the mud into the fresh current. But eventually the water dropped, and trash drifted into the sinful shallows where once again it stuck and rotted. "The man who has found a flat path to heaven," Slubey said at the end of his sermon, "may have an easy walk, but he'll pay a hell of a toll when the asphalt begins."

"Pickering," a reviewer wrote recently in a Baton Rouge newspaper, "seems the kind of writer Thoreau might have been if he had married and fathered children." No one is the character he appears on paper. Sometimes I think the children fathered me, giving me life and personality, not I, them. Still, in part the reviewer was right. Place matters to me as it mattered to Thoreau. When I walk ridge and pasture, I try to seize the neck of place in hopes of feeling the panting earth. In August the beaver pond shrinks, closing like a bruised eye. Simultaneously, the Fenton River, pumped throbbing by spring rain, collapses into a stringy rivulet. Like nature people experience season. For two weeks at the beginning of August, I roamed hill and field. Instead of slipping quietly into a narrow, dry bed, I swept over the confining banks of desk and paragraph.

I've lived in Connecticut for two decades, long enough to notice change, not simply the broad transformations of seasons, but differences between years. The first week in August Joe-Pye weed rumpled across the Ogushwitz meadow. Under the bright sun the blossoms exhaled, heat cooking the purple, baking it into fragrance. Thickets of Jerusalem artichoke dappled shadows between field and wood, and in open patches monkey flower bloomed, its blossoms loose blue buttons. In 1987 Mother and Father sold their house in Nashville and moved into an apartment. Forty years earlier Father dug belladonna lilies from the side yard of his parents' house in Carthage. In Nashville Father planted the lilies behind the garage. During summers the lilies bloomed, the stems bursting from the ground almost overnight. After Father and Mother sold the house,

Philip, who worked for Mother, sent me five bulbs. "From Carthage to Nashville to Connecticut," he wrote, "maybe the flowers will bring your parents to mind." Mother died in 1988, and Father in 1990. Each spring fountains of leaves spray promising from the bulbs. Not until this summer, however, has a bulb blossomed. One morning in August a leggy stem appeared. By the end of the week six pink trumpets twirled around it. "I love this flower," Eliza said. "Does it remind you of your old home and your Mommy and Daddy?" "Yes," I said, "it's part of nice August."

Canada goldenrod bloomed at the beginning of the month, the blossoms draping over the ends of stems in loose yellow mittens. In contrast buds on lance-leaved goldenrod remained tight as gloves. For tonic I chewed leaves on my walks, those of goldenrod, then Virginia mountain mint, and mugwort, these last deeply cut and as stylish as eighteenth-century wallpaper. I also ate handfuls of blackberries. The berries seemed bland, perhaps because I remembered spicy childhood and Mother's warning me about snakes. "Be sure you and a black snake don't reach for the same berry," she told me.

I spent afternoons in the meadow. Flowers on Canada thistle shredded into fluff. From a distance seed heads appeared gray and gritty. Up close the gray turned silver, and instead of gritty seed heads were as smooth as lanolin. In August I overturned walls of rocks in hopes of discovering a brown snake. Only once have I seen a brown snake, and that was in June. Under rocks I found ants, snake skins, then paper wasps and yellow jackets. A juvenile spotted salamander dozed under a mildewed cardboard box while a marbled salamander lurked under a rotting log, his eyelids blue splatterware, at first making me think him blind. Beneath another log fifty-two nightcrawlers curled together like entrails. In woods south of the cattle pens, farm workers bulldozed brush, creating glades in which they buried animals. Workers dug holes with backhoes, but bits of hide and bone worked proud through the dirt. While flesh fermented into other lives, the smell of death hovered in the air like thick batter.

Often I sauntered along the Fenton River. Amid dry stones near the water cardinal flowers grew. I counted six plants, the first I'd seen in Storrs. Before swelling into blossom, buds looked like curtains gathered then tied. In bloom the flowers became long-necked birds, startled and leaping up and back, the lower lip petals flaring into tail feathers, the upper two petals, wings frantically beating flight out of the air. Along the river bank fox grape twisted through trees. While sweet-scented bedstraw tangled across the ground, knots of virgin's bower fell from branches and loosened into flowers. I plucked blossoms from button bush and waved them about my head, sugaring the air.

Walks separate a person from others, both in distance measured by miles and in that marked by attitude. One humid afternoon I counted eleven turkey buzzards in Valentine meadow. While the ends of their bills shone like brushes dipped into white paint, their feet were dandified, gleaming like spats. Across the meadow Morgan horses switched their tails, polishing their flanks. Seeing such sights made me even less a goer. Forever on the move, the goer misses life. Wood and field oil ambition into silence. Instead of harkening to desire one hears a red-tailed hawk rolling *r*'s from a dead tree, turkeys rattling under spicebush, or at dusk a great horned owl calling from a white pine.

Along the cut for the power line behind the sheep barn, an indigo bunting scolded me, leaping from limb to limb, flicking his tail like a switch. Four blue bird fledglings perched on the line itself. A woodcock burst from ferns, light dyeing its breast orange. At the top of Ski-Tow Hill deer thrashed out of high grass and snapping through locusts pounded down the slope. Because I have aged, I walk slowly and pause frequently. As a result I now see more than I did in past Augusts: woolly leaf galls on burr oak, the galls small pink powder puffs half an inch in diameter and five-sixteenths of an inch high; a dead mole on the shoulder of a trail, burying beetles dropping it out of sight and form; under hemlocks downy rattlesnake orchis, leaves of the flowers shards of molding, light green lines wrinkling across midveins.

Beside a marsh I discovered a green plastic tub. Growing in it were two marijuana plants. In the tub I dropped a scrap of paper on which I wrote, "Mary, Mary, quite contrary, how does your garden grow?" Later that afternoon I watched a Virginia rail forage the edge of the beaver pond, slipping between clumps of tussock sedge as if playing hide-and-go-seek. Mountain laurel was healthier than in previous summers. Not only were fewer leaves yellow, but *Cercospora* spots hadn't dried many leaves. Beyond the spring at the foot of Ski-Tow Hill red chanterelles grew along the woods. The cups of the mushrooms turned up, and the edges rolled over fringed, gills pressed into bright pleats. Sulfur shelf clustered fluffed and almost feathered on a rotten log. At first the mushrooms were yellow, but time bleached them white, almost as if they had tried to lift the tree off the ground and the effort had drained their quickness. Three amanitas stood demurely beside a path. Their caps changed color, yellow suddenly welling and fading. While I thought the caps straw-colored, Eliza labeled them "champagne," and Vicki, "frosted chamois."

Peppering Tecumseh's hide with green-eyed horse flies would have turned the mule into a goer. Instead of prodding me into a gallop, however, insects slowed me. In August I spent more hours observing insects than netting stories. The more I watch mankind, the more bugs appeal to me. "If you waste days looking at creepy crawlies," Josh once advised me, "you won't go far in the university." "That's fine," I said, paraphrasing a statement I found in an old book, "I'm holding my own. I hadn't accomplished anything when I came to Storrs, and I haven't done much since." Such high banter aside, in early August I perused insects not words. In Tennessee walking sticks are almost as common as twigs. This August I saw my first northern walking stick, a light brown female. A dragonfly dipped and flicking her tail, deposited eggs in a sink near the beaver pond. As she skipped off the water, a bullfrog sprang from the mud, barely missing her. Cherry-faced meadow hawks zipped over the meadow. A black-tipped darner sliced between flowers, cutting quick blue lines. An immature spangled skimmer pasted itself to gravel, at the ends of its wings black-and-white epaulets, yellow braids falling off its back and twisting along its abdomen. A bluet clung to elderberry. While the tip of the bluet's abdomen burned into ash, the sides of a black-winged damselfly shined metallic and oxidized.

A hummingbird clearwing moth shimmied above Joe-Pye weed. A pearl crescent puddled beside a path, and ringlets dipped blinking through grass. When I walked the road crossing the meadow,

Carolina locust beat up from the sand. For a moment the grass-hoppers' hind wings spread in black and yellow fans, but then they closed, transforming the insects into twigs. In contrast to past summers, monarchs and viceroy butterflies outnumbered fritillaries. Unlike the bigger monarchs, who flew higher and more leisurely, gliding in orange glory, viceroys staggered through flowers, their flights nervous, their wings lopsided. Near the wolf pen a clymeme moth dropped into briars. The moth's forewings resembled keyholes, brown binding creamy centers like tarnished brass. One night a large moth landed on the screen outside the kitchen window. Because the window is high above the back yard, I had to climb a ladder to see the moth clearly. The moth was a laurel sphinx. When my flashlight played across the insect's forewings, the tips seemed dusters of minute gold and brown feathers.

In August caterpillars appealed to me more than moths or butterflies. "People are caterpillars who delude themselves into believing that someday they will become butterflies," Eliza said. One evening after a walk I found the caterpillar of a blinded sphinx clinging to my sweat pants. The caterpillar's body was bright green, and its dorsal horn, a candy cane of red and yellow. Now the caterpillar is in a jar on my desk, munching leaves of field birch. Also in a jar on my desk is Henry, the caterpillar of a Luna moth. A biologist gave Henry to Eliza. One morning Henry escaped. I searched for him for two hours, eventually finding him sleeping beneath the seat of my chair. While looking for Henry, I found the caterpillar of a silver-spotted skipper crawling along the baseboard in the hall. "Willy" is now chewing locust leaves in another jar.

Near the Fenton River I found a pandorus sphinx caterpillar. Green rather than brown like many *Pandoras,* the caterpillar was fatter and longer than my little finger. When I touched the caterpillar, it rolled toward me, then pulled its head and the first two segments of its body into the third segment, swelling and looming threateningly over my fingertip. A virgin tiger moth caterpillar bustled across milkweed. The caterpillar's body was dark purple and speckled with pink. Around it bristled twelve disks of stiff black hair. A colony of newly hatched milkweed tussock moth caterpillars reduced a leaf to a skeleton. Sawflies ate dogwood. While the bellies and legs of the caterpillars were pale yellow, their backs were white and woolly, so changing their shapes that they seemed tufts of cottony scale.

In a sermon Slubey Garts once said, "If you want to see divine light, snuff your candle." For me heaven is a meadowy place. Jewelweed and wild carrot, boneset and burdock adorn the New Earth. Caterpillars drift under leaves in rainbows. A small river circles the meadow in a halo. On its banks fox grapes grow ambrosial and blue. During dry August cardinal flowers leap from the stream bed and flutter into birds. A pack of angels occasionally trundles across the meadow on mountain bikes. No longer damned to hunt sinners, they stop and turn over rocks, exposing necklaces of snakes. Sun and Moon don't roll above the meadow, breaking time into days. Consequently no soul is a goer shackled to schedule. Instead, souls lounge and tell corny stories, tales transparent as the streets of Revelation's heavenly city. On that day when Josh arrives in the meadow, the first tale he tells will be the one he told me yesterday. A farmer in Chaplin, Josh said, obtained a marriage license. A week later he returned to town hall and asked the clerk to change the name of the woman on the license. "I can't do that," the clerk answered. "You have to buy a new license." "How much will that be?" the farmer asked; "and do I get a discount on a second license?" "This isn't the month for discounts," the clerk said. "The fee is twenty dollars." "Is that the law?" the farmer said. The clerk nodded, and for a moment the farmer was silent, thought plowing wrinkles across his forehead. "Shucks," he eventually said, stuffing the old license into his pocket, his forehead smoothing out fallow. "The first gal will do. There isn't twenty dollars difference in them anyway."

Most Embarrassing

Todd is Edward's friend. Two weeks ago at the Middle School, Todd's mother Sue spoke to me. "Sam," she recounted, "last night at dinner Todd said you were the most embarrassing parent in Storrs." "Yes," I exclaimed, bending my right knee then extending my right arm and jerking it back as if I were a baseball umpire signaling a runner out. "I have succeeded at something." That evening I pondered my number-one ranking. Perhaps being an idler, indifferent to popular doings, contributed to my success. When zeal urges belief and commitment, my ears play truant. As a child I ignored slogans stenciled above blackboards, phrases that turned classrooms into bully pulpits sounding brassy calls for industry and discipline, maxims declaring "Footprints on the Sands of Time are not made sitting down." More congenial to my taste were aphorisms which suggested shuffling rather than marching, "Don't trouble yourself to do what isn't worth much thought when it is done." Instead of harnessing myself to diligence and ploughing up difficulty, I spit out the bit. "The wise," Josh declared recently, "often spend their wisdom trying to undo the folly of the good."

Never is an idler so busy he can't be distracted. Idlers have too much vitality to bind themselves to tasks. Because their imaginations range widely and randomly, idlers are not dogmatic. Consequently idlers are rarely believers. "Reading the Ten Commandments once is not dangerous," Josh said in May. "On the other hand studying them puts bad ideas into a person's head and undermines Christian conduct." Thoughts that celebrate waysides far from paved accomplishment irk high achievers. So that better colleges will admit them, high school students stamp themselves out of individuality into grades. Instead of abacuses of the ordinary, children become mother boards. Students hammer tinny programs onto days and so short-circuit their sensibilities that they lose not simply appreciation for the odd and the embarrassing but their natural, wayward appetites.

Late in August Francis and I went to a picnic at Williams College. While prospective students sampled classes, parents attended meetings chaired by admission and financial officers. The brain is as strong as its weakest think. In place of means, I inherited a fee simple of wandering genes. The drive to Williamstown wore me out. While other parents spent the afternoon calculating tuition, I roamed the campus. In the basement of Sawyer Library I read graffiti on the walls of a carrel. Much of the scribbling meandered aimlessly. To the right of "Dance of the Free Women" appeared "I AM LONELY RIGHT NOW." Under the desk some one carved, "Fuck Mickey Mouse." No man, not even the idler, can saunter beyond profession. Lying on my back beneath the desk, I remained English teacher. "Not bad. B+," I muttered after reading, "Few people get dizzy doing good turns." The grammar of students in Massachusetts was no better than that of students in Connecticut. After reading "Rachel Gatta is gods' gift to man," I removed a pencil from my pocket. "My children," Vicki once said, "must not associate with people who misuse the possessive." Francis liked Williams, and so I scratched three lines under the g then drew a circle around the apostrophe. To the top of the circle I attached an arrow which curved over the s and pointed to the space between the d and the s, thus changing gods' into God's.

The minds of students are not open but blank. Because schools teach similar lessons and the classroom is responsible for many of the jottings which disfigure youthful pages, students are conformists. Only after memory fades and the mind becomes a pad of erasures does a person become eccentric. One wall of the carrel resembled a page torn from the Book of Common Prayer, the phrase "Carrel of Perverse Obsession" provoking a litany of responses:

"Carrel of Eternal Digression," "Carrel of My Dark Confession," "Carrel of Misplaced Aggression," and finally in red letters, "YOUR WRITING MAKES THIS A CARREL OF ENDLESS DISTRACTION."

On the way out of the library I perused the card catalogue. Williams owned six of my books. "Were any checked out?" Francis asked later. "No," I said. Two days earlier I received a letter from a man in Arlington, Virginia. He had just finished reading *A Continuing Education,* a collection of my essays published in 1985. "The card pocket of your book," the man wrote, was "inexplicably spare of date stamps." "Before I pulled the book from the shelf," he continued, "borrowers had returned it on Oct. 13, 1995; May 14, 1994; Aug. 12, 1993; Feb. 14, 1993 (a good year!), and March 8, 1992."

It doesn't take much reading to brighten days, and years. While I was in Williamstown, the *Frontgate* catalogue arrived. After dinner I read the catalogue. Susceptible to extravagant dream, youth covets. I have aged beyond dream into mulling. Not since our house was built in 1942 had much been done to the upstairs lavatory. The plumbing having grown long in drip and the asbestos tiles on the floor flaking like psoriasis, Vicki renovated the room this past summer. Alas, *Frontgate* arrived the day workmen left. If the catalogue had appeared in June, perhaps the bathroom would be different. For $695 I could have bought a "Brass Aktiva Shower Head with an Extension Arm." "Too fine for your plated skin," Vicki said after I showed her the picture of the shower head, water drizzling from its "72 individual spray outlets." "Nothing," I replied, quoting the catalogue, "relaxes, rejuvenates, and refreshes like a truly fine shower."

Vicki rolled her eyes upward, whites lapping the shore of the sockets, making her resemble a dying cod. I said nothing, however, when she left the room. People who fish choppy domestic waters are liable to hook, as Josh punned, two sailors, or a tar tar. After Vicki's departure I resumed studying the catalogue. For $155 one could purchase a Chantilly soap dispenser and for $90 a rollerless Toilet Tissue Holder, both items containing "hefty portions of brass." If I wished to "individualize the appearance of every bath in the house," I could buy a miscellany of soap dishes and toothbrush holders. Brass, chrome, and satin nickel dishes cost $65, $75, and $85 respectively. Forged from the same materials, the holders were slightly more expensive, costing $75, $85, and $95. There being but one bath in the house, not a commodious many, I did not long indulge my fancy for fixtures. Still, before leaving the room, I screwed a "solid brass knob to the bottom of the toilet seat using the screws provided, and voila" for only twenty-five dollars provided Edward and Francis with "an easy, sanitary way to lift the seat."

After I finished the lid of the pot and was testing the Chantilly Dispenser, George and Penny, the dogs, began rumpusing on the landing. My children love the dogs. Fortunately the children are not quite so fond of animals as was little Dwaine Purdy in Carthage. Dwaine's passion for animals was so great that instead of sending him to the Male and Female Select School, Dwaine's mother Phronie apprenticed him to Dinwidder the butcher. Animals and culinary matters being on my mind, a hook of black type in the catalogue snagged attention. "Ceramic bowls and wrought iron stands create five-star dining for dogs," the type announced. While a personalized twelve-inch bowl cost $39.50, a wrought iron stand cost $64.50. Penny and George presently dine off six-inch plastic bowls purchased by Vicki at Caldor's for eighty-nine cents a piece.

"Glance at this advertisement," I said to Vicki, ambling into the kitchen as she sprinkled Cascade into the dishwasher. "These ceramic bowls contain none of the allergens of plastic bowls, do just fine in the dishwasher and handle large amounts of food and water for less frequent filling," I read. "The canine equivalent of fine china, they're hand-painted with a big, friendly paw print and, for those who like a personal touch, your dog's name. When bowls are elevated on the optional wrought iron stand, your dog can feed in a relaxed, upright posture, reducing strain on muscles and joints caused by bending to reach bowls set on the floor." "Dog bowls alongside dinner plates," Vicki said, slamming the door to the dishwasher; "that's too personal."

Frontgate hawked improving items for every room in the house. For the bedroom one could buy a "hand-crafted" trunk made "from genuine hardwoods and rich, supple, topgrain leather with an antique finish." Forty-two inches wide, twenty-eight deep, and thirty-five high, the trunk weighed two hundred and forty pounds, cost $6,200, and was built to contain a twenty-seven-inch television. A remote control started a "powerful motor," manufactured "by the supplier of windshield wiper motors to Mercedes Benz." The motor raised both the lid of the trunk and an inner platform on which the television rested. In the catalogue a trunk stood with lid raised and television elevated at the foot of a bed, this last covered by a quilt, across the top of which swirled a garden of orange flowers. I bought Vicki's and my television fifteen years ago, the day after Edward's birth. Time has blotched the picture tube, and pastels occasionally gather then swell red and proud before breaking and flowing into black and white. "Maybe we should buy a new television," I said, looking at the trunk. "Genteel people," Vicki said, "do not place televisions in bedrooms. A lady cannot watch television in bed without indelicacy." Although my writing has not padded a bank account, it has influenced Vicki. On my looking puzzled, she alluded to Carthage and characters in my essays. "Remember," she warned, "that after Slubey Garts bought cushions for pews in the Tabernacle of Love, Malachi Ramus accused him of transforming the church into a woman of easy virtue."

Occasionally an idler slips out of mood control. Hands on his timer whirl; his accelerator pedal sticks, and his ventricles clack. When anxiety makes thought buck, I walk. Like a flywheel smoothing pistons, hours in field and wood soothe my running. The first week in September I roamed fields behind the old police station. Forty-two turkeys hurried out of a gully and scooted across a lane. While a solitary sandpiper tripped along the shore of Unnamed Pond, a peewee lingered in the curtain of an alder watching for insects, cues that drew him bustling into sight. Big darners shifted back and forth above corn like prompts. Startled, a heavy groundhog lumbered into the ropy offstage anonymity of high grass. In the broken land above the dump ribbon snakes dozed under rotting boards. On being exposed to the clatter of sunlight, the snakes snapped like crisp dialogue then vanished, almost as if I'd turned a page. Running down the new page were decorations, ladies tresses, the tips of their petals icy white shavings, and a butterfly bush, a monarch clasping a finger of blossoms, its wings clapping slowly, the orange and black setting of an autumnal ring.

The next morning I wandered fields behind the sheep barns.

Blossoms of Joe-Pye weed clumped soiled in damp dishrags. In contrast goldenrod bloomed in dusters, the feathers of flowers wiping lints of insects from the air. A tree hopper jutted sharply from a stem, and a locust borer shook a tablet of blossoms. An ambush bug lurked nearby, the upper portion of its front legs steroidal. September seemed insect season. Strings of bees vibrated above Japanese knotweed. A red-banded leaf hopper dropped onto a leaf then vanished. Lady bugs doubled themselves on milkweed. While nursery web spiders tied leaves into gloves, caterpillars of monarch butterflies scalloped edges, turning themselves into taffy. A black-horned tree cricket dozed on a leaf, the angular veins in its wings sharp as slats on a garden fence. Looking as if they had been bound to plants, bandages of orange aphids clung adhesive to stems. A katydid perched on wool reed grass, hind legs jacking its body up. In the Ogushwitz meadow eleven cabbage whites spiraled around each other, rising and falling, sweeping like the fringe of a curtain tossed by a breeze.

A pair of fawns curled behind trees, and a great blue heron beat up from the beaver pond, its flight heavy and slow. While I studied woolly aphids on brambles, a pickerel frog sprang from a tuft of grass. Expecting to see nothing and everything, I idled through the day. For six minutes I touched fruit capsules of jewelweed, delighting when they exploded, shooting seeds like fireworks. I scratched an itch with barnyard grass. Near a mound of rocks I smelled the oily melon aroma of black racer. Under a slab of plywood I found a milk snake then near the beaver pond a northern water snake. On the bank above the Fenton River I discovered three marijuana plants. In hopes of finding ways to describe season I munch plants. I chewed a leaf of marijuana. I didn't chew long. The juice burned my tongue, and I rinsed my mouth with a wash of wild mint and goldenrod. While cardinal flowers in the gravel along the river had melted out of color, wrists of turtlehead bloomed white and vital. *Calligrapha* leaf beetles clung to the undersides of grape leaves. Dark lines scrolled down the centers of the beetles' front wings. Beyond the lines black sprayed over the wings like ink shaken from fountain pens. When I touched leaves, the beetles dropped to the ground and hid in litter.

I caught a beetle and took it home to show the children. The children have reached the age at which a television in a box interests them more than a leaf beetle. In truth my enthusiasms may be a source of embarrassment. On nights I don't pull a beetle or a caterpillar from a pocket at dinner, I talk about things occurring in my essays. Carnivals forever crawl across my pages nibbling holes in the coin purses of Carthaginians. After freeing the beetle, I described the latest additions to Hollis Hunnewell's side-show: armor worn by the ghost of Hamlet's father, a living mummy, a basket containing the shells of oysters eaten by George Washington the night after Cornwallis surrendered at Yorktown, and "The Heroic Hog." Having smelled smoke, the hog broke out of the piggery and risking his bacon, bowled through the front door of his owner's house, "yodeled" and awoke the family, saving them, as Hollis phrased it, "from a fate worse than crackling." Stuffed, the pig rested on four roller skates and resembled an inflated sausage, his owner, notwithstanding the animal's devotion, having put the hams to nutritious rather than instructive use. Causing a sensation in Carthage, however, was "The World's Smallest Giant." People flocked to view the "monster." "He was only five feet eight inches tall," Loppie Groat told the crowd at Ankerrow's Café. "What was amazing was that he looked like a normal fellow. If there hadn't been a sign over his cage, I would have passed right by." "That shows the importance of education," Googoo Hooberry added. "If you hadn't been able to read, you wouldn't have knowed he was a giant and you'd have missed a once-in-a-lifetime sight." "Would you spend a quarter to see the show?" I asked Vicki after I described the exhibits. "Not a penny," Vicki said, standing to clear the table. "Not even," I said, "if you could purchase a bottle of Leghorn's Spiritual Hair Tonic and Rejuvenator? After only three doses, Hollis told spectators, the Ancient of Days woke up one morning, and after looking at the clock on his bedside table, turned to his wife and shouted, 'Quick, Mammy, hand me my satchel. I'm going to be late for school.'"

Hollis's side-shows are too demonstrative for the gravity of children. That which causes me to erupt into an esophagus-rending guffaw, disrupting digestion and dignity, provokes a nervous twitch in my progeny. Believing that much can be accomplished and that accomplishment matters, children take life seriously. Laughter is the affectionate, promiscuous consort of age. Only after living years bumblingly rich with failure is a person capable of uncomplicated, spontaneous laughter. Because youth imagines the world to be rational, a landscape across which discipline and virtue beat paths leading to rewards, children are conservative. They fear surprise, suspecting, correctly, that it undermines order. In contrast surprise delights me, in great part because it buckles and disrupts. Or as Turlow Gutheridge said after attending a philosophy seminar at Vanderbilt, "if so, so; if otherwise, otherwise; at any rate, not exactly. However."

Rarely does purpose flatten my day. The *if so*'s of life jostle hours. Last Monday a package arrived from Iowa. For years a friend has written me from Ames, most of the letters supposedly the work of Mrs. Neeoscaleeta Pemberton, founder of The Carts for Wienie Dogs Foundation, a charity established to aid crippled dachshunds. Two years ago Mrs. Pemberton and the Reverend Russell "Rusty" Zwanger attended a convention in Kansas City. Following an evening of unseemly activity in the Raphael Hotel, Mrs. Pemberton and Reverend Zwanger vanished. Pining for the comforts afforded by right religion, Starlene Zwanger hired Merle T. Oderman, a detective, to find her "ram of God." Although Merle's efforts to locate the wayward spouse have not been successful, they have led, a letter accompanying the package explained, "to discoveries which Starlene Zwanger has understandably called a grief and a heartache."

Addressed to "Proff. Pickelring," the package contained an extra-large red tee-shirt. Printed on the front of the shirt was a white medallion. Scrolled around the rim of the medallion were the words "CHRISTIAN NUDIST CHURCH. AMES, IOWA." A fleshly Greek maiden appeared in the middle of the medallion, pouring wine from an amphora. Although the girl's ankles and haunches were trim, her chest was robust. As she leaned over the amphora, her bosom swung out from the rack of shoulders and navel like a brace of Rehoboams, not scratchy and piny with retsina but undulating with *Blanc de Blanc*. Members of the Reverend Zwanger's former congregation, Ivadell Teaverbaugh Naslund explained, wore similar shirts on Sunday outings. The shirt, Naslund continued, "speaks for itself as to the nature of the church, only confirming what Starlene has always described as rather odd worshipping techniques that Rusty asked her to practice in their mobile home in those days in which he lived there. Mrs. Sponsler across the road from them confirms this as her grandson Ricky Dean reported what he has seen through the windows at the back."

In the absence of Neeoscaleeta Pemberton, Mr. Naslund assumed the mantle of "Fundraising Chair Pro Tempore" for The Carts For Wienie Dogs Foundation. Stapled to Naslund's letter was a two-age addendum, listing one hundred and fourteen people whose membership payments to "TCFWDF" were overdue. Included on the list were: Alpha Sandage, Cheeping Kuok, Orlando Penrod, M. T. Shuey, Luis Poffenberger, Dianta Bustamante, Phu Luong, Fabian Dekok, Larry Ray Arn, Lyle Scogland, Eastside "Eddie" Hoover, and Jamalia Rogene Habhab-Beisch.

The delinquents brought Carthage to mind. Like Heaven and Hell my Carthage is well-imagined but non-existent. In August Slubey Garts began renting funeral clothes. Customers could select outfits, denoting full, half, one-quarter, one-eighth, and one-sixteenth mourning. For congenial mates of long-standing, spouses usually rented full mourning. For a close relation whose will proved unsatisfactory, family members might choose half, or, if the leavings were disappointingly puny, quarter-mourning. One-sixteenth was subtle, for surviving males consisting of ankle-length black socks held in place by dark garters, each with two silver tears stitched into the elastic. Someone who had committed an indiscretion of the intimate kind with the deceased might find, Proverbs Goforth explained, "fractional mourning appropriate." "Committed on some stormy night after the dearly departed swallowed a little too much bilge water causing her keel to wobble—usually before," Proverbs explained, "she sailed into matrimonial dry-dock and modesty scraped away the barnacles of reputation."

In my Carthage more people live in graveyards than they do in suburbs. Not to hone a phrase too vigorously, but in September the whetstone of cholera ground Hink Ruunt's eighth wife Anonymia into dust. Hink asked Loppie Groat to serve as a pallbearer, the funeral being the fifth occasion on which Loppie assisted in burying one of Hink's wives, a matter that disturbed Loppie considerably. "In this world," Loppie told Turlow later, "a fellow should give as well as receive. I just can't keep accepting Hink's invitations without paying him back. I feel so guilty." Hink was an experienced widower, and Loppie's guilt lasted longer than Hink's grief. The weekend after Anonymia's death, Turlow met Hink at the meat counter in Barrow's Grocery. "Hink, how're you feeling?" Turlow asked. "Anonymia's death was a great shock to me. It was so sudden, but time heals all," Hink said. "And I'm feeling right pert—perter than I've felt in months. Anonymia was a superb wife. She was a good-looking woman and a fine housekeeper, and she always done her duty by me and the kitchen. Up until this last spell she won't sickly, and even then she never complained. But somehow, I didn't care much for her, and now that she's with our blessed savior, I'm feeling pretty pert." "Turlow," Hink continued, seizing a fryer by the drumsticks and turning it first left then right, "I appreciate your asking after me, but don't you worry none. With the Lord's help I'm going to weather this blow."

Idlers have active imaginations, and lives. Rarely does a task so occupy moments that I forgo an opportunity to embarrass the children. In September the local high school fielded its first football team. "I hear E. O. Smith is starting football," Michael said in the English department. "The school will have trouble finding players. No one in his right mind will let his child play." "Actually," I began, "Edward is starting quarterback." I did not tell him that Edward weighed only one hundred and thirty pounds and had never played football before. "What does Vicki think about Edward's playing?" Michael asked. "She's eager to see the first game," I said. "That surprises me," Michael said. "You don't know Vicki," I said. In truth no one knew the Vicki I described. The enthusiastic football mother smacked more of Carthage than of truth. "I can't wait for the season to end," Vicki said before the first game. "I'm terrified Edward will be hurt." "But you'll come to the games?" I said. "No," Vicki answered. "Football is for Martians, and I'm no Martian."

Parents of players formed a booster club and putting together a program sold it at games. For me flat, lined surfaces are playing fields, be they grass with white slicing across them or yellow paper, blue running from margin to margin at intervals of three-eighths of an inch. For a hundred dollars I bought the back cover of the program. Next I brought four ringers from Carthage to Storrs, and after adorning them with the soft cleats and helmets of words trotted them onto the cover to advertise my essays. "If Pickering's new book doesn't win the Heisman," Turlow Gutheridge declared, "I will eat a football." "When this man's verbs juke, I get the all-over shivers," Clevanna Farquarhson said. Having exercised his vocal cords in my books for years, Googoo Hooberry was in better shape and consequently was longer-winded than Clevanna and Turlow. "All Pickering's sentences spiral," Googoo said. "Each paragraph is a touchdown and a two-point conversion. Move over Dickens, Ohio State, Notre Dame, and Shakespeare." As coaches perennially testify, teams are composed of practice and game players. "After the kickoff," Floyd Moles, inspirational coach of the Ames Apostles, wrote me, "some players dig deep and step and suck it up, and becoming all heart, bark, and give one hundred and ten per cent effort. When the yards get tough, the tough become tailors and measuring themselves don't cut the cloth short." On the cover Abner W. Clopton seized his game pencil and declared, "Bump and run prepositions, two adjective wide outs, drop back conjunctions, hit the crease nouns, gerunds at tight end, beefy bench-pressing participles. Pickering's new book is a cinch for the Fiesta Bowl."

The program reduced Edward's height by two inches then pumped him up with ten additional pounds, making him resemble teammates. I suspect the cover so embarrassed him that he engineered the cosmotological touch-up. At home games I sold programs. Fortunately doings on the field so occupied Edward that he did not observe my technique. The program cost a dollar. Buying a program, however, entitled a person to purchase a kiss from me, "five dollars for women, two-fifty for men," I said. "Not a single person bought a kiss," I told Josh. "I suppose fellows who cruise football games aren't real sports." "No," Josh exclaimed, "pastures are ideal for affection. The beige must have come off your helmet or perhaps your hip pads were a little baggy."

Smith's first game was against Sheehan High School in Wallingford, seventy minutes from Storrs. I went to the game alone, Vicki deciding to stay home to avoid blood and Martians. I arrived an hour before kickoff and spent time chatting with people. "I went to the other high school in town," a policeman said. "We are Sheehan's rivals, and I hope you win." The mother of the Sheehan quarterback sold tickets for the gate prize. "I don't care who wins," she said. "I just hope our boys don't get hurt." Sheehan had fielded teams for decades. On a fence hung a black flag, a white skull and crossbones in the middle. Sixty students played in Sheehan's marching band, and the cheerleading squad outnumbered Smith's sixteen to one. During the game cheerleaders sold seat cushions for five dollars a piece in order to raise money for a trip to the Citrus Bowl in December.

I bought a hot dog and a Coca-Cola and sat on the home side of the field amid parents of the Sheehan players. If Edward had been a lineman, I would have watched the game from the Smith stands. Because Edward was so visible, I hid among strangers. My diffidence did not last long. I sat on the top row of the bleachers and leaned against the bottom of the pressbox. Sheehan kicked off, and after Smith received, Edward loped on to the field. "Pinkerton, no Pickelring," the announcer said, "leads the Panthers out of the huddle." "Pickering," I said, turning around, "the name is Pickering." Rusty Zwanger, Merle Oderman recently discovered, now preaches under the pseudonym of the Reverend Zevs Cosmos. By the end of the game Edward needed an alias. In the first quarter alone the announcer said *Pickering* fourteen times, on each occasion enunciating carefully and loudly. "I've never been so embarrassed," Edward said at home that night. "Why did that man keep shouting *Pickering?*" "Beats me," I said. "Let's look at the prize. At half-time my raffle ticket was drawn. The prize was in the pressbox, and after I picked it up, the announcer said, "Pickering, the father of Ed Pickering the quarterback, wins the raffle."

I won a wicker basket crammed with goodies. Twenty-three inches above the basket floated a brown balloon shaped like a football. Inflated with helium and attached to the handle of the basket by a silver ribbon, the balloon was a foot and a half long. Inside the basket a brown plastic dish stood on end, ready to kick off snack time. A foot long and seven inches wide, the dish was shaped like a football. Eight plastic laces stitched across the bottom of the dish. Between the laces a star shined, the words "FIRST DOWN" radiating around the points. The dish served as goal post, keeping knickknacks from tumbling out of bounds: two cans of Coca-Cola; a "Big Poppy Bag" of Pop Secret Popcorn; four one-ounce packets of "Lays Classic Potato Chips"; then a twelve ounce bag of Fisher "Salted In-Shell" peanuts. While an ounce of the peanuts contained 170 calories, 120 of which were "from Fat," a pack of Austin Toasty Crackers with Creamy Peanut Butter contained 190 calories, 90 of these being "Fat Calories." The basket contained two packs of Toasty Crackers, "Baked With Pride." Sketched on the wrapper of each packet was a red mill shingled in black. In front of the mill water spread creamy, falling over a round cracker-like grinding wheel.

Anticipating that the raffle winner would fumble crumbs, boosters of the Sheehan football team included sixteen, three-ply "Football Stars" napkins in the basket. Across the front of each napkin a quarterback, wearing an orange helmet, a white jersey, numerals stamped on it in green, and orange trousers with green stripes trailing down the outside of each thigh, tossed a football over a mound of red shirts and blue trousers to a player with *81* stamped on his jersey. Printed across the shoulders of the quarterback's jersey was "RIEMOS." I scrimmaged with the name for two quarters, searching for a hidden message. Suddenly a desperate "Hail Mary" led to inspiration. *Mori* is an Indo-European root meaning "body of water." When the two remaining letters of Riemos, *s* and *e,* are added to *Mori, Mories* results, clearly an attempt by the manufacturer of the napkin, the Amscan Corporation located in Elmsford, New York, to transform a body of water into spills of liquid, say those running like milk into the lap of an athlete, just the stuff to be absorbed by a bulky three-ply napkin.

Hunkered in the bottom of the basket like a middle guard was a Teddy bear dressed in a white plastic helmet and a sweater. While the body of the sweater was black, its sleeves were red with white cuffs, the colors being those of E. O. Smith. Sewed on the right front of the sweater was the letter *E.* On the left appeared an *S.* Between the two letters a round white button cinched the sweater together, in the process forming the abbreviation *EOS*. On my suggested that Teddy Smith should hibernate in his locker in the school gymnasium, Edward growled.

On the first three possessions of the game, during two of which the ball was in Smith's hands, Sheehan scored. At the end of the fist quarter the score was 32-0; at half-time, 46-0. The game ended 52-0. After the game the Sheehan coach talked to the Smith team for ten minutes. He congratulated them on starting football. He found matters to praise and in the process so cheered boys and parents that defeat lost bite. Three weeks have passed since the Sheehan game, and Edward's team has not won a game. Defeat does not upset Edward. Last Saturday he passed for 261 yards. "We didn't win," he said that night at dinner, "but now I hold all the school passing records." Embarrassment, if not over losses on the field, however, is part of the teenage day. Edward plays piano. On Tuesday afternoons he leaves football practice early in order to take piano lessons. Before the season began, I told the coach about Edward's music. Nevertheless, Tuesdays make Edward nervous. Two weeks ago when I picked Edward up at school, he was jumpy. "Daddy," he said, "I lied to the coach. In front of all the players and other coaches, I just couldn't say I was leaving to go to piano, so I said that every Tuesday at this time I had an appointment with a psychiatrist."

Football may have kicked Edward through the goal posts of sanity, but his is not a serious disorder. At times the genial idler surfaces. Fall has arrived, and leaves have blossomed. Last Wednesday during a lull at practice Edward glanced across the field and noticed a stand of yellow hickories. "Look at those trees," Edward said, turning to a tackle standing beside him. "Aren't they beautiful?" "Trees? Beautiful trees?" the tackle said, looking puzzled for a moment before exclaiming, "You Homo!" "What did you say?" I asked Edward. "Nothing. I laughed," Edward said. "In fact I laughed so hard that on the next play I fumbled the snap."

Life is repetitious. Because doings are rarely freighted with meaning, repetition doesn't irk the idler. For an idler living is not an art, formal and learned, but just living. Knowing that the frown curving over the top of a circle will eventually roll into a smile, the idler enjoys spinning time. Columbus Day was cold and rainy. I spent the morning behind a concession stand at a soccer tournament. Eliza's team had played three games, losing them all by the cumulative score of 10-0. I peddled counters of candy: Tweezlers, Snickers, Roll-Ups, Jolly Ranchers, and Smarties. I sold four colors and flavors of Power-Aid: purple grape, green lime, yellow lemon, and red cherry. While Subway sandwiches cost three dollars, coffee and hot chocolate were fifty cents a cup. Initially doughnuts were also fifty cents. Once rain soaked them, though, collapsing the dough and sweeping frosting and sprinkles into sticky washes, I gave doughnuts away, usually to girls whose teams lost games.

The next day was sunny, and caterpillars appeared: woolly bears along roadsides and by the back door an American dagger moth caterpillar, the four pencils of black hair on its back sharpened, its other hairs dusty yellow. Last week eastern stinkhorn mushrooms broke through mulch near the university library. This afternoon the *Frontgate* Christmas catalogue arrived in the mail. Eight and an eighth inches wide, nine and a quarter inches tall, and fifty-six pages long, the catalogue was smaller than the autumn issue which consisted of sixty-eight pages, each measuring nine by ten and three-quarters inches. Despite the paper shrinkage the hand-crafted leather trunk had bulked up, putting on seventy-five pounds and so increasing in size that it could contain "a full service bar." The price was also more muscular, swelling from $6,200 to $9,900, the sinews of this last price chemically enhanced by "6 red wine glasses, 6 white wine glasses, ice bucket, champagne bucket, whiskey de-canter with 4 glasses, and cognac decanter with 4 glasses."

After Words

Words, Turlow Gutheridge once said, make fine clothes for the rich and riches for the poor. From the view point of the first Cause, Josh declared last month, a little muscular help amounts to more than a load of wordy sympathy, no matter how well-expressed the latter. Earth is far from heaven, however, and the first Cause is old and suffers from cataracts. Nowadays words open doors faster than biceps. Syllables have become blister substitutes. This spring Francis took the Scholastic Aptitude Test in writing, the SAT II, as it is called. Included on the test was an essay, the topic being "The nail that sticks out gets hit on the head by the hammer." Francis made a perfect score, and I asked him what he wrote. "Look Dad," he explained, "graders spend two minutes on an essay. To ace the test all a student has to do is use big words and furnish socially appropriate examples." I asked Francis what examples he cited. "I started with Martin Luther King Jr. then skipped to Jesus Christ. I was home free after those two, but for good measure, I tossed in Galileo, Charlie Chaplin, and the French Revolution."

"Writing isn't life," Francis said. "Have composition courses only taught cynicism?" I asked Josh later. "No," he said, "Francis has learned craft. He knows the hard truth that ornament matters more than content." Josh was only partially correct. Writing, even ornamental writing, creates life. At times I think light and dark don't exist until a pen marks a page, forcing them into being. This past Saturday I was bored until I grasped a pencil. Almost immediately

I noticed beggar ticks in the side yard, the plant's leaves toothed, sharp enough to shred seeds into splinters. Above the beggar ticks hung kerria, each bloom now a minute star-shaped platter, five green seeds heaped upon it. Stems of ox-eyed chamomile wound low across the dell until they twisted into sunlight and burst into yellow disks and rays. A grisette mushroom shouldered through grass, its gray cap tinted with silver and pleated around the edges.

I walked through the woods behind the house and down Fairfield Road to Mirror Lake. Purple loosestrife bristled around the lake. Tops of the spires dangled limply like gloves. Below the fingers spires hardened into wrists then forearms hairy with flowers. I hadn't walked around the lake in six months, and I said the names of plants aloud: soft-stemmed bulrush, wool grass, fox and hop sedge, and touch-me-not. A green heron grasped a broken limb. Along the shore, water willow slipped through grass, its leaves in crisp threes resembling the footprints of a large bird. I sat atop a flat rock. Across the lake, dodder unspooled into orange mats, blades of iris scissoring through them. Vervain bloomed in forks. While the tines of blue vervain were hard with blossoms, those of white vervain were soft, appearing melted, the blossoms themselves slight and unleavened.

Until I write, the world seems shredded, pages torn out of sentence and paragraph. "He meant to live, but he died," an epitaph in Carthage states. From my perspective words not only create but they also order life, enabling a person to enjoy existence. Silence, be it on tablet or tongue, perpetuates chaos and may destroy. As I sat on the rock, a comma anglewing tipped along the shoreline, light slipping through the orange upper half of the butterfly's wings in needles. Japanese beetles chewed grape leaves into lace. Golden brown above the edges of the beetles' abdomens, the elytra shined like jewels set in black and white. Eastern amberwing dragonflies swarmed above the water. Like a harrow yellow disks sliced through their bodies turning over brown furrows. The insects' wings were the color of weak tea, and as the dragonflies beat above the lake, they wrung ecru out of the air.

The amberwings were beautiful, and I did not think I'd see their equals again this year. Words, however, dung hours, and in the afternoon near the beaver pond, brown-spotted yellow wings perched atop timothy. When the dragonflies stirred the air, brown rolled the yellow into bars, creating shadows. As I looked at the dragonflies, I imagined myself inside a church, light sifting through stained glass windows, dappling a ragged stone floor.

Much that I saw on the walk wasn't pretty. In grass by the beaver pond a star-nosed mole rotted into maggots. A squirrel lay dead on a trail, the skin of its face black and leathery, its body unzipped by dermistid beetles, the fur spilling like down from a pillow. By Mirror Lake itself a mallard slumped into the ground, its skull smashed by a rock the shape of a turtle shell. Green bottle flies washed across the head, tumbling gold over each other, appearing so suddenly they seemed panned from the air. A Virginia ctenucha moth hung lifeless from milkweed, an upper leg pinned in a blossom. The moth's body was bright blue, and as I looked at the milkweed, I noticed a great golden digger wasp bustling across another flower. Later in the afternoon I found a cache of black racer eggs under a board. I brought three home to incubate. "Eggs?" Vicki said. "Yes," I answered. "I want to unscramble them into words."

The next morning Vicki, Francis, Eliza, and I went to the Unitarian Universalist Meeting House in Manchester. In May Eliza competed at History Day in Hartford. She finished second in performance, portraying a girl talking to a younger sister in the 1890s and describing the career of Elizabeth Cady Stanton, the suffragist. In June Vicki and Eliza went to College Park, Maryland, for National History Day. A fortnight after their return the Unitarian society invited Eliza to visit their "Meetinghouse" and discuss Stanton, "one of our great UU foremothers." The morning was humid, and the walk about lake and pond having tired me, I considered staying home and missing Eliza's presentation. Words invigorate, however, and I accompanied the family to Manchester. Once there I prowled the meeting house. In a blue box in the kitchen lay three empty bottles, all having contained 750 milliliters of Martinelli's Gold Medal Sparkling Cider. "100% Juice From Fresh Apples," the label assured apple bibbers. "Contains No Alcohol." Pasted on cardboard throughout the kitchen were instructive signs, all printed by hand and the words in capital letters: on a cabinet near the sink, BEWARE—KNIVES HAVE BEEN SHARPENED; above the sink, PLEASE WASH, DRY, AND PUT AWAY ALL THE DISHES AND UTENSILS YOU HAVE USED—THANK YOU!; and on the front of the icebox, PLEASE BE SURE THE FREEZER AND REFRIGERATOR DOORS ARE CLOSED TIGHTLY—THANK YOU! "When life gives you lemons," a placard in the women's lavatory instructed, "make Lemonade." "In contrast," I said to a member of the society, "walls in the men's lavatory are bare." "How did you know there was a sign in the ladies' bathroom?" she said. "I went in. Essayists are adventurers," I said. "Of course I was invited inside. Ceremony matters."

The service itself was less ceremonious than comparable doings in the Episcopal Church. When the minister said, "Good morning," the congregation responded, saying "Good morning" in unison. "A short version of the litany," I said to Vicki. Next a woman wearing a white baseball cap, a claret polo shirt, blue jeans, and white sneakers reminded parishioners about a picnic at Camp Newhoca in Vernon. Another woman described attending the general assembly of the Unitarian Universalist Church. From the woman's neck hung a sling. In the sling dozed a baby girl, a yellow pacifier in her mouth and her head as big as a softball. Unitarian Universalists, the woman said, were fast becoming a "force in the world." Following the announcements the society sang "Rise Up! Rise Up! O Woman." I recognized the tune as that of "Stand Up, Stand Up for Jesus," one of my favorite hymns. "Rise Up! Rise Up! O Woman," Ada Bowles wrote in the 1880s,

> No longer sit at ease,
> The banner of thy freedom,
> Is lifting to the breeze.
> Be ready for the morning,
> That breaks thy long dark night.
> Shake off the ancient bondage
> And hail the coming light.

"A Time for Sharing" followed Eliza's performance. A neighbor described a gash a child received when she tripped. Two women announced that they were proud of their husbands. While the spouse of the first woman adapted a short story by Anton Chekov for the stage that of the second had rowed twenty-six miles in a twelve-foot boat. "Now's your chance," I said to Vicki. "I ask only that you say nothing about my astonishing capacity for affection." Alas, Vicki remained silent and Episcopal. Next members of the society introduced visitors from Greece and North Carolina. "Daddy," Eliza said later, "the morning seemed more like the meeting of a support group than a religious service." "At its best religion supports people," Vicki said, "and didn't you like the people?" "Yes," Eliza said, "they were really nice."

Unlike essayists, some people use words sparingly. Last summer Elnathan Davis had a gall bladder operation at Baptist Hospital in Nashville. The suture became infected, and Elnathan stayed in Nashville thirty-two days. At the end of the fourth week his wife Joelean wrote him. "Red Boiling Springs is quiet," she recounted. "Our son Tom is dead. Cherry calved, and parsnips are middling. P.S. Bring back a bottle of Carter's Spanish Mixture."

Words, of course, can undermine worldly success. "If you want to sleep in a whole skin," Josh once advised me, "stop writing." For years Monroe Dowd cooked his neighbors' chickens. In February Sheriff Baugham caught Monroe in Maury Stonebridge's hen house. The county prosecutor Shubael Sterns had recently become susceptible to political ambition. Instead of simply assigning Monroe to the road gang for ten days, Shubael brought the theft to trial and oratory. "When all Nature was rocking in the bosom of Morpheus," Shubael declaimed, aiming a long middle finger at Monroe like a rifle, "this wolf slithered out of the briar patch and leaping the fence sheltering the fold devoured whole litters of chickens."

A drinking, not dining companion, Abner W. Clopton defended Monroe. After listening to Shubael, Abner tuned his pipe to a higher pitch. One evening decades ago, Abner recounted, when Monroe was poaching in the womb, his mother Tidence got a wishbone caught in her throat. Because Dr. Sollows and his obstetrical forceps were assisting the birth of triplets in Maggart, the bone remained lodged in Tidence's craw forty-three hours. Children in the belly hear and feel, maybe even see things, Abner asserted, declaring that the forty-three hours caused Monroe "to be born with an insane appetite for chicken."

"Only the blessing of God Almighty prevented him from sprouting tail feathers ere he ceased to be oviform." Sadly, Abner continued, Monroe's family was too poor to buy chicken. "The tonsils of the growing boy never glimpsed a pullet's breast. Drumsticks never played 'Dixie' on the adolescent's adenoids. No capon ever took the young man's esophagus in his wings and danced 'The Tennessee Waltz.'" Only in braised imagination did Monroe taste dumplings cooked in pot likker. Never did hot buttered biscuits, string beans, and cornbread pucker the infant's lips. Little Monroe never saw chicken fried in a black skillet sweet with bacon grease. Not once did the tiny baby hear the magical words *broiled, stewed,* and *barbecued.* The Dowds were so poor, Abner said in the peroration, that they couldn't afford two-day-old giblets. Having quaffed, as Turlow put it, "the Demosthenian draught," Abner cooked a fat-free meal of culinary poverty, one unfortunately that stuck in Monroe's craw. Just after the word *giblets,* Monroe interrupted the proceedings. "Poor, yes," Monroe shouted, "but not so damn poor, neither." Abner lost the case, but Judge Rutherford let Monroe off with a warning, telling Turlow later that Abner's oratory went down as smoothly as a roll of Brandreth's Pills and cured a stubborn pummeling in his bowels.

For some people words are life-and-death, not simply gustatory, matters. Two years ago Josh's colleague Winnie retired from teaching. Winnie moved to California and began to frequent the society of the young, something that is always dangerous but especially so when a person is a remnant of himself. Even worse, Winnie started writing poetry and conceived a passion for a chippy. "Happily," Josh reported, "the passion did last full-term. Winnie wrote a poem entitled 'Bird of my Heart.'" "What species of bird did he have in mind?" I asked, being curious about symbolic matters. "Booby," Josh answered. "Anyway the bird was not in mind but heart. It nested in Winnie's left ventricle. Shortly afterward a cardiovascular storm tore through Winnie, knocking the nest loose, downing life lines, but at the same time providing Winnie with wings, transforming him into a lyrical angel." "It just proves," Josh concluded, "that if you don't take love to heart it can't hurt you."

Occasionally words don't come easily, and I rummage the university library in hopes of hot-wiring Pegasus. Three weeks ago I read the *Southern Literary Messenger,* a journal published in Richmond, Virginia, in the nineteenth century. On 19 December, 1837, George Tucker, professor at the University of Virginia, the *Messenger* reported, addressed the Charlottesville Lyceum. "A taste for literature," Tucker argued, "affords to individuals the best security against vicious and immoral habits." "Tucker is right," Josh said. "Unlike the illiterate classes, readers don't have the leisure to indulge in the high pleasures of theft and larceny." Certainly books keep me occupied. Last month I read *The Heroine: or, Adventures of Cherubina* (1813) by Eaton Stannard Barrett, who, by the by, occasionally wrote under the name of Cervantes Hogg. I have so aged that I enjoy lyricism more than action. Sheaves of verse enlivened *Cherubina,* the most poetic leaf being "Sensibility":

> Dear Sensibility, O la!
> I heard a little lamb cry ba!
> Says I, so you have lost your mamma?
> Ah!

> The little lamb as I said so,
> Frisking about the fields did go,
> And frisking trod upon my toe.
> Oh!

George Tucker believed literature shaped character. When the professor spoke, the nation was young and optimistic. Now the country resembles me and is middle-aged. The less useful literature, the more I enjoy it. "The more sophisticated the writing," Josh said two days ago, "the more superficial the content." Be that as it may, I wandered margins of the *Messenger.* Pasted to the binding of the twenty-first volume was an advertisement two and a half inches square. "Joseph Funk & Sons' Cheap Printing and Binding," the advertisement stated, located in "Mountain Valley, Near Harrisonburg, Va." "Books, Pamphlets, Circulars, Handbills, Business Cards, Labels, Blanks," the ad asserted, "Printed with Neatness & Dispatch And At Reduced Prices." Glued to the right of the advertisement was a book label. Adorning the left side of the label was a wrought-iron post, ferns and grapes swirling around it. Jutting out from the post pointing toward the right edge of the label was a rectangular sign. On the sign appeared the words "This Little Sign Means Book-of-Mine." The *Messenger* belonged, the label noted, to the library of Henry E. Harman, who lived at "Mildorella."

Several appealing poems roosted in the *Messenger.* "The birds that sing, in the leafy Spring, / With the light of love on each glancing wing," the first stanza of "The Bird Song" trilled,

> Have lessons to last you the whole year through;
> For what is "Coo-Coo! te weet tu whu,"
> But properly rendered, *"the wit to woo?*
> Coo-Coo! Te weet tu whu, *the wit to woo—*
> Te weet tu whu!"

"The Bird Song" appeared in the December 1857 issue and was ostensibly written by Adrian Beaufain. In truth Beaufain was William Gilmore Simms, an accomplished regional novelist, much of whose poetry, though, was addled. Initially I thought "Bird Song" dreadful. Once I discovered Simms was the author, doubt began to chirp, and I wondered if the poem was meant humorously.

I haven't reached a literary conclusion. Remaining undecided about matters has a distinguished intellectual history, at least in Tennessee, the precedent in Davidson County, for example, extending from 1797, the year Tennessee became the sixteenth state in the Union. A controversy over a prolific sow brought two prominent Nashvilleans to court. The quarrel was so hot that five justices of the peace heard the case. Arguments lasted four days, after which the justices debated for another day. On the morning of the sixth day the chief justice, a local chandler, reconvened the court. "Gentlemen of the bar," he announced, "this court am hung." "With five justices hearing the case a hung decision is mathematically impossible," lawyers shouted. "Gentleman of the bar, order in the court," the chief justice said, placing a pistol atop his desk after which he gestured to the left then the right. "These two gentleman justices to my left is in favor of the plaintiff while these other two gentleman justices to my right is in favor of the defendant. As for myself I is half in favor of the plaintiff and half in favor of the defendant, and so this court am hung."

The last Saturday at camp Edward led his team to victory in Capture the Flag. The following Tuesday I received a postcard from Mook, an old friend and counselor. "Capture the Flag," the card recounted. "His Nibs executed three jail breaks—How do I know these things—I was the jail warden—They should have picked someone faster with better eyes, . . . etc.—Love, Mook." On the front of the card appeared a photograph taken in South Bend, Indiana, just before the start of a football game. "It's generally 'standing room only' at kick-off time in the Notre Dame Stadium," the caption stated. "Nearly a quarter-million football fans watch the 'fighting Irish' perform on their own gridiron each Fall. Every seat provides an unobstructed view of the field and the press box is regarded as one of the finest in the nation." Age had browned card, and the picture appeared taken in the 1950s. "What ties Indiana in the 1950s to Maine in the 1990s?" Vicki asked. "Mook," I said, adding that life blended the incongruous. Only in fiction did words and sentences slide smoothly together. Still, I added, thinking about this book, "if the writing is good enough then after the words come satisfaction and sometimes happiness." "What do you mean?" Vicki said. "I'm not sure," I answered. "An ancient Chinese proverb says that it is easier to mount a tiger than get off his back once you are seated. Once I start sketching life, it takes a lot of buck to bounce me from a page." "Do you know the letter-writer's blessing?" I asked, seeing Vicki looking puzzled. "We thank thee O Lord for what we are about to receive, and having no more to add, remain truly yours. Sincerely, Amen." "Good God," Vicki exclaimed, "what a noodle you are!" "*Noodle*," I said, picking up a pencil, "what a wonderful word."

A Little Fling was designed and typeset on a Macintosh computer system using PageMaker software. The text is set in Adobe Garamond and titles in Hepcat and Beanstalk. This book was designed by Todd Duren, composed by Kimberly Scarbrough, and manufactured by Thomson-Shore, Inc. The recycled paper used in this book is designed for an effective life of at least three hundred years.